THE

GREATER

FOOL

BRAD GOBRIGHT
and the Blinding Shine of Originality

The Greater Fool: Brad Gobright and the Blinding Shine of Originality
is published under Catharsis, a sectionalized division of Di Angelo
Publications, Inc.

CATHARSIS

Catharsis is an imprint of Di Angelo Publications.
Copyright 2022.
All rights reserved.
Printed in the United States of America.

Di Angelo Publications
4265 San Felipe #1100
Houston, Texas 77027

Library of Congress
The Greater Fool: Brad Gobright and the Blinding Shine of Originality
ISBN: 978-1-955690-20-1 / 978-1-955690-38-6

Words: Lucas Roman
Cover Artwork: Franky Cardona
Cover Photograph: Samuel Crossley
Cover Design: Savina Deianova
Interior Design: Kimberly James
Editors: Ashley Crantas, Elizabeth Geeslin Zinn, Willy Rowberry

Downloadable via Kindle, iBooks, NOOK, and Google Play.

For educational, business, and bulk orders, contact
sales@diangelopublications.com.

1. Biography & Autobiography --- Sports
2. Sports & Recreation --- Extreme Sports
3. Sports & Recreation --- Rock Climbing

THE GREATER FOOL

BRAD GOBRIGHT
and the Blinding Shine of Originality

WRITTEN BY
LUCAS ROMAN

FOREWORD BY
ALEX HONNOLD

A NOTE FROM THE PUBLISHER

Growing up in a climbing family, my love for adventure plays a large part in the projects we choose to take on as a publishing firm. With that also comes an appreciation for the unique characters that the world of extreme sports attracts. I know this because I am one of them. While learning to BASE jump, one of my mentors, Matt Blanc, sent me an article on *Medium* titled The Greater Fool, written by a young wordsmith, Lucas Roman. Lucas' ability to capture Brad Gobright's character immediately drew me in with the analyzation of an anti-hero, while simultaneously offering an alternative perspective of who our heroes should really be. I only had the pleasure of meeting Brad one time; we were at Camp 4 in Yosemite, and we met through some mutual friends. In that interaction, Brad mesmerized my very being, and I followed him closely thereafter. The initial conversation with Lucas about turning the *Medium* article into a full biography didn't quite go as expected. Lucas was hesitant, for he felt that he didn't have enough content to do Brad's full life justice—I begged to differ and managed to convince him that if written correctly, this would be one of the most powerful stories ever told. I cannot express the enormity of blood, sweat, and tears that has gone into the creation of this book, including the cover. The cover conversation brought a lot of contention among the climbing community and those who knew Brad best, and there was opposition for the

hardback cover to be a painting—especially considering the title was already obscure. Franky Cardona's art is synonymous with portraits of the best in their field—from athletes like Kobe Bryant, Carloss Carrera, and James Harden to legends like Stan Lee. Franky's style was unique and modern, and I knew it would make for a challenging cover, which is what I wanted. After all, Brad's character was challenging. He was the antithesis of everything you think a high-caliber athlete should be. An alternative view to a preconceived notion of what should be. What a cover of a climbing book should be.

With that being said, a paperback version was also created for the climbing community and features a beautiful photograph by Samuel Crossley.

The reason I wanted to publish this as a book wasn't for Brad's many climbing accomplishments—it is because of Brad's unique character.

I started this publishing firm to help share powerful stories with the world in an attempt to alter perspectives and inspire. *The Greater Fool* encompasses both of these initiatives, and I could not be more proud or thankful of the team that helped bring this project to life.

—Sequoia Schmidt, Founder of Di Angelo Publications

To Jim, Pamela, and Jill. To those who knew and loved him. Thank you for allowing me access to the corners of your heart. Thank you for giving us your pain, that we might see more of his light.

CONTENTS

INTRODUCTION

Brad Gobright's eyes were categorically disarming. For those who knew him, especially those who loved him, to be held by his undivided attention and to be the recipient of his cherubic smile were among life's most righteous affirmations. There was a certain assurance in his gaze, and, as his closest loved ones speak of it, his smile offered the type of stillness found in an alpine meadow. It was not the assurance of tall and mighty and endless forests; it was not an indomitable thing. It was something precious, unlikely, and beautiful, often unseen by most. Full of light, delicate and generous, those were the attributes of Brad's love cast upon others.

Overflowing with love, Brad Gobright's life was also full of devotion and what I can see now as a great sense of ordinance. The truth is, while often fox-holed into a profile that was comic, absurdist, and even unintelligent, Brad's life was flush with these broad and glorious and, ultimately, very human plots. He was a most unique, truly inimitable person—something I learned in friendship with him, years back, and learned again through the process of writing this book. But as unique as he was, he was also strikingly familiar. Seen by most people as an outrageous climber—as the subject of mostly sensational climbing media—there was a lot about Brad that the world did not know; that most of us did not know. It wasn't anything overtly secret, as there was no shameful list of liabilities. Instead, behind the shroud, unseen to most, was just the good stuff, the best stuff. At the underbelly, Brad's life had richness and humanity and, at times, exquisite vulnerability. The crux of it, as I came to find out, would be how to present this delicate love, this endless devotion, this great ordination, on the pages in a book.

In early 2020, after having read a short piece that I had written about Brad online, Di Angelo Publications reached out with an offer. Due to Brad's unlikely heroism, his lightness of being, and his quizzical, sometimes inscrutable persona, they were transfixed with him. A more detailed, full-length biography, they suggested, was needed. At the time, I was just beginning nursing school, and having never written anything beyond the length of a short story, I was largely overwhelmed. The truth is, up until 2020, I had only ever written to personally practice what felt like a discipline of mindfulness. Having a project at scale, deadlines to meet, and the thought that any of my work could suddenly turn into something up for public review, felt largely nauseating. Still, after suggesting we first publish a collection of short works to help ease me into the landscape, I agreed—with one caveat: Brad's family needed to be on board. That summer, while shaping the rough drafts on what would become *Aperture Alike*, I met with Brad's parents, Jim and Pamela Gobright, to discuss the prospective book.

After a few fond get-togethers and my being the beneficiary of Jim and Pamela's great hospitality, we had spent enough time learning about each other to issue what felt like respective votes of confidence. Little did I know these would be the fortuitous beginnings of a deeper friendship. With profound love and encouragement, they told me that two of the greater lessons they had learned from Brad were to never shy away from an adventure and to always lean into the long journeys of the human heart.

Lights green, we looked ahead. Quickly, a year passed, *Aperture Alike* was published, and nursing school went into its second season.

In January of 2021, with Pamela's help, I was given a list of Brad's closest climbing partners and friends, which led to even longer lists of contacts and acquaintances. Beginning a thorough process of data collection as the contacts naturally lined up, I began to arrange phone-based interviews, meeting in person whenever possible. Unfortunately, considering many of these partners and friends of Brad's lived across a variety of state lines and latitudes and there were the ongoing realities of a pandemic to surmise, face-to-face interactions were limited. For ease of documenting, I recorded nearly all of the interviews, with each person's permission, on my old iPod. By the summer of 2021, and on a short break from school deadlines, I had what I believed to be sufficient content to begin composing a first draft. As with any work, before words went to the page, I first had to navigate a process of framework and scope. The primary questions I had to address before writing this book—before I even conducted any interviews—were, what is the purpose of a biography, as a genre? And what is the story I am attempting to tell?

After some thought, I concluded that a biography ought to be, at least idealistically, about all of our lives. In other genres, that notion is often underwritten. Human stories apply to all of us—heroes, heroines, and lay folk alike—and therefore, so do the truths implied. But in certain biographic works, we lose that same undertone, which makes us feel we are only learning of someone rather than taking a journey with them, or better still, taking a journey for ourselves. Thus, in writing this, I very explicitly aimed to show how Brad's truths were, and are, fit to be ours also. With what may be called a bit of foolish optimism, my aim with this book was that upon finishing it, the reader would feel they learned as much about their own life—through moments where I have inserted places to pause and see how the protagonist's arc parallels our own—as they did about Brad Gobright.

The story I was expressly trying to tell was, therefore, about more than Brad alone. It was not just going to be a text about Brad supremely living and then tragically losing his life. It was going to, in some measure, ask each of us how we might be sadly or lamentably not living our own. But as much as it would ask of our lives, it would also celebrate them. Brad showed us the brilliance of life in ways that few could. He saw light shine from the center of the universe, he saw wildflowers in spring, he saw abundance and glory and the might of existence, and he wanted us to see it too. So that became the story I tried to tell. What I aimed for was a view of life—of all our lives—that would refresh us; a story that was about a young and intrepid man, but also about each of us. A story that might, all at once, make us cry for the acknowledgment of what and who had been lost, and have us weep for the sheer joy, enlightenment of, and surrender to all that had been found. I wanted the reader to close the book and, even if only for a moment, take nothing in their life for granted. Even more, I wanted them to want to live it as never before. I wanted all of that not because I thought I was qualified to deliver it, but because I thought that's what Brad would have wanted—a space where we could hold his life and our own lives together in wonder.

And so, after a few drafts, re-drafts, and revisions, which have passed the likes of Di Angelo editors and Brad's family alike, we've come to *The Greater Fool*. On the title, some context is owed.

For me, there is a certain magic in foolishness. I for one have always romanticized the function of folly, and I don't think myself alone in this matter. Look close enough and it can be seen throughout human history, from the first painted caves and scrolls to the scripts of Hollywood today. Whether it be the village idiot, the errant knight, the town fool, the noble fool, or, of course, the greater fool, humans have always had a fascination with the edge of reason. From time immemorial, studying the way of the foolish has been the way of the wise. Precisely because it is counterintuitive and challenges our epistemology, we find treasure not by writing off, but by leaning into the dissonant parts of life.

For the first handful of years that I knew Brad, his brilliance was not as obvious as his charm, but by 2015—largely considered his breakout year—the pieces were adding up. Brad wasn't just a misfit with a deeply pure heart, but a blooming wildflower keeping company with the icons of the climbing world.

As his first few features in magazines began displaying a happy-go-lucky, nonchalant version of the kid, an entire slew of curmudgeons somewhere in Brad's old life looked on from afar, quite honestly confused. This is partially because Brad had more than a handful of stories in local lore that were not bright and shining, and for those events, he was rightly chaffed. Certain folks couldn't let go of that old image of him; they simply couldn't believe he was onto something so grand and so clued in. But Brad kept being himself, his own northern star, and in short time, even the skeptics had to admit the kid was tapping into exceptional frequencies. Those who were first exposed to Brad from 2015 onwards would've only known him as a spritely, zealous crusher—part underdog, part goof—who, when stuck in a jam, could just buckle down and pull through moves with a strength that was only outsized by his massive risk tolerance. But those of us familiar with his early years saw him as something else entirely; we'd seen the transition, the pupa, the cocoon, and, yes, the unlikely, beatific result.

Whatever it was that got him to where he was, I felt compelled to decode it. I had a sense there was more to his magic than his lucky charm, his spriteliness, or even his incredibly strong fingers; I just needed to find something to hold it up against.

By 2015, Brad was already being compared to the mighty Alex Honnold, whom he had already befriended, and with whom he would eventually share many historic, highlight-reel days. The thing was, Alex already had the market cornered on almost everything iconic in climbing except for foolishness. Rather, he was the spitting image of poise—the collected, mindful climber. Hell, he was a humanitarian and an environmentalist, but he was no laughingstock.

In fact, I can remember reading a primary profile piece on Alex between 2008 and 2009. The article was published in *Climbing* magazine, and he had the centerpiece; the title of it ran as, "Nobody's Fool." The piece, one of his earliest appearances in press, painted Alex in colors that he'd keep for his entire life. In the text, he was portrayed as a mythic climber, not without his own idiosyncrasies, who was as sculpted and high-functioning as he was deeply aware of his place—and climbing's place—in a world of global inequities and larger plots. Truth is, it was a great article, and an accurate one. It was a contrast to the long-overused tropes of recklessness that accompanied any talk of a free-soloist's mental framework in that day and age. It put to rest all the bullshit notions of death-wish thinking and the slopping remnants of the 1990's bygone era of "Xtreme" this and "No Fear" that. Alex was, indeed, nobody's fool, and nobody's adrenalin junkie either. In so doing, he turned a much-needed page, essentially ushering in a new era for the outside world on model characters and character types. If, in 2009, any stragglers of the

"Go Big or Go Home" era remained, after Alex, they vanished.

Then, in 2015, came Brad: a breath of fresh air arriving at just the right time. His model was almost a perfect antithesis to Honnald's, and his timeliness came at just the right inflection point—not only for the climbing world but for my world, too. I'd always been prone to a certain lens on life, a bit too in my head and hard-pressed to find connection in the heart. Consistently afraid to go and live the full life that I deeply desired—both in climbing and beyond it—I could barely get myself out of the gates, let alone out of my own head. And perhaps I wasn't the only one stuck in fear and analytics, flummoxed by the vacuum of self, unable to unlock the secret joys of life. Others around me, it seemed, operated on the terms that the modern world had handed down, and did so with the same baleful results. Collectively tripped up by certain idioms—like the notion that you could somehow think your way toward right, or good, or valiant living, rather than needing to live your way into clear thinking—I sensed most of us had, at least in some form, gone awry. But Brad was not most of us. For years he'd been putting action first and watching joyfully as the desired mood and result followed.

Finally, after years in his operating system, Brad was getting some proper comeuppance. His spotlight was not only well deserved but also, like Alex's, redefining. Failing hard, tackling giant objectives, going in over his head—Brad's path worked. It didn't depend on smarts, wit, tact, or guile, nor did it hinge on the precision of the master's path. It simply required an elementary, almost childlike reboot of curiosity, and a willingness to go in the direction of uncertainty.

So, given Brad's model, especially compared to Alex's, I needed to pin a title on him tha fit for the praise he deserved. The climbing world had already drawn so many comparisons between them—sometimes even pitting them against each other as rivals, when in fact they were spirited friends—that I figured I should, too. While Honnold was decidedly Nobody's Fool, Brad was, for me, the Greater Fool—three simple words packed neatly into one homely epithet. Folly, a notion that Alex could fully distance himself from with his mastery, was the exact thing that Brad could use as a defining strength. It felt uniquely fitting and somewhat true to the analog of its economic etymology.

In the finance and business world, the greater fool is the person whose troubled scenario comes down to one essential problem: by some lack of insight, they've mistaken the perceived value of something for the actual value of it. If the stock or asset they've bought in on is, in the eyes of the market, seen as spurious or over-valued, a sell-off always occurs. After the herd running wild and the ensuing market correction, the worth of that stock or asset can, in a matter of minutes, sink to absolute zero. But standing there, unphased as ever, after the dust and the punchlines settle, is the greater fool—the one poor chap out of touch with reality just enough to hang onto something when all others let go. When the world around them sees only an empty promise, the greater fool maintains there is worth to be discovered after all.

But every now and then, markets are wrong. And every now and then, presumptions on lifestyles and people are, too. As it turns out, the climbing life—Brad's climbing life—offered more than ephemeral dances with delight. In fact, the way Brad took it, its value stands without question. That means, yes, it is something at least partially derivative of the boulder fields, the disheveled sleeping holes, and the homeless, dollar-a-day living trends that he maintained. It was not the result of a cozy Sprinter Van and a well-paying remote work lifestyle, fine as those things may be. It was deeper than that.

Brad's paradigm did not depend on a person selling all their possessions and casting them to the poor, it only asked them to become poor in spirit—to be open. That was the needle's eye, after all. To come to a place in life where, for the sake of a new experience, one might ditch all the tricks, tools, presumptions, targets, and even the operating systems. That was the only requirement. From that point forward, it was simple. At the heart of Brad's climbing life was a devotion to this perfect blend of an ascetic, ego-deflating practice mixed with an overtly aesthetic, bound-to-nature's-bosom, steady state. It was about curiosity, dedication, and a willingness to believe that you didn't need to see the next step to take it. So long as you took it—in fact, *because* you took it—a step would indeed arrive at your feet.

The opportunity costs were high, sure; stuck in minimum wage jobs, Brad wasn't getting any standard earning power, nor was he keeping certain important relationships close. But with time, those relationships did come. He would learn by his own forge and his own pain precisely what was missing in his life. He would learn about imbalance and ratio, and how even in poverty there can be plenty of gluttony. That is precisely where the details of his story come in; it's what fills the pages that lie ahead. But as for the model—and the asset which the traditional greater fool would not sell—by 2015 and beyond, there was no disputing its value.

It wasn't all glory, of course; nothing ever is. But it had magic not only for him, but for anyone willing to follow. So follow we did—at first in magazines, films, and on social media, but eventually in small doses applied to our own lives, we followed with action. I'm not suggesting it was delirium or anything like market pandemonium, but in speaking with his climbing partners, friends, loved ones, and romantically beloved, I can tell you that everybody took on parts of Brad's approach on life. In the years since I published my short story on him, from many conversations at campfires and parking corrals, I can also tell you that his reach went far beyond his immediate circle.

Brad inspired hordes of people to live anew and put a light in our lives that we didn't even realize had been missing. The beauty of it, from the Greater Fool point of view, is that he was always destined for it. The Greater Fool, at least in economics, is a lot more necessary than any one of us as individual bystanders are, for they are the prime movers. Truth is, the market relies on the Greater Fool not only to hang onto that asset in the dump cycle, but to sell others on it too. It's how commerce is driven and how markets stay fluid; it's how ideas translate off the page and into the heart. The true nobility in the Greater Fool isn't that they can see value in something that we can't, and it's not that they can endure a host of mocking bystanders while they're busy making bricks without straw. It's that after all the scorn, they're the ones with magic in their pockets, the ones selling us on something we pawned off to the rubes. The sweet irony of the Greater Fool is that every good thing that's ever lasted the test of time in the human experience—love, charity, compassion—was founded by one of them.

That was it, clear as day. What John Lewis was for the notion of "Good Trouble" all those years ago, walking across the Edmund Pettis Bridge, Brad Gobright was for the notion of "The Greater Fool." More than anything, he could restore the conversation of why foolishness is not so foolish, after all.

For the rest, you've got to just get in there and turn some pages. If anything sticks, it will not be because I wrote it but because Brad or one of his many loved ones lived it. I invite everyone to take a journey with Brad and with the people who loved him, if for no other reason than to see if he might also be a Greater Fool for you, too. Follow along to see if he might soon have you relearning how to embrace the whims of your inner delight and how to listen to the words of your inner voice—the one that is, so often, just sitting there, wishing to fully exist.

In the chapters that follow, you'll find the narratives are told as much from others' perspectives as they are from Brad's. His many adventures—and misadventures—are seen as much from the cameras, eyes, and hearts of his partners as they are found from the remnant crumbs he left us in his musings on social media, in passing conversation, or in B-roll cuts of footage. In many places, it may well feel as if we're living Pamela's journey as she reminisces on Brad's life with glittering pride and, at times, painful despair. Large swaths of the book are devoted to his relationship with his mom: a beautiful, rare glimpse at a heartwarming bond. In the small details, in the choices he made, and even in the routes he named, we'll find love letters between the two of them demonstrating how some things just carry past space and time. In some places, we'll explore truly tall tales that are flush with joy, while in others we'll cradle into the pits of fear, loneliness, and anxious disconnect. Some parts are savage, outrageous, animalistic—as one must be in order to climb at the scale Brad did—and others are patently light, whimsical, borderline absurd. But whether it's in the details of the day that Brad first crawled out of the womb, or in the day that more than five hundred friends and loved ones gathered in a small church in Orange County to remember him, what you'll find in Brad's life is the same thing tucked under every corner of your own. It's about love.

A NOTE ON APPROACHING THE OUTSIDE SAFELY

In the past decade, climbing has taken on a completely different shape. Recently, with blockbuster documentaries starring the likes of Alex Honnold and Marc-André Leclerc and climbing's inclusion in the Olympic games, the scale of it has multiplied. With that growth has come entirely new eyes and many new branches of participation. It is no longer just an ethic of the outcast. The idea that climbing is now nearly a household, cultural trend, and that it has so many new participants— especially of the inner-city and ethnically diverse populous—is a joy. Most of us who've been toiling away on the rocks for years are actually quite refreshed, as parents would be, to see such great learning occur in so many new participants. Whether it be on the level of pure sport, a mind-body practice, a simple means of release, a pathway into a community, or even a pathway to a spiritual framework, climbing offers a host of rewards. But it also comes with unavoidable elements of risk.

Climbing—especially the outside variety—is, by nature, a dangerous affair. The consequences that come with moving freely over great sections of the earth are as much a reality of it as the joy that it brings. It simply cannot be eliminated. While thoughts and diatribes could carry on for days in these forums, the simple intention here is that we focus for a moment on bringing awareness to that risk. As with anything else, it is in the learning and transition phase that one is most likely to err. In climbing, by and large, one of the highest risk areas is the transition stage from the indoor gyms to the outside experience. It should be no surprise then that the majority of climbing accidents occur not upon giant oceans of granite, but at smaller crags. Additionally, by the numbers, the most dangerous element is not the upward ascent but in lowering and rappelling. As was the case with Brad.

The work of this biography is, by far, more a focus of his character than his cautionary tale, for that is where we find his humanity and our inspiration. But for purpose aside, it's worth noting that in Brad's case, his partner was, relatively speaking, newer to the outside multi-pitch system of rigging and lowering than he was. With that novice scope, he did not have the ability to apply a cross-check on the team's safety. That's not to issue any fault, but only to note that a team is only as strong as the wisdom they share. Traditionally in climbing culture, people operated in small groups and mentorships, which meant that not only were skills passed down in active learning scenarios but they were also passed down with personal care. Friendship, community, mentorship—these were powerful elements of the old ways that made the teacher-to-student bond tighter than it is today. These days, where much can be learned on YouTube, and much of theory is for hire—whether by climbing guides or weekend tutorials simulated at indoor gyms—gaps in applied knowledge can emerge.

Quickly it becomes obvious to most that what works in the gym does not work as easily outside. Pumping music from a set of loudspeakers is no longer on the menu at a crag, nor is trusting that your partner "has you" without bothering to look at their system. While that list of dos and do-nots could also extend *ad nauseam*, the point is that for the baseline elements of safety to continue in climbing, the entire culture needs to maintain focus on it. Risk, danger, and the like are each person's to define for themselves, but to allow people—communally speaking—to the outdoors without efforts to educate them on those risks is a fallacy of omission. The safety of the newer among us is a burden we all carry. While it's also clearly the burden of the individual themselves, most people simply don't know what they don't know. Asinine as it may sound, these platitudes have real-life consequences in the climbing world.

So if you are new, newish, or new to a part of the sport that is different from your foundations, please seek guidance from a community, not just a person, as you venture forward. If you are not new and have been climbing for some time and have, by any means other than dumb luck, managed to not injure yourself or your partners, then odds are you have some wisdom to share, and someone around to share it with, either at the gym or the crag. I have no interest at all in policing others' behaviors or telling people what they must do, but for the sake of human decency, mutual respect, and broadening climbing's growing spirit, let's just try and exercise broader awareness. Let's take care of one another. I have complete faith that we can encourage community safety and rear life-long climbers who, in large number, will not court the risks and dangers chosen by the bold, but who will celebrate them and even identify with them all the same. I see no threat to the wildness of climbing's heart, to the grittiness of its forefathers, or to the renegade spirit of its chosen heroes and heroines. We can grow in more than one direction at once.

FOREWORD

by Alex Honnold

Brad Gobright and I used to meet up at three or four in the morning to climb El Cap together. He was camping illegally in the boulders, so he had no tent or stove. He would just wake up, eat a cold muffin, and meet me on the side of the road. He'd stand there in the freezing fall weather, alone, in the dark, with his climbing bag ready to go. He never complained, he was never late, and he was always ready to do some of the hardest climbing in the world.

I can't specifically remember the first time I met Brad Gobright—we were both dirtbag climbers, living out of cars and occasionally running into each other at various climbing destinations across the Western U.S. during the mid-2010s. I was at the beginning of my journey as a professional climber, having just become known for a few big free solos that had earned me my first sponsors, but I was living out of an old Ford Econoline and doing nothing but chasing good weather and new climbs.

Brad was on a similar trajectory, but he was living out of a beater '94 Honda Civic. We were of similar age, but to me, Brad represented the next generation. He was the climber coming up in the wings, the one you heard stories about from those in the know. Maybe not so groundbreaking as to attract mainstream attention (that would come later), but impressive enough that you heard his name around the campfire. "Did you see that kid send Air Sweden today?" or "Did you hear that Gobright soloed The Rostrum?"

It would be years until we routinely climbed together, though I'm not sure why it took so long. We were inspired by the same kinds of objectives and often worked on similar projects. Despite this, I only saw him consistently when we both began wintering in Las Vegas. I always really liked Brad. He had a refreshing earnestness about him that I appreciated; he didn't talk up his strengths or hide his weaknesses. He was just Brad.

One of the big breakouts of Brad's climbing career was the release of the film *Safety Third*, which showed him doing some mind-bending free solos in Eldorado Canyon and a devastating ground fall that broke his back. There are several interviews in the film where Brad struggles to articulate his thoughts and experiences, often to an amusing effect. In fact, Brad's lack of eloquence on camera was used as comedic relief in Reel Rock's *The Race for The Nose*.

I vividly remember the two of us hiking up to the top of El Cap one morning to rappel in on The Nose. He had just read *Sapiens: A Brief History of Humankind*—which is not exactly light reading—and was telling me what he'd learned. We hiked by headlamp, the sun barely brightening the eastern horizon. We were both panting heavily; Brad always set a stern pace uphill. We were talking loudly to make ourselves heard over our breathing and the crunch of granite underfoot. We were rambling about the future of humanity, the rise of China, the rise of artificial intelligence—all kinds of random topics—when we disturbed a team of climbers bivvying on the summit of El Cap. I remember thinking, *What a strange way to be woken up in the mountains—two men musing about esoteric topics while panting like dogs.* Brad was often portrayed on film as a simple soul, but he read, he was curious, and he was always good company.

Lucas Roman had known Brad for far longer, since their early days of working together at Rockreation climbing gym back when they both dreamed of Yosemite's big walls. I was glad to hear Lucas was writing a book about Brad. Lucas spoke with virtually all of Brad's family as well as his climbing and romantic partners, and he's used those conversations to craft a complete portrait of Brad. There are many film clips of Brad out there; it's not too hard to find footage of him climbing at an elite level, but it's much harder to understand how he got to that level and what he struggled with to get there. With humility and grace, Lucas digs into the heart of what made Brad such an amazing climber.

That was the interesting dichotomy of Brad Gobright: by the standards of mainstream society, he was a slacker. He never finished college, he worked as little as possible, and he lived out of a car that often looked like a trash can on wheels. But that belies his true strength of character and his incredible motivation. It negates his early morning meetups and how he was always ready to tackle seemingly blank faces of rock. That level of commitment and dedication is hard to reconcile against the Brad who didn't quite fit in the modern mold, but that is exactly the contrast that Lucas so skillfully navigates throughout this book.

The Greater Fool includes most of my favorite memories of climbing with Brad: our various link-ups in Red Rock, our back-and-forth speed records on both The Nose and Epinephrine, and even a particular day of sport climbing outside of Las Vegas. When Brad talked about his climbs, he was always so nonchalant that they didn't seem too outrageous. But now, seeing all that he achieved compiled in one place, it's hard not to be blown away. He free-climbed six different El Cap routes, each in a day. Most parties spend three to five days climbing a route on El Cap; Brad never spent a single night. He preferred to do all his climbing in lightning-fast blitzes, which is ironic since it's not like he was trying to get down to a warm meal at home. He was setting speed records just to get back to his illegal bivy in the boulders.

Despite all of our big adventures together, I learned a lot about Brad from this book. Lucas helped me understand the other sides of the incredible climber: the loving son, the proud brother, the directionless dropout. Brad struggled with things in life that we rarely talked about as climbing partners. I generally saw him at his best: calm, composed, unburdened, and doing things that he was uniquely good at. But life is more than just the highlights. There are always moments back on the ground when you have to grapple with the mundane: how to make a living, how to come back from injuries, how to maintain relationships while traveling full-time. We were always so busy hiking quickly or climbing like madmen that we shared precious few conversations about the rest of life. This book serves as one last deep conversation with Brad.

Thank you, Lucas, for sharing such an honest portrait of our dear friend.

And Brad—thank you for all the incredible climbs and for the continuing inspiration. When I don't want to greet a cold, early morning, I just think of you and hit the trail.

Alex Honnold
January 2022

BLOOM

Fall, 2015.

High on the historic Naked Edge of the Redgarden wall in Eldorado State Park, Colorado, a lone climber emerges from shadow into light. Perched some 650 feet above the canyon floor, flanked by walls of Fountain sandstone speckled in a brilliant spattering of yellowjacket lichen and wild moss, he climbs. He is more anomaly than hero, more elusive vision than visionary. Up in the death zone, he moves with grace across the undulations of stone, without a rope and above certain death. He moves by rote memory, guided only by the tactile impressions of each hold and the exact, familiar muscle contractions which come with each action. His motions are so ingrained in his psyche that from the ends of his fingertips to the chain of his entire nervous system, they translate in the psychological and emotional landscape of his execution as homelike, spacious, and even grounded. Ropeless, with gravity and mortality beside him, he is slave to neither. Instead, he looks, he feels, he senses. He arranges his every move by intuition alone. Much as in his life below, up high there is no place he will position himself to which he does not belong.

Far above the scattered pines and junipers that rustle below, he deftly sways out from the chimney formation of the penultimate pitch, and then a moment later over the final crux segment, past a tricky bulge onto a small slab of rock. He shifts his balance delicately until he is directly under the final, glorious headwall. A single, hand-sized crack, formed eons ago by the forces of the South Boulder Creek, is all that remains above him. One last fissure of rock that leads to the open face of the headwall above it, which lays bronzed in an afternoon cut of sunlight. Up there, it's just glory waiting for him, no further difficulties to surmise.

It's a worthy frame to pause on because, contrary to the common opinions about his character, he's quite clued in. Arguably, he always has been. Up there, he's connected—both to his own nature and to the earth's nature. To the land, the air, the elements of life itself, he is true. He is true to the uncanny inner tuning that calls him to such harrowing ropeless passages. Up there, he is in and amongst a cornucopia of natural history, biology, and elemental expressions of the universe. Up there, he knows—better still, he *feels*—that both his nature and Earth's nature are the same. His beating, untamable heart and his wild desires to live an adventurous life are coupled together with the outcrops of wildflowers sprouting beside him. Even ropeless, he's completely tied into it. Connected. It is simply a matter of fact.

It's also a worthy frame because, whether he knows it or not, this ascent (just one of the twenty-five-odd times he has climbed the Naked Edge without a rope) is the one that will change his life. It will validate on paper and in the fickle slab of public opinion all the years of inglorious and derelict waywardness he's been born from. Brad Gobright, the elusive vision in the scope of our focus, dressed in a banged-up pair of grey pants and a sky-blue base layer, is on film right now. Down below at the canyon floor with the cinematic B-shot is a new friend and filmmaker, Taylor Keating, while above him at the crux headwall is the multigenerational climbing legend and filmmaker, Cedar Wright.

Wright was one of Brad's heroes long before he became one of his friends—especially for the grit and no-frills style with which he chopped at a slew of America's boldest climbing routes. For the past twenty years, maybe more, Wright has forged a reputation and brand on big adventure. It's a climbing style that dates back to the beginnings of climbing itself, before it was about conquering mountains, before it built a history of expeditions on the backs of colonial infrastructures in the high peaks, before it was a golden era of privileged rebels from Western society, and well before it became a lifestyle sold in magazines, films, and social media. Climbing anything of consequence from the stone age was always about the great instinct for exploration of self and environmental setting. It was an expression of the human condition which burns for rapture and revelation in a universe beyond comprehension.

Wright has always climbed with this ethos, and Brad the same. Sadly, the atavistic approach does come with certain costs. Wright has seen many of his contemporaries and, more importantly, his closest friends go out by tragic circumstances in such pursuits. But even with the pain and bone-chilling gravitas that comes from such loss, the value of an adventuring approach to life—the need to maintain a familiarity with the edge—is fundamental for Wright. He too is wild at heart, and for that reason, he now has Brad—a cut of the old cloth in a modern generation—ropeless above Eldorado Canyon, directly in frame as he enters that burst of sunlight on the final headwall.

This is the first shooting day of what will become a landmark film for both Brad and Cedar: *Safety Third*. It will sprout from a small project and go on to be picked up by the Reel Rock Film Tour. It will win awards and accolades. It will merit Brad multiple sponsorships which will take him out of the frozen boulder fields and the phone booth-sized cabin of his janky Honda Civic that he's been sleeping in for the past seven years. It'll bring him and his inimitable charm, coupled with his inscrutable Greco-cynicism, straight into the hearts and minds of the collective climbing consciousness. It'll make him familiar to many; it'll put him in magazines and future video features; it'll lead to articles of both praise and critique (things about which he does not and would not care); and most importantly, it'll give him a modicum of stability. Instead of a singular concern about where and how to pinch a meal after his next climb, Brad will ponder how to fill his life with further purpose. Perhaps that part would have come on its own with enough time. But no doubt, *Safety Third* will change the course of Brad's life.

Right there, shit-grinning ear to ear atop the Naked Edge in the afternoon alpenglow of another flawless climb, Brad Gobright is completely and finally in bloom. With Wright behind the camera beside him and a new precipice outstretched before him, Brad's life is traversing into a higher order right before our eyes. He wouldn't know it then, not with the wind lifting his soft, satisfied gaze, nor with such an immaculate sunset on the bow at the close of day, but his life was about to change. From that moment, from that film, from that friendship with Wright, and from the thousands of hours Brad had invested in following his wild heart, a bloom as bright and rare as a field of California poppies was in season. All of it was in gentle motion, unfolding quietly before him. Suspended, like the very oxygen in his lungs, upon the inspiration of his next deep breath atop the Naked Edge.

For a man with such a legendary, incomprehensible course on this earth, it's a fitting place to begin. To decode Brad's operations, most of which may at first seem cryptic, I believe that we need to adjust our aperture. So much of what makes Brad remarkable can be lost if we strictly apply a lens of the rational mind alone. In changing this lens for a wider, more holistic one, I do not intend to suggest that Brad's life, or any of ours, is beyond accountability. I only suggest that we at least attempt to see a person openly and fully before forcing them into the boxed shapes of our own frameworks and failsafe rubrics. To see Brad's shine, we ought not yet ask our character by what means he has come to such a situation in life, or ask upon what exact principles he has composed his oeuvre. We will lose the beauty of that deep, full breath he took atop the Naked Edge if we do. His brightest moments, all the personal and soft nuances that touched his spirit while he lived a life upon high, will be lost on us if we think too long on the *hows* or the *whys* behind his actions rather than open our hearts and see the *whats*.

What he was doing up in Eldorado Canyon that day was magical—perhaps not for any of our lives, for we are not him. Saying it is magical, or beautiful, is not saying that we have any business to do as he does. Brad stood on top of the Naked Edge in that moment, not us. His life was in bloom up there—ours, only time will tell. He is not climbing as a dissertation; he is not up on a wall to defend a doctrine or much less a thesis. He is in the realm of expression more than explanation, of art more than examination—a reason I propose that Brad, so beautifully, is more like a koan of Zen than anything of a Western archetype. His life was somehow so uncorrupted, so original to himself, that it challenges our own frameworks, even as bystanders. Up there on the Naked Edge, basked in a ray of sun, it is on us, not Brad, to see the brilliance. He was already bathed in it, raptured by it, filled by it. If we hope to be also, then we must openly, honestly observe. And to observe is less to think as it is to feel.

If one were inclined toward legend, you could say that the tale of

Brad Gobright began with the close of a gas cap on his horrendous, beater-old early nineties Honda civic. In June of 2008, Brad began the trip of a lifetime. With a muted, silver-to-blue, paint-chipped exterior and the seasoning of a hundred and a half thousand miles of disrepair, Brad's car was a hollow, sunbaked shell of its assembly line origins. It was the perfect vessel in the perfect state of abandon, primed for his unilateral quest at full speed toward utter ignominy. Or perhaps it just seemed that way to many of those around him at the time, myself included. But neither fate nor the judgment of others was in Brad's purview, not then, and rarely ever, in fact. After a final session at the old climbing gym he'd grown up in, Brad closed the lid at the nearest and cheapest Arco station off Katella Boulevard in Orange, California, and set off for the rest of his life. All he could carry and all he would need from that point forward, the whole of his material existence, was cast astray in no sensible order into the cabin and trunk space of his trusted steed.

Brad always burned for adventure in the kind of way that made you want it, too. Maybe his means of getting there were questionable, but his desire wasn't. If you could see past the trainwreck of what I prefer to call his unique approach to the divine, you got the feeling that he was on to something. Exuberant, unstained blue eyes alight, Brad had both a confounding and magnetic aura even back then. The truth is, very few people that knew young Brad ever really understood what he was up to. Most of us figured that he wasn't all that clued into it himself, but everybody agreed that for whatever reason, you probably had a shot at becoming someone better if you kept him close, or at least gave him a chance. I remember that look in his eye when he set off that non-descript summer day, and I remember feeling, against my better judgment, that whether he knew it or not, that kid was shining a light for all of us. Ahwahne (Yosemite) bound, Brad was finally moving in stride.

Stride, as in with grace, was not the norm for Brad Gobright. Truth is, Brad struggled his entire life to find place and purpose, much like any of us. But Brad's struggles were specific, and ever since childhood, he seemed unmoored in ways that were elusive to all of us—his nuclear family, his childhood friends, his future climbing partners, and the climbing community alike. For a kid becoming a man, capable of such grit and sticktoitiveness on the stone, he struggled hard to pass milestones most cruise through during adulthood. Brad and his becoming were concepts interwoven, sure, but only by threads of nylon cord and not by the trappings of society or its usual pathways. He had tried honestly and to his best ability to gel. He gave community college a chance. He went to class and showed up mostly on time. He didn't become a drop-out on the context of thinking he was better than or too cool for school; he bought and opened the textbooks, per instructions, and gave them the best attention he could, line for line.

After two semesters, in the fall of 2007 and the spring of 2008, he'd found an inner truth: this just wasn't for him. Likely, it never was. Brad dropped out of school, assured of himself and his choices in ways that few of us ever are. His path was not in academia, and he knew it in his bones. What is fascinating, as best as others recount it, is that pure willingness he possessed to step face-first into the unknown. Brad had talents in climbing, having been doing it since he was six years old, but he didn't have them in spades and he didn't yet have a community. In a world where we find our best selves by merit of relation to others, Brad yearned for connections but found himself mostly wanting—a fact that makes his leap of faith even more striking.

Nearly every "great" in our sport's legacy, nearly all climbers who've made the annals, have had similar moments. Many lives have been defined by paramount tipping points, single instances where destinies hung on a dime just as Brad's did. Many climbers also dropped out of school and many fell slave to a general obsession with the outside life, but as far as accounts go, they could do school, and they chose their obsessions. For example, from what he shared, Alex Honnold didn't struggle for concepts at university, he struggled for direction. When he commandeered the family van to begin his own hero's journey, Alex was arguably more fit than Brad, physically and psychologically, for what was to come. By the time he took to the road and the dirtbag culture, Alex had climbed harder grades, taller walls, been on more teams, done more solos, and had truly found the makings of his own expressions—on and off the wall. Alex consciously knew the type of life he wanted to live on the merit of principles, concepts, and aesthetics. He had a framework.

Most climbers in our history have been similar. If they didn't have a defined credo to strive for, most, if not all, at least had a credo of what they were rebelling against. Many among us who take to the road to ditch the facades of society in exchange for naked exposure to the outside life do it to fulfill an ideology. Many have read the historical narratives of climbers and non-climbers alike, from the likes of Siddhartha Gautama to the Desert Fathers, to accounts by Muir, Thoreau, Emerson, Pratt, Robbins, Chouinard, and especially the Beat Generation. Brad, remarkably, came from no such place. His wasn't an anti-establishment quest any more than it was a mystic one. To be clear, it's my opinion that Brad was capable of and did, in fact, live all those paths in what he found outside regardless of his approach. He surely found revelation and experienced joy through both ascetic suffering and deep hunger, and he transcended himself in ways only found through engaging with a power bigger than himself. But my perception in 2008, and now, is that he wasn't after any of it the way the rest of us were.

In the wake of a childhood that was full of love but short on vision and connectivity, in the wake of a young adulthood that flummoxed more than it thrived, in the midst of a vague disillusionment but a great desire for life to mean more, Brad followed his pure heart with a singularity that would later become his trademark. Pointed north, Awahne bound, all of what and who Brad Gobright would become was finally, for the first time in his life, truly in season. Knowing full well that he had his parents' love but not their financial backing and charity, nor anybody else's, Brad burned all the bridges available to him. Knowingly or not—a fact less important the longer you ponder it—Brad forced function by that single act of embarking on his own journey.

Brad set off into the world the way we all at some point must; delving into an environment where the only guarantees we get in the process of our becoming are true encounters with pain and deepening uncertainty. With the close of one single gas cap, an unlikely journey into the heart of adventure—a place reserved for all to one day take for themselves—lay before him.

Of course, it wasn't all so glorious at the time. This is Brad Gobright, and he comes with quirks. Rich, complex, riddling quirks.

To save up for the rest of his life, as it were, Brad worked as a belay slave at the climbing gym for children's birthday parties, which usually occurred on weekends. I know because I was also there, toiling on the belay assembly line with him during my own quest for as many road trips as I could fashion. At the time, he didn't have many climbing partners, but if he was going to find them, it typically would have been during the weekends when everybody else in the social order gets permission to imbibe from life. And so, the realization that he had to work while others were off to play ate at him often. For minimum wage, he'd stand there, two hours at a time, four cycles per day, and grind out an eight-hour shift by hauling crying children up and down the walls on a rope. It was the closest thing to an honest job he could fashion.

The mindless drudge of it, though, and the understanding that his skills in life were only good enough for such menial compensation, did not settle well with Brad. In addition, the fact that the climbing gym was located just next door to the posh neighborhoods of Newport Beach did not help. The fact that it was commonplace to see high-end sports cars rolling in and out of the parking lot, operated by the bourgeoise who were dropping off the children that Brad grew to loathe for their absent work ethic and entitlement, made for covetous circumstance. Sometimes that envy got the better of Brad. Like many of us, when frustrations boiled over, he could live on the reactive side.

For Brad, in the early years, those reactions usually took the form of an increase in danger climbing and petty theft, both of which were meant to demonstrate, if only to himself, that he could have any experience or individual thing he wanted as much as the wealthy could.

We all worried for Brad in our own ways. As Cedar Wright later said, "In the early years, he was obviously too stoked for his own good. He climbed too long, too hard, without rests, and he climbed dangerously." Most people worried about this side of the coin and its consequences, but often, I worried about how he was getting there in the first place.

At that stage in life, Brad was already stealing whatever he deemed necessary for his ambitions, even if he knew better. And he did know better. Usually, that was something small, almost unnoticeable. A candy bar here, a carabiner there. Occasionally, though, he ramped it up. From my guessing, it never really sat well with him, but for his age or his compulsions or whatever reasons, he could see no other way. On the day Brad set off for Ahwahne (Yosemite), the rest of his life sitting right there on the dime, that urge came one more time.

On the last kid's belay party he worked before filling up his gas tank, Brad buckled right in front of me. In walked some unfortunate, sports-car-driving soul with a brand new Arcteryx superlight (AR) harness—the ones all the fly professionals had been wearing in the magazines at the time—and Brad just couldn't stand it. Another mindless, wealthy bloke buying a high-end harness because some sucker at the gear shop told him to, only for it to be used a handful of times and then end up sitting in a closet for years. It was too absurd not to intervene, Brad figured. That harness needed to be rescued.

By the end of that rich bastard's climbing session, when he went off to the bathroom to change, Brad had thought it over for long enough. His decision was made, and the only window he had was rapidly closing. Operating on all the wrong premises, Brad walked over to the cubby, did a quick scan for danger, then swiped the harness out of the man's duffel bag. Instantly, a full sympathetic takeover came, and Brad bolted to his car, which was impressive because categorically, Brad never ran. Ever. But, like a track star off the blocks, Brad blasted out to the parking lot, hid the evidence in his trunk, and returned to his post on the birthday detail, rope in hand, to finish belaying the kids. A minute later, the rich fella went to his cubby, grabbed his duffel bag, assuming it still had his harness, and drove off never to be seen by Brad or myself again. The deed was done. This was how the "Next Great Free Soloist," as Devon O'Neil of *Outside Magazine* called him, was starting the rest of his life—primed for glory but oft derailed by absurdity.

I was no moral authority and would later find myself in life stealing more than I'd like to admit in order to get my vices, but for whatever it was worth, I told Brad to watch it.

"Don't fucking do that shit, man. It's not okay," I said to him. "You're gonna get caught at some point, dude, and that'll fuck up all your climbing."

"Ugh, uuhm." He shrugged uncomfortably, conceding that he knew better; that he wasn't raised with sticky fingers. "I know.

You're right. But, man, I mean, it's just that I'm going to the Valley today, and it was easier than picking one off at REI."

I hung my head, lacking understanding, worried, and—let's be honest—amused. Nearly everyone who knew Brad had too many moments just like that with him. He would do things on the wall that most couldn't, then would do things in life that most shouldn't. He would get from A to B by first going to Z, and often without asking why. He pursued huge, heroic feats in his outside life and then jeopardized them all in these idiosyncratic, back-ass-wards ways on the home front. Yet somehow, it all made sense. He was confounding to the point of comfort, even laughter. Regardless of Brad's penchant for petty theft, I could never look at him for too long without just appreciating the way his inner dialogue narrated his own script.

With a newly stolen harness in tow, Brad got in his car, pushed the pedal to the floor, stopped at his parents' house one last time to toss a pile of rubbish into the backseat and trunk, and filled up his gas tank. All that philosophical and spiritual insight aforementioned was there too. No doubt, he was in touch, he was connected to the earth, he was the light and the boundless vision of a wild heart—regardless of whether he or any of us knew it at that time. But that's the part of life we usually only find in the rearview. Rarely apparent in the fabric of our contriving minds and our human drama are the deeper truths and broader themes, though they ride with us all the time, even when we insist we're the ones at the wheel.

The legend of Brad Gobright began driving up the non-descript arteries of the Interstate-5, northbound, past Los Angeles and into the haze of agriculture country spanning from Bakersfield to Fresno. But his true origins, the roots of his becoming which were just as unlikely and always at the razor's edge, began long before.

On the morning of June 16, 1988, after two weeks of the Saint Joseph Medical Center staff's best efforts to keep a certain underdeveloped child in the womb, Brad Gobright—for whatever choice he had in the matter—could wait no more. Eight weeks early, barely scratching in at four pounds soaking wet with the amniotic envelope, Brad entered this world with all the sacred splendor a mother could wish for, but also with no defense against the outside world. Brad's birthing sequence had glimpses of the precious animus one sees in slow motion, as hidden flower petals uncurl with a time-lapse to life under the sun, but it also carried all the impossibility of becoming.

Making it a month into life itself seemed herculean, surely one of his many labors to come, when the sum of his thoracic respiratory capacity alone was equal to the passive volume contained in a single adult nostril. With such low odds, such frailty, one might have thought that for all that this life requires of us, for all its weight, so much as a gust of wind in the wrong direction could have done away with him right then and there. Even with the privileged situations of his birth considered—his sex, his family structure, his economic circumstance, his country of birth, his ethnic background—Brad was always an underdog at becoming one's best. Pamela and Jim, his mother and father, watched for more than a week as baby Brad lay in the incubator, incomprehensibly small, sheltered from a world that would threaten even the next cycle of cellular generation. In the heart of Orange County, California, a most unlikely hearth for a future outdoor elite, Brad came into our world just the way he left it: well ahead of his time.

Four pounds. How on earth could anything of might or magnitude, let alone an indomitable human spirit, ever arise from such humble beginnings? His life was always a most unlikely affair, an arrangement of the cosmos which ran counter to all sense of the norm, the sensible, the assured—something very few, if any, were ever really prepared for.

During a spring afternoon get together at their house in Orange, CA, I asked Pamela and Jim if they thought that three decades, a few movie films, and many media spotlights later, their son would have chosen to define his life by a pursuit of the vertical world and the community that comes with it. "Absolutely not," they both agreed.

"The last thing we thought he would end up as when he was in that hospital was a strong man of the outdoor field, that's for sure," said Jim. "As babies go, the kid wasn't even a flyweight, you know?"

The images of Brad, years later, that would make cover shots and poster spreads, high on To-tock-ah-noo-lah (El Capitan) and at his best, were unimaginable. Brad barely ate, let alone thrived, in his first few weeks of life. Looking down in the incubator at this child of theirs, whose minuscule keratin beds glossed his toothpick-sized fingers, neither Pam nor Jim would have suspected that those fingers would later grasp all the earth in its vertical glory, to heights and in ways that exceptionally few ever do.

"He was a fantastic child once we got him home," Pamela reflected from her backyard. "I was so afraid for him, though, that Jim and I actually got a social worker assigned to us. But turns out that's just because I was such a Nervous Nelly. It took no time before she took herself off the case. She told us we had everything set up exactly right. But, you know, when it's your first kid and they're that small you just can't help it. You just can't imagine how little he was."

Pamela, who I've had the honor to spend time with since Brad's passing, sat back, the wind rustling through embers of her now-gray hair, and reflected further. "If I could do anything over in the whole process, you know, I'd worry less. God, I worried so much," she acknowledged.

As her hair danced with a rise of wind across her face, I saw why that was an important lesson for her. It's not a regret as much as it is a reminder. Since losing Brad so tragically, and just a couple of months later adjusting to the wake of life under the pandemic and a breast cancer diagnosis, Pamela has had to live this truth. How are we to worry less? How are we to be present with all that is uncertain, when ultimately so much, if not all of it, is truly out of our hands?

Time, perhaps, and fellowship with others, are beginnings. Pamela, no doubt, has learned that to worry less is not the same as to care less. And there is freedom in that fact. There are big freedoms that come of this—ones that let you follow your heart more than any other dial—and small freedoms, even ones as small as leaving her hair dye in the vanity closet and embracing all the gray on her head. A gray that wafts across her forehead as she reflects on her son's life. A gray that worries less. A gray that finds new beginnings even across the worst thresholds of pain and human loss.

Pamela, Jim, and I were enjoying an afternoon on the backyard porch, which was festooned with patio lights, décor, and a small herbal garden beside the deck and terrace, which Jim, as a landscape architect by trade, had made himself. Sitting together, it became apparent that their entire home, the whole of their local daily environment, is a living testament to their nearly four decades of life together. In each corner, at every bend in the house, the deck, and the hallways, shards of Brad's life and memories of him would unfurl. Seemingly everywhere Pamela looked to gather her wits and clear her head when conversation became difficult just brought another flood of memories. However painful, it's clear that their home is a special place, one to which she and Jim still both belong. That afternoon, as we shared food and memories, Pamela did not run from her son's ghost; she sought it. It's something she seeks every day in her joy and her pain—surely an example for all of us when it comes to holding up the people we love so dear.

"You remember the time he spilled oil all over the driveway when he tried to change the motor oil in his car?" Jim laughed lovingly through the remnants of his midwestern drawl. "You know, he had this way of just not seeing things the way a lot of us saw them. He'd nitpick and know everything about the sequence of a rock climb, you better believe it, but the stuff that drove us mad, you know, it was all the other parts of life. I mean, how do you forget the oil filter? Or think it's a good idea to leave oil on the driveway and brush it onto the pebbles? He was just his own guy, that's for sure."

Jim added, "A lot of this goes back to those compulsions he had. It was always there, you know, he could focus on one single thing in ways nobody else did. It became a strength with climbing, but the poor guy had a hard time with growing up. For a lot of people, it just seemed like he was in outer space."

From the beginning of Brad's time on Earth, two things were clear: he was always going to be a bit behind the curve developmentally, and he really could wrap his attention on things to the point of singularity. As Jim said, he was compelled in many ways. From the get-go, milestones most kids pass on the way to other feats became fixed points, places to stay, perhaps for just how fascinating they really were.

Brad took his time to crawl, not finding its mechanisms until the middle of his seventh month, and he stayed for a while, too. For whatever reason, Brad crawled longer than most and didn't find walking a useful means of exploration until somewhere between sixteen and eighteen months. He spent nearly a year crawling. Pamela shared that there was a three-foot-high ladder-and-slide apparatus at their old place, and Brad spent most of an entire lunar cycle on it during his waking hours, putting in laps. Quickly up, quickly down, always crawling, whole-body. It may be conjecture, but as crawling is closer to climbing, I prefer the notion that he stayed there knowing he'd need the skillset later, or that after walking, he always yearned at some biological level for a return to those ingrained musculoskeletal patterns. The notion that crawling was always something of a return to his original state is, for me, also echoed in his climbing.

"He also showed that early sense of awe for things that were high up," Pamela said. "He was always fascinated by things that stood much taller than he did." Pamela remembers that Brad gawked at anything as tall as a tree when walking around the neighborhood. And whenever they passed big commercial buildings or took road trips into the woods, there was Brad, fixated, never so taken as he was when in the presence of things of the taller order.

By all the other measures of growth and development, Brad was always behind the mark. Unlike his sister, Jill, who would come to the family a year later, Brad struggled for concepts and language. Quietly, Pamela worried what this might mean as he would sooner or later be forced to integrate, play, and move into learning environments with others. Jim, seeing Brad's disadvantages, set to task to firm the boy up. Brad would need to be tough, he'd have to take some good knocks, and he'd need to be able to deal with difficulties. He was, after all, a puny kid, and it looked like that frame wasn't going to change much heading into adulthood—one more reason why Jim, who had endured leagues of physical and emotional difficulties due to losses in the family in his youth, rolled up his sleeves. Meanwhile, Pamela did everything possible to seek alternate means of education.

For all his difficulties in development, Pamela shared that Brad was still an ideal child: not a crier, not colicky, not full of bad moods or ill temperament. Brad was a joy, a goof, a happy kid, an image that lights up Pamela's face. Even as a superstar in his later years, Brad had a childlike purity that shone from the well of his blue eyes, a spark of life that never extinguished as he grew up and went into elementary school, where his real trials to gel into the world around him began.

By the time he was in kindergarten, which he started a year late, Brad was already facing difficulties. He didn't get excited the way others got excited; he didn't focus the way others focused. He couldn't keep attention in learning environments, yet he always seemed fixated on something, often on things most would consider trivial. He was already expressing notions of that singularity, that unchosen sense of obsession, which even then was often interpreted as aloofness. The earliest version of this compulsion, according to Pamela and Jim, was as a preschooler, when he was taken with an obsession with keychains.

"He just couldn't get enough of them," Jim shared. "Like they were going out of style. It probably lasted a full year, too."

Agreeing with Jim's point, Pamela laughed. "He was so into those damn keychains. One day when we were in an elevator, Brad swiped a lady's keys right from her purse like a car thief! The only problem was the keys made a bunch of noise and he was caught in the act.

"He was in trouble, sure, but you can't imagine how embarrassed I felt about it, too," she added. "It didn't stop in that elevator, either. He kept that obsession for a long time. In fact, that same year, during Christmas, Jim and I pinched a pretty penny to get Brad a train set that we thought he'd fall in love with. But of course, no gift stood a chance against a good keychain. We unwrapped it, set it up for him, showed him how to keep all the pieces moving, and then to our complete surprise, we watched that train set spend the whole week until New Year's on the floor doing nothing while Brad tinkered with his keychain collection."

Reflecting with all the joy a mother could muster, Pamela giggled, "We could've had a much cheaper Christmas."

The second phase of Brad's singularity came at age six.

"Mom," he exclaimed in epiphany, "I'm going to be a deep-sea diver!"

After a trip to O'ahu, it was settled. Brad Gobright was to become a marine biologist. For my money, I think there's an alternate narrative in a parallel universe where he became just that, where all the achievements he'd made and all the ways he blew our minds were done in the ocean. A narrative of wild adventures surrounded by the ocean's best cast of sea creatures, out there in the deepest trenches.

It all started when the family took a trip to the mythic Hanauma Bay on the southeast coast of O'ahu, Hawaii. Stuck right there, among the thousands of visitors on any given day, among the three million annually who wade in the waist-deep waters, was a young gumby called Brad Gobright. A reminder that for every tourist overrunning a natural resource, a true, lasting change of heart often resides side-by-side with every selfie you want to roll your eyes at. Hanauma Bay, with its clear, intoxicating aquamarine water housing hundreds of species of native sea life, did something to Brad on a heart level. It transfixed him. Face down, snorkel up, Pamela says that Brad looked God—or what we'll call revelation—straight in the face the day he went to Hanauma.

"He floated in that bay long enough to get skin cancer on his back," Pamela laughed again. "But it was a whole new world for him."

From that day on, Brad was set. No questions left to ask of this world or its direction for him. He was going to be a scientist, a biologist, a whatever-it-took to be the guy who gets to stay right there in that shimmering blue, underwater kaleidoscope.

In one of our early get-togethers, Pamela kindly shared a vinyl-sized, grenadine-red school binder from Brad's early years, fashioned during the post-Hanauma Bay era. It was made as a school journal project in first grade, where the prompts were for Brad to devote a page to self-identifying issues such as: Who are you? Who are the members of your family? What do you like to do? What do you like to study? What do you want to be when you grow up? The answer to the final question, of course, was a given.

This was before Brad succumbed to his learning difficulties and before he realized how much math and science it would take to live the Jacques Cousteau dream. It's a snapshot of him before many of his troubles set in. It's Brad at six: premature, idealistic, with all the world before him.

It is not only perfect as a sentimental relic, but it's also laminated, preserving all the skeleton figures and crayon-stained images that young Brad Gobright once devoted himself toward. Pamela, being the worrying mother, confessed that she helped him the entire way through it. Concerned the rest of the kids in his class were going to produce a neatly composed journal project, she didn't want Brad's messiness and lack of apparent order to stand out. Pamela helped cut out images and place the printed photographs of Brad and his friends into a collage and glued them to the page. In other words, she gave it a mother's touch. But the drawings, the words, and the heart of it are vintage Brad—including what would become his trademark spelling errors.

There are photos of his friends from his Cub Scout troop, and he has notes clearly distinguishing regular friends from best friends. There are sketches of the house he lives in, of his mom and dad. The note next to dad says just one thing: "Dad plays rough." It was testament to the fortitude and toughness Jim had always been trying to instill in him, firmly but with love.

Also included in the family drawing is Brad's younger sister, Jill. There are photos of him and her together, the close bond between them visible behind the cloud of his shaggy locks and her wildly curly hair in the spunk and rambunctious joy lighting up their blue eyes—lights of a childhood experience not yet squandered by the pains of life.

Being religious in upbringing, there's even a page devoted to Brad and God and their relationship. Aside from the formalities you'd expect, it's clear that what Brad believes in—what he always believed in—was something or someone behind it all. A magic maker, if nothing else, benevolent enough to put all those fish in the sea among all those bright tapestries of coral.

Turn the page, and scribbled onto a wide-ruled sheet of paper is Brad's mission statement on life. Here he declares his intent to be a deep-sea diver. Beside the text is a drawing of Brad, done by himself, enveloped by the sea and its creatures as he sinks toward the ocean floor under the protection of an old DESCO air hat. In the text of his writing, he recalls his first trip to Hanauma Bay and the way it struck him smitten. He talks of sea life, of the feeling of water on his body, speaking articulately of the whole experience in notes of colors and textures. It is a surprisingly well-composed tribute. It shows us just why he was so captivated for so long.

But the hard facts of the school binder do not paint the whole picture. Brad was already struggling to keep up, partly due to difficulties processing and retaining information, but also due to that single-mindedness that many mistook for absent-mindedness.

Brad struggled his entire life with formal education. It was no easier for him to read than it was for him to speak with confidence. Brad was not graceful in learning or expressing whatever it was that he had learned. He was also not good with a pen, rivaling physicians with his chicken scratch. All of this meant it was difficult for him to integrate with others. He was aware of it enough to know that it concerned those who cared about him and to understand that other kids who didn't struggle saw him as lesser-than. He knew, with a certain pain, what it felt like to be the brunt of jokes. But whether by naivete or the deep kindness in his heart, he didn't let it get to him, at least not too deeply.

"Besides," Pamela says, "he was just too fascinated in his own world to care that much about it."

That's where he was protected, in part, from the scoffs of the world around him. He was safe in his compulsions, with his exquisitely detached focus that took him worlds away. He could always plug into another space when things got tricky; he could always resource the sublime when he needed it most, a life skill that the wise among us struggle for in the high spaces we like to call mindfulness and meditation.

"You know," Pamela began with a smile, "there were so many times when Brad would come to me at that stage—having trouble reading, pronouncing, and spelling words, dealing with kids in school—and he'd just have this tired look, like he was giving it his very best. He wanted to do well; he really did. He'd come to me all the time and just say, 'Mom, I try hard to pay attention, I really do. I try in school, but every time I'm trying, next thing I know I'm right back there, in my submarine, with all the sea animals, and it's just so pretty.'"

The submarine, like the walls he'd later come to climb, was a sanctuary, a free space, a natural orientation of the mind where order and fascination were held. Brad talked for a few years about that submarine, perhaps more frequently and with more depth than an imaginary friend. When life was hard, when a teacher asked for a response to a question by calling Brad's name in class, when a softball pitch was coming his way from the baseball coach in Little League, when Brad was at the dinner table with a coil of spaghetti on his fork, or when staring at the ceiling while lying at night, Brad Gobright, the child who came long before the famous climber, teleported into his submarine, safe, surrounded, and alight, perfectly steeped into a world of wonder around him.

Perhaps that's the first lesson he can teach us, among the many. The kid who struggled to read, who didn't fit in or know how to play and laugh like the rest of them, found that above the opinions of others, the first principles of life dictated that he not ever forget that we inhabit such a magical space together on this earth. We are surrounded by revelation, always. It is always available, calling us, inviting us, wooing our hearts.

What began as an unchosen distraction, a compulsion—first with keychains, then trees, then sea creatures from the view of his submarine—became a means to weather the storm. This was Brad's way of focusing on elements of mystery and beauty in a society that convinces us that our time is better spent attending to who we shall become rather than first asking who, and what, we really are. We are holy, lest we forget it. We are the raptured hearts, the manifestation of light. We are children of this blue spinner, this wild planet, this burst of atoms and consciousness and sea creatures and elements that we call life. Something that we often desperately need to remember, Brad never forgot. Brad, the wild, unformed Zen precept, was always there in that fact, perfect in what we labeled as his aloofness. He was free of the shackles with which we chain ourselves in our rational minds.

Since birth, eight weeks early in that hospital bed and barely passing an APGAR evaluation, to the beginnings of his education, Brad Gobright's life was drawn with struggle and colored by confusion. As much as he didn't—couldn't—think and process the way many of us do, he was equally misunderstood in what he *did* value from life.

In the years to come, it would continue. Brad would often be made fun of; he would struggle in academia; he'd be shuffled through the educational system, taken to counseling, put on medication, prayed for, worried for, left out of cliques, and laughed at by every group of people who should've taken him in.

But for every time Brad struggled, he also soared. He was always too taken by the beauty of the earth around him to be weighed down by our condescension. You could almost see him out there somewhere as a misled kindergartener and all through elementary school, at times without friends, aware of his deficits, but in large part not caring either, just pleasantly in attendance to the world around him. Happy to see it all with such a unique scope. Teaching us, even then, that it's not so important if others don't see the revelation at hand: if you keep it in focus, it'll shine off of you and back toward them soon enough.

ROOTS

In June of 2007, I turned the corner of the Ahwahne (Yosemite) Tunnel View for the very first time; I was twenty-four years young, and Brad Gobright was beside me in the passenger seat of my almost-overheating, air condition-less, dusty Chevy pick-up. Brad, just out of high school and a week shy of his nineteenth birthday, had his handheld disposable camera at the ready, instructing me to turn a quick left and park the car for a shot of the Valley, majestic in all its Californian—better still, its indigenous—splendor. Like a bomb detonating in close quarters, the corridors of my mind were dismembered into shrapnel and cast amok in the wilderness as I struggled to consolidate a framework, let alone words, with which to entertain such grandeur. Overtaken, devolved to childlike incompetence, I finally parked the car and walked with buckling knees to the cobbled retaining wall where tourists and dreamers alike lose themselves for just a minute to the embers of a living piece of perfection.

Brad, unlike me, had already been there, and in certain terms knew exactly what he'd come for, whereas I only knew what I was running from. I'd had a very different childhood than Brad, which, while not filled with bullying or being cast out from cliques, did have a lot of aimlessness and pain, and perhaps more than anything suffered from an environment where the outdoor life and a relationship to the earth was simply not a part of who we were nor what we identified with. Our lease on life—a slanging hodgepodge of Mexicans we called family—was the type of generational economic struggle you get with immigrant peoples and the generational mental health struggles that co-signed it. In the wake of that and a conservative approach to adventure, relationships, and any worldview altogether, my first visit to Ahwahne was made only to run away from things. Away from the clutches of my past, away from family trauma, away from a relationship with a woman who wanted something of a domesticated life that I knew I couldn't deliver. Away from any commitments that might interfere with finally finding a life outside.

Brad, to my surprise, was a hero in this regard. He wasn't running away from life as much as he was, at last, running directly at it. In our six months of climbing together, I'd already seen him as the brunt of many a foul punch in joke form. I'd seen him dismissed, heckled, and struggling for his own identity. But I'd also seen him lead-climb where I would only—and barely—be able to follow. I'd seen him push beyond fear, and I'd seen him call high places home. For that, for his courage and inability to let failure be defined in the negative, for his constant pursuit to be falling from climbs at his limit rather than standing on summits that scarcely tested his inner thresholds, he was my unlikely guide and dissonant hero.

"How's that for a view?" he said with his classic smirk.

Brad was already lost on To-tock-ah-noo-lah to exacting detail. I knew about it only as a projection, as phantasmagorical energy where men tested their metal. I knew its indigenous legend about a first ascent that was a humanitarian mission to save two stray boys, and I wondered if I might one day be a small worm rather than a bear or lion. At the same time, I knew about its American history, about the Harding and Robbins rivalry, which pushed Harding up the historic 1958 first ascent of The Nose. I knew of To-tock-ah-noo-lah like I knew about most of life: from other people's accounts rather than my own experience. I knew about John Salathe, Pratt, Chouinard, Rowell, the Huber Brothers, Paul Piana, and Todd Skinner. I knew about Sibylle Hecthel, Bev Johnson, and, of course, Lynn Hill. But Brad knew of it better than I did, even then, with neither of us having climbed it. He knew it by its crucibles.

While I was wiping the tears from my eyes, the other hand trying to steady my quivering knee, Brad was quickly pointing his way around the massif.

"See that?" he shared. "Those are the dihedrals that make up the Muir Wall. Just right of the Heart, which is just right of the Salathe, which you can spot by the Monster offwidth..."

Brad kept on with the type of expertise his loved ones had always hoped to see him manifest somewhere in the halls of academia, in perfect expression, in the one place that truly educated him both to himself and the world around him: Ahwahne.

"Next summer we'll climb it," he flagrantly suggested. "You'll see."

In disbelief, I followed Brad back to the pick-up truck, started the engine, and drove down the road, past Bridalveil Falls and the famous Leaning Tower, to the clearing in the meadow where you realize that God made a stone so big that it will not remotely fit into your windshield for a full view unless you scootch absolutely to the edge of your seat, hunch over the steering wheel, and extend your neck past the limits of your first two cervical vertebrae. Eventually, humbled into obsolescence for my course in this universe, I parked the car at Camp 4, the hearth of American climbing legend and birthplace of many historic ascents, and set foot in the Valley proper.

It was an impossible situation. I, an urban kid from a broken home, born from a plot of immigrant folk and socioeconomic discord, fresh off the coattails of a misled youth, standing side by side with Brad Gobright, an apparent anomaly to most sensible order, a kid whose uncanny strength and might on the wall were only outdone by his awkwardness in life at large. Together we stood in the land of giants, packs in hand, all the world before us—no plan, no place to stay, and no more than a hundred bucks between us.

This was our beginning.

The reason it is important to pause on that frame is because it is one of many moments throughout life where we can actually see clearly what we'll call in this narrative The Impossibility of Being. And to be perfectly clear, more than Brad's story, it is this, The Impossibility of Being, that connects the dots.

It is a truth of the universe, just as it is a realization of the heart. A fact as operant as a force of nature, such as gravity, and also a truth—a comprehension, an experience, a realization—to be had and felt on an emotional level. It is the fullness present at every moment of our existence as conscious beings. It is the impossible combination of events and circumstances that lead each of us to single moments of connection with others—to parallel paths with few precious people we call friends, family, acquaintances, or partners in this great adventure we call life. It is always there, and yet it always hangs on such a gossamer-thin line, sometimes in such desperate abandon, at the very edge of possibility. It is the realization that so much of what we call the here and now, our present condition, should likely have never occurred. It's the understanding of our exact past, and the aggregate of all our choices and the choices of those we could never exert control over, for so many reasons could have, almost should have, been something other. It is the understanding that there were almost always greater odds for the alternate, for another inevitability among all the permutations of direction. So much so that it startles us to the unlikelihood of the now. It awakens us to the profundity of what truly is. It is the emotional, heart-level understanding that we have no other conclusion of the present moment than to see it for what it is: miraculous, inexplicable, impossible.

Often in our busy, hurried lives, we pass these precise frames without pause even though they are full of incomprehensible splendor. Our course and greater awareness are deterred by pain, trauma, and our need for exact order and rationale in the dark moments of our lives, but the pains and insensibilities of life do not betray the great gift of it. Hurtful as they may be, they affirm it. The Impossibility of Being—nuanced, delicate, and yet fuller than a flywheel in its momentum—is always as present as our beating hearts and involuntarily breathing bodies. It works for us.

Without a full appreciation of this, without acknowledging this miraculous lens on life, Brad's story—all of our stories, perhaps—can only be as sensational as the superficial details we define them by. Without this perspective, we are but the things we do, not the reasons for which we did them. And by that I do not mean the cursory reasons; I mean the unseen reasons, the ones which are only available in retrospect, the ones which show us the connections life has always had planned for us behind our very contrivances. Without this, we are but a rock falling into water, not the force which preceded it to fall in its exact place nor the elements which formed it, nor, most importantly, the wake and ripples by which a beautiful design and an exponential effect are initiated. Without this perspective, our stories are only things told rather than great, sacred, and dynamic forces which were always meant to intersect.

And so, with that addressed, I can distinctly recall looking at Brad standing at the plaque at Camp 4, which lists it on the National Registry of Historic Places, while at the same time looking at the beaming pillars of endless pines. I remember thinking of my father and the smallest fragments of indigenous direction he always sought, and I remember being overwhelmed by it all. It felt as if Brad and I both were there for a reason, though we couldn't yet parse the forest from its trees.

"Let's just ask the first person we see if we can open-bivy on the floor of their campsite tonight," Brad suggested, "and then we'll wake up at four a.m. and hop in the line at the front gate."

Unlikely as it seemed to work, it did. And, as once mentioned, we spent the next few hours during sundown collecting cardboard we could use as sleeping pads for our bivy. Upon a fair harvest, Brad and I laid there on the dirt floor, osmosing history and courage as Brad played an endless series of *Masters of Stone* DVDs on his handheld screen while seemingly every other soul in Camp 4 surrounded themselves with the convivial wafts of firelight and warmth, burning what seemed like endless spliffs of cheap marijuana in cycle with the swashing of King Cobras and bottom shelf swill.

For whatever it was worth at the time, neither of us could have been happier. I remember looking up at the struggling blotches of stars, barely visible behind the spired wings of the tall pines, and thinking back to how Brad and I met in the first place.

Before my parents divorced, around the age of twelve, I walked home from school one non-descript day, opened the mailbox, and had my mind blown much like it was that day at the Tunnel View with Brad. At the time, my father had taken a casual, layman's interest in rock climbing, only to the degree that he and my uncle had a few pieces of gear, a set of carabiners, a cordelette, and one 10.2 mm giant of a rope. They had read a couple chapters in *Mountaineers: Freedom of the Hills* and had taken a course at a local outdoor shop on how to set up a top-rope anchor. Once, maybe twice that year, they went out to Joshua Tree and top-roped what must have been a limit of 5.4 while I stayed home with a child's imagination that inflated their rockcraft to the highest peaks. Soon after, my parents divorced, and with my uncle and father on opposite sides of the rift, they never climbed again.

While I didn't climb with them, the very thought of it for that entire year burned my soul alight. But that day, walking home from school, that's when it truly struck. Given that my dad and his climbing gear had moved out at that point, I'd almost forgotten about the bug. But before moving out, unbeknownst to me, my dad had signed up for a one-year subscription to *Climbing* and *Rock and Ice* magazines. And, in the fortune of the universal order, smack on the cover when I opened the mailbox that day was a shot of Thomas Huber freeing the Salathe Roof pitch with all the world beneath him. Obviously, a wayward kid down in Southern California was the last thing on Thomas Huber's mind when he came straight from Bavaria and made history on the wall, but connections are precisely the point.

It took another twelve years to come to fruition, but the seed had been planted. January of 2007, on another non-descript day where I couldn't say why nor how the thought entered, I found myself driving from the unsung streets of Fullerton, CA, to Costa Mesa, where the only rock gym worth a damn was in operation. I cashed out my bank account, all $700 of it, and signed up for a year-long membership, ready at last to meet the mysterious fragment of my childhood imagination.

Engrossed by the complexities of the movements and

romanced by the culture of its members, I was hooked—so hooked that it took less than two weeks for the gym owners to see I was one of the unfortunate, smitten kind, having attended the gym every day for two weeks straight. As one can imagine, my girlfriend at the time raised her concern about my change in behavior and asked why I wasn't visiting her as much. This I diffused by lying immediately out of my lack of any other life skill. Honesty wouldn't be a suit that fit for another seven or eight years. But, as fortune would have it, those owners offered me that aforementioned belay job at those kids' birthday parties, and I celebrated the offer as a win altogether when I had my membership money refunded and the prospect of a real excuse to be at the gym. I didn't have to lie to the lady anymore, at least not as much. Obviously, I was now just at work all day.

It was with this context that I met Brad Gobright for the first time a week later. I can still see him, completely in his zone, with his staff shirt that he would occasionally tuck in. Those shirts were a thick, over-starched cotton blend in an alarming purple color. For all the hate he often mustered on those entitled kids, Brad was also their energetic equivalent, a mirror to the most rambunctious and awestruck among them. Brad made those parties better for the kids in ways I simply couldn't.

Being a freelancer on life, I walked in a few minutes late to the shift, sporting my staff shirt, which I had already managed to style into some obnoxious version of a V-neck with a pair of scissors, because, well, I was just a bit special in my own mind. The outfit, along with the rest of my mannerisms, begged for recognition that Brad, to my surprise, happened to hand out.

"Hey man," he called out above the clamor of the kids. "Cool shirt."

I'd already seen him in my previous two weeks at the gym,

working the hardest route we had up—a gymnastic 5.14a on a 45-degree overhang—and was both intimidated and impressed by his gusto. I replied with a bashful, "Thanks."

"Hey, you're new here, aren't you?" he asked.

"That's right."

"So, like, what kind of climbing are you into?"

With no reference or vernacular to resource and having no idea of the sub-disciplines and styles that differentiate climbers, I unwittingly replied with a shit grin on my face: "Tall climbing!"

Brad rightfully looked flummoxed and, hoping for more clarification, asked, "That's cool, but what style?"

"Oh man." I blushed red. "I have no idea what you mean. But I'm pretty sure I want to climb El Cap. Does that help?" *Does that help?* I may as well have said the apostles' creed to the minister. Brad couldn't contain himself.

A few weeks later, we were in Joshua Tree, another place that overwhelmed my soul, for our first of many miniature expeditions. With its mystic twilights, erratic alien trees, coarse formations, and drastic contrasts of shadow and light, it welled up within me generations of hidden deoxyribonucleic coding—a sense of aboriginal belonging to a landscape that had long laid dormant in the maze of a messy Mexican history. Joshua Tree was where we learned to climb, but it was also the first place where I began to learn more of who I really was.

But where I was busy on my vision quest, Brad was already on his unlikely path to mastery. All the things I tried to find about myself and my roots when I climbed and sought the pathways of nature, Brad in many ways already had. Perhaps not as mindfully as you'd like, but he was already home in ways I was only learning to be. I tried to hold the magic of my human ancestry when I held the stone out there, as if it were a magician's orb or a storied mirror into a parallel universe that would show me who I was and what I was to become. Brad held it much better. He held the rocks the way Hendrix held the guitar; he didn't think for mystic engagement; he manifested blood and guts with every interface. Brad had elemental connections with climbing that would take me many, many years to understand.

But those were the days, from January to May; that's how we cut some teeth. Next thing I knew, it was summer, Brad was out of high school, and the flatbed of my pickup was filled with a bartered spattering of clothing I called 'outdoor wear,' a guitar, and the lot of Brad's climbing gear, which was perhaps the largest his rack would become, considering how few pieces he'd use to run up his grandest ascents. Beneath it all, to tie the two of us together, a single rope, now twelve years old but only used a few times over, which once belonged to my dad.

I remember passing through Fresno on the freeway, just past the heart of its downtown district and beneath another nondescript bridge, at which point you can see a placard framing the logo for Highway 41 Northbound, with one single word beneath it: YOSEMITE.

Brad pulsed into a sudden glee, snapped a picture—the first one on his camera roll—twisted his thumb beside the shutter to wind up to the next frame, and looked over at me from the passenger seat with a grin bigger than his giant forehead.

"It's going to blow you away!" he laughed. "God, I'm so psyched."

When Brad Gobright and I crossed paths that day in that Costa Mesa climbing gym, it was one hundred percent a simple relationship of happenstance—nothing more than a short-term, mutually convenient engagement. No way you could have convinced either of us there was something like design stitched between the nylon cord that held us together those first days in Joshua Tree, Tahquitz, and the Royal Arches in Ahwahne. But years later, perspective changes.

In fact, when it comes to roots and Brad's entire act of becoming, our intersection was only the tip of the iceberg. As unlikely events go, Brad's parents take the cake. And, for the sake of further context, to dig the roots and put hand to soil, the story of Pamela and Jim is just as compelling as the last climb Brad ever fashioned in his time with us. Their story is as much a part of Brad's story as anything. In fact, it *is* his story. Who they were, how they met, and the life they set out to live had everything to do with who and what Brad Gobright became.

Summer, 1980. Disco was dead. New wave was on the radio waves, punk, reggae, stadium rock, and everything in between was on the rise. Stevie Wonder sang "Hotter than July," U2's "Boy" was debuting, as were albums by The Cure, Joy Division, The Gap Band, Donna Summers—the list goes on. Smokey Robinson, who Jim had lived next door to growing up back in Detroit, was one year on from the release of the summer ballad of the decade, "Cruisin'," which was still the slow dance of choice. Somewhere in the mix, on any given night at the Red Onion, the local discothèque and beach bar at Huntington Harbor, CA, you could dance to all of it. Wild, unabashed, sweaty nights with neon lights, jerry curls, and miles of denim were *en-vogue*, and at the Red Onion, you could get it all in spades. Modern kids, eat your hearts out; while society at large was naïve and less than inclusive, in a lot of ways this was the era you'll always wish you had.

Jim's mother, his anchor point since losing his dad at the young age of four, lived just behind the car park of the bar, and Jim, a space rocket of vitality at the ripe age of twenty-four, single, and fresh out of college, was on the prowl.

"I went down there that night because why not? You know," he recalled with a grin. "I figured I'd just hang with the locals before the music got on. But then, Jesus, in walks this girl, and, wow. A minute passed, you know, enough time for me to think about it, and when she passed by again, I was set. I knew I had to talk to her."

Jim introduced himself first upon meeting the twenty-one-year-old Pamela. Surprised but equally enamored, Pamela, who was on a happenstance summer vacation in Southern California where her dad and stepmother lived, obliged for a drink and a dance. As a girl from the east coast, a hot fling in the heat of summer out on the west coast was just the cliché she'd have imagined for anyone other than herself. But here, neon lights and new wave soundtrack bouncing off the subwoofer, greyhound or California chardonnay in hand, a summer romance was exactly in front of her.

"We really danced that night away," she laughed. "We exchanged numbers, had a ball, and ended up going on three damn good dates that summer."

If it sounds old-fashioned, that's because it was. But it was real, too. There were three wondrous dates, one of which was on a boat in the local marina. Pamela and Jim stayed on deck until sundown, which is how the Golden State gets its name, when the epitome of romantic vision strikes in the form of long shadows cast over the endless Pacific Ocean at twilight. Pamela was enamored.

After that, Pamela went back to university in Ohio and finished her last year of study, during which for the first handful of months she and Jim stayed in touch the old-fashioned way, by snail mail. Jim, who lived a frisbee's throw from the Newport Beach Pier in a bachelor's apartment, often took pictures of the view from his headboard, which looked directly out over that same Pacific Ocean they'd sparked their romance from. Pamela recalls how she and her girlfriends would work up into a frenzy back at school when the mail came in and "that hot flame from California" would write in with those warm photographs.

After a few months, though, the flame cooled, and nature took its course. Both began seeing other people, many of whom had the potential for a serious long-term suit. By Christmas, the well had run dry; no more contact, no flame. Neither of them, it seemed, carried a great concern for their course without one another. But, as fortune would have it, 1981 had plans. Pamela, once out of school, found a job posting in California, one she felt unqualified for compared to the hundreds of other applicants. Still, she applied on the off chance. It wasn't just Jim who'd left his mark on her—California had, too. It was new, exciting, different, and she still had her father and his wife to visit anyway.

In the course of a few weeks, Pamela got the one-in-a-million job offer, took it, and on one of those non-descript, one-in-a-million days, happened to be walking around Newport Beach with her dad and stepmother for a promenade.

"I just happened to mention to my stepmom, 'Hey, this is where that guy I met last summer lives,'" Pamela recalled. "My stepmom insisted that I leave Jim a note, and God knows, otherwise I'm certain I wouldn't have. So that's what I did, I wrote him a note and just said, 'Hey, it's me, Pamela from last summer. I'm here in California now, working, and you should call me.'"

Jim called, quicker than expected. Though contact was restored, it was a delicate kind. Both were protecting their hearts. It had, after all, been a full year. In that time, they'd both made connections with others. And, as it turns out, it was exactly Jim's relationship with another woman that would help steer him back toward Pamela.

Of course, with much of life, it didn't seem that way at the time.

It was a Saturday during peak wedding season, and Jim had invited Pam to be his plus-one for a friend's wedding in town. Pamela, elated at the opportunity, had her dress and her accompanying accessories—her purse, earrings, and necklace—all sorted and at the ready. The only problem was, when she called Jim that morning and asked when to come over, Jim fumbled.

"He just rolled right over his own tongue," Pamela laughed, "'Urrg, uhmm.' Turns out he had invited two of us to that wedding. Me and some other girl he'd been seeing, and when he told me about it, especially that he was going to be taking the other girl, you bet your ass I'd had enough. I was done with him. He made it easy at that point." Pamela smiled.

But, sure enough, that fumble of Jim's was the needed impetus for the love story to spark. A week later, Jim called Pamela on hands and knees, penitent as your first confession, and begged for another chance. It's a shameful plea, and everybody has their own version of it, so fill in your own imagery, but begging for another person's heart is just a fact of life. We all do it.

For whatever reason, kindness perhaps, Pamela took Jim at his word and gave him one final shot, which created the space for them to get together a few times over several months. During that time, they kept guarded hearts, Pamela especially. Eventually, the critical mass had to go one way or the other, and once again the pendulum would swing from an unlikely outside force.

Jim had invited Pamela to join him for a company work party, one of those old-school, all-day hangouts at a park with Bellini's, wine spritzers, and grilled hotdogs. Categorical as it may have been, it was there that Jim first introduced Pamela to his mother. And while Jim took a break from that awkward first conversation between the three of them by stepping off to join his mates for an impromptu baseball game, his mom was the one loading the bases.

Pamela recalls, "Jim's mom just came right out the moment he left us together and said it, 'I'm just so glad to meet you, dear. You know, you are all Jimmy talks about these days!'"

Jim blushed as Pamela retold the story, then deferred, saying, "You know, Mom was the ultimate marketer, a real matchmaker. Because, you know, she was just lining it up for the grandkids."

But it worked.

"I got way more aggressive with Jim after that," Pamela continued, adding, "I called him, a lot. I made sure we went on dates often. And I let him in." An easy thing to do when Jim swept her off her feet in ways she'd never known.

Growing up on the east coast, Pamela recalls, the closest thing to an outside life was going to the pool in summer. Often, time was spent in air-conditioned public spaces like the mall, the movies, or a museum. Her folks weren't the type to adventure outdoors, and for that reason, neither was she. But Jim was the opposing force, a compass pointing outside. He was also a meticulous planner, and the preparedness he kept when planning their hikes went great distances to convince Pamela that she could have adventure, too.

Jim's knack for adventure and his attention to detail were born from trials. As mentioned, Jim's father passed when he was only four, which left him solo for the task of his becoming. He was mostly alone in his youth, which gave him a space to explore his curiosities and learn to be self-sufficient. Not the self-sufficiency that fails us all in the end, when we realize our powerlessness to reverse the hands of time or to avoid the pains of life, or to move the mountain of our own inner turmoil. Jim learned the self-sufficiency of discipline and the necessity of creating order to manifest your goals in life. This engineer's mind, which eventually plotted him a course in landscape architecture, enabled him to explore the outside world successfully.

As for his wildness of heart, according to Jim, that, too, came as a result of the pain. I can testify personally that many of us who are drawn to the outside revelation are driven so because we lack both the structure and the guidance of more traditional family circles. We go to it for lack of another place to learn of ourselves, of who we are, of where we fit, of what we must become.

Jim's best traits, those gathered in the wake of life's calamities, made a huge impact on Pamela. In the first year together, they hiked the cable route to the top of Tis-sa-ack (Half Dome), they hiked to the top of Tumanguya (Mount Whitney), and they trekked a dozen miles into the heart of the Grand Canyon, the epicenter of Dineh (Navajo) and many other indigenous lands, at Havasupai. Pamela and Jim fell in love inch by inch, one milestone at a time.

Years later, while Jim and Pamela would both hold a strong tension bordering on disapproval of what Brad did and how we went on living (mostly the stealing), much of it was reflexive. There is a clear line in the ethos of how they met and what they did together that is connected to who Brad was and how he best found self-expression. They raised him with it. Not long after Brad could walk, even, they went back to Havasupai, where Jim hiked the trail out and back, some twenty-odd miles, with Brad and their camping gear saddled on his back.

Jim even said, "Well, thinking back on Brad, I'm completely sure now that he got that spirit for adventure from the both of us. I mean, he took it to a place we couldn't imagine, you know. But there's no doubt we gave him the spark. We planted his roots."

FOUNDATION

A week before what would have been Brad's thirty-third birthday, I took a trip up to Ahwahne (Yosemite) to find a parcel of his presence. So much of who he was and what he did—not just what he climbed but also the people he forged relationships with—all started and sustained itself here. Springtime in the Valley is majestic. Always has been. Lengthening days give light to vibrant new shoots of pine needles, which reach out with flickering fingers to the sky. Sunbeams crisscross the corridors from north, south, east, and west at the end of the day as one long timelapse, while the Merced River feeds outcrops of brush, the occasional maple, and the tall California sequoia. The walls themselves, the living fragments of eons of natural history, glow almost distinctly, each in their own fashion, appealing would-be suitors.

With the help of a handful of Brad's longtime friends, namely Jim Reynolds—with whom he climbed The Nose faster than any human at that point had—and Mason Earle—with whom he established the Heart Route on To-tock-ah-noo-lah (El Cap)—I've triangulated his old bivy zone. For years, beginning not long after the close of that gas cap in 2008, Brad made these rockpiles, which sit a five-minute hike from the main road, his home. For me, being within days of his birthday and having spent the spring with his family and friends, collecting interviews, it didn't feel right to pass within one hundred miles of the Valley and not make a visit.

More than a climbing sanctuary, the boulder field Brad called home is a climber's sanctuary, and historically, Brad was not the only one to put it to full use. As sure as you'll find a drunk on the same barstool sloshing the same pint every day at your nearest dive, you'll still find a dirtbag-in-the-making every year, every climbing season, up in these boulder fields. According to Jim Reynolds, who has spent many a night in the same outcrop, at peak season there's even something of a 'musical chairs' between bivy sites. That's because, even with all that real estate, there are only so many plush caves, flat bedding spots, and agreeable post holes that aren't too far a hike from the car park. In peak season, it's common for a good dirtbag to swipe into your spot during the night or two it would take for you to climb a big wall such as To-tock-ah-noo-lah.

But where for many seasons over the prime bivvies of the boulder fields were stolen and used for trade, Brad's spot, humble as it may be, was almost exclusively known as his. In his own way, Brad was a legend out there. And, short of Fred Beckey, most the kids up there saw Brad as the all-time dirtbag—so much so that when planting a flag in the Valley for a season, most everybody knew better than to swipe in on Brad's home base. That said, Brad was always on-premises before anyone else, often arriving a full month ahead of the recognized climbing season. More times than not, he'd keep camp longer, too, usually staying well into the hot weeks of summer and well past the cold spells of fall. Combine that with the fact that Brad almost exclusively climbed everything, including the innumerable ascents he took up the Big

Stone, in a push, in a single day, and there wouldn't have been time for anyone to swipe in on him anyway. So, for years running, that little plot of granite and soil was as close to his in ownership as anything could be.

These days, Brad's bivy still stands as its own outcrop of history. Cast away from the famous sites of Camp 4, the boulder field—quiet, humble, astray—has both an eerie nostalgia and the comfort of a place he called home. Like any historical site, there's a certain energy about it, a magic that's easy to romanticize. But if you spend a few minutes with it, especially on a hot summer's day, you might feel otherwise.

In fact, the first thing you'll learn about Brad's bivy, as I did, is that it doesn't take long for the mosquitoes to overthrow the romance. Second, if you crawl down into the bivy and lay for long enough that the rocks start sticking into your back, you'll notice there are hordes of ants with bodies bigger than the nuts in your trail mix, all too eager to start comingling with you in their rightful home, which you've clearly mistaken as your own. But that's not the main event in this domicile. Those ants, of course, are only the preamble to the ashen, ghostly-looking bark spiders that slip in and out of the nooks where you'd lay your head—where Brad laid his head—night after night. That's what Brad called home. Often, even when he could have gone elsewhere, when he had other options, that was his abode.

Like that moment up on the Naked Edge, if we are to understand him at all, we've got to lay right there with him. We've got to take that all in, consciously, then imagine doing it without a dollar to our names, for years on end, all while sore, tired, and with open blisters on our hands and feet most days of the week. We've got to remember that just sleeping in that bivy was an act of illegality. We've got to consider that Brad must have always slept with one eye open, hoping that sunrise would come sooner than the glare of a ranger's flashlight in his face, and sooner still than when a black bear would wake him by curiously clawing about the den.

I sat in the boulder field that day thinking of him, of our first climbs together all those years ago, overwhelmed by what he managed in such a short period of time. I asked myself if I ever once burned with as much desire for the high and lonesome expression as he did. I asked if I would have ever been willing to burn all the bridges behind me for this rocky piece of real estate.

Laying in his bivy zone at high noon on a June afternoon, I felt Brad close. I understood that to fully appreciate Brad's course and his outstanding *curriculum vitae*, you've got to be in touch with a modicum of high-performance climbing. You've got to hang out in high places, you must, to some degree, know what it is to execute desperately hard moves over small protective gear, to touch incomprehensibly small nubbins while stuck in a cold sweat, to pulse with your entirety at the next hold above you. You've got to know at least a taste of what it all requires physiologically.

But you've also got to dig, not just climb. Just as important as it is to dwell in the remote, high spaces he called home, you've got to sink into ground level. To understand Brad Gobright and the light he brought to Earth, you've got to lay your head where he did.

Nothing happens overnight, of course, and neither did Brad's becoming. When he set out from Orange County in 2008, he managed to land a job working with the Delaware North Company, who up until 2015 had exclusive rights to concessions and hospitality services in the Park. It was, and remains today, one of those multi-faceted, international, white-collar manifestations of capitalism with teeth. It wasn't exactly a charitable organization. With a profile like that and a character like Brad in the shuffle, among the 50,000 other employees, it is amazing that he lasted as long as he did.

In his first season as a bellhop and room cleaner, Brad had a strong working relationship with his immediate supervisors and the hotel management, but it did not assuage the contempt he held for the job and the corporation itself. Of the corporation, Brad felt it was at least partially to blame for Ahwahne, his beloved sanctuary, becoming something like a public theme park. Ahwahne was sacred for Brad; it was where climbers came to bridge the expanse between gods and men. For Brad, corporations in the Valley tainted that dimension because, in addition to the throngs of tourists, they also brought in the stench of profit-hungry business models; he became intimately familiar with the artifice of overripe, Candyland smiles and see-through sincerity folded behind the starched collars of the hospitality industry. Corporations brought not only the layfolk to the Valley, but the suits, the lawyers, and the c-suites, too—a branch of society that Brad had *apriori* decided was not for his course and which did not manifest anything like light into this earth.

On the job itself, Brad did not enjoy much of his workload. The people he worked with were the glue, or at least the grease in the machine, and he got on well with most of them. Often, because their suffering is shared, coworkers in any form of the service industry are bound by their co-misery. But while cleaning rooms, sanitizing toilets, cleaning puke, and even cleaning soggy excrement from the floor, Brad was short on co-workers to lean on. Stuck on hands and knees with the end result of a stranger's emesis crusted into the carpet, Brad, as any of us would have, struggled for that wax on, wax off perspective. The menial wages he received did not help, either.

Workload considered, it was a challenge for Brad to prioritize a punctual record or even attendance at every shift. In his first season, things managed fine. But, by 2009, on his second anchorage at the Ahwahnee Hotel, Brad was running out of motivation and running into disciplinary actions. It's one thing to hate your job, but when your hated job is prime in the center cut of the climbers' universe, there's only so much you can take. How would a surfer feel about smudging a tourist's shit off the floor while a ten-foot pipeline is thundering down the block? Or a ski-bum, not pouring drinks, but cleaning toilets, at the chalet while blankets of new powder cascade across Squaw Valley? Of course he was conflicted. He wasn't trying to be a rebel, with or without a cause. But with tourists recycling in droves each weekend, with the endless supply chain motoring in by semi-truck all night, he just didn't know what to make of the whole circus. How could he passively watch the place he called home move toward such disrepair?

Brad, of course, wasn't the first to call Ahwahne home. The Ahwahneechee before us knew all too well, and still know of this pathos. While respect for human history, the aboriginal lands, and its caretakers has come to some inflection point in recent years, a focus on humanitarian equilibrium has not historically been a function of the Western rock climber. The truth is, climbers were not always the best caretakers, nor land-stewards. In many ways, we, too, had teeth as sharp and track records as offensive as the institutions that not only Brad, but many of the outdoors community, have come to loathe.

Respect for the indigenous peoples, their histories, and the ecological balance they kept in what Westerns call climbing spaces was not a part of traditional climbing history. Western rock climbing has a deep history akin to Western colonial history, where the white, Western protagonist looks, at least in one lens, a lot like the entitled kids Brad so loathed and the devilish company he so bitterly worked for. I'm not sure if Brad ever thought about his pursuits of climbing between these broader storylines; just like most, up until recently, I hadn't either. I do think he was as respectful to things of the sort as he could have been. He spent most of his childhood, largely his life even, as an outsider, which gave him a natural empathy for those deemed "less than." At the same time, he'd later call himself a "near-sighted dirtbag" for much of his life, indicting himself as having assumed many of these Western entitlements.

What Brad *did* know was that every time he had a job, whether belaying kids or cleaning hotel rooms, he was a part of something that ostensibly took the soul out of the lifestyle he so loved. For my money, that was at least a contributing factor to why he went so hard and fast out there. There are many such accounts of people in the service industries doing exactly as he did. In the restaurant industry alone, entire histories and traditions have been born from people who, whether as chefs, line cooks, or servers, ran wild in all kinds of directions, determined to party harder and live louder, or just completely apart from the lifestyles of the wealthy they were subservient to. On plenty of occasions, that has landed many a man, woman, or non-binary person into despair. Whereas for Brad, it mostly only led him up and away. It drove him, near obsessively, not only to seek the highest walls but also to pursue all the rudiments of a wild life—elements in his story we'll soon cover. It drove him to camp anywhere he could, to eat whatever it took, to take pride in the beater Honda Civic when he had every opportunity to upgrade along the way.

Brad's exposure to the consumer side of the outdoors kept him, at least partially, on the plane of the contrarian. He was the antithesis of corporate America. In his own way, there was always something deeply rebellious about him. The essentially punk rock thing to do would have been to work within the system, to *change* the system, which, because of the compassion, patience, and tact required, few ever do. But in his own way, just by holding pattern until the day he died, he kind of applied that function, too. That's where the Greco-cynicism came in.

In recovery circles, they tend to say that you wouldn't let your vice do all that it does *to* you unless you've first felt what it can do *for* you. Why else would you work for a company you despise, end up stealing as a lifestyle, or abandon the morals and etiquette endowed by your family for a life in the boulder fields? Why else would you rent literal closet space from a band of stoners for a few hundred dollars a month, live off a donut diet, and keep your bills, your credit line, your car, and all else of duty in disrepair? Why else sleep as an outlaw on the run? To climb, of course. To take gravity and life itself to the hilt.

For Brad, though, to climb—at least superficially—was not just about the act of moving one's body over a vertical expanse. It was about more than ascent alone, just as it was about more than a simple escape. It was to *feel*, to be, something different, something more than what he knew as normal. Giant walls and ropeless climbs notwithstanding, I think nearly every member of the human race can understand at least that much of its appeal.

To understand what drove Brad, though, we've got to understand what it did for him. We need to know what it made him feel, which is to first understand what he felt without it. *Before* it. We need to also understand how he first came into climbing. We need to learn what the first outside experiences were like for him so we may see what kind of foundations they laid.

Often, the larger the character becomes, the more their achievements are celebrated rather than their reasons. In Brad's case, climbing media couldn't help but look at his results—all those ridiculous free-climbs up To-tock-ah-noo-lah, for instance—more than his internal targets. It's just a function of the industry. But family and those who watched his entire arc were able to see behind the veil. For that reason, it is at the family level where much of his story will be shared.

By his early twenties, it was Brad's penchant for theft, combined with his habit of getting caught doing it, that worried his parents most. Pile that on top of what his parents saw as his lack of meaningful friendships, his listless approach to pursuing a purpose in society, and the thought that any next climb, especially his growing number of solo climbs, could be his last—it plagued them. Pam and Jim worried, because while at that time he was indeed a "near-sighted dirtbag" and could not look beyond the next bend in the road, *they* could. They didn't want him to change course completely, as it was clear that climbing did for him what so many other sports, relationships, creative outlets, and institutions could not. Instead, for the sheer singularity of his quest, they worried that somewhere far down the line, he might just come to regret not reaching out for the other spoils life had to offer.

The beginnings of Brad's full expression out on the walls, to Pamela and Jim's despair, was also the beginning of what Brad himself would later call his misdirection. Pamela and Jim had raised Brad to embrace an adventurous lifestyle, but not to fall slave to the trappings of the dirtbagging culture that came with it. It was in these parts of his character formation, in the swindling, derelict, and at times unlawful scope of the climbing culture that concerned Pamela the most. She reflected that while she understood Brad must get his wings and fly, she worried—given the direction of his mannerisms and by what she saw as the forming of a dishonest character—if he'd ever come back.

Recall, Brad wasn't out there in open rebellion against his parents. Though all of us reject parts of what we are born into, this wasn't about that. Brad hadn't come from a broken home and he didn't have a credo that he was specifically for or against apart from climbing and what it did for him. He wasn't on a purge against society, nor was he desperate to free himself of his parents or their best intentions. Even if those things were true, his parents would have seen them as understandable causes. It's healthy for all to raise certain questions of life and to forge their own identity, Pamela and Jim believed. It wasn't the questions they had issue with, anyway. Being loving parents, wanting only the best for their boy, it was his lack of direction that scared them the most. How had he gone from that sweet, imaginative boy to the one pinching food, homeless, and struggling to keep a job?

Jim often thought back to their first expedition together, and the many other times he'd guided Brad outside, with a certain confusion. He'd only ever had the best intentions of getting Brad to love the outdoors. Hell, he was the first one to take him there. He never expected it would drive Brad so unilaterally; he couldn't have seen it then. Just as Jim and Pamela also couldn't have seen, in 2008, 2009, and 2010, how Brad's path would inevitably inspire so many others. The dots rarely connect facing forward.

There was nothing memorable about the day that changed Brad's life, right up until the point at which it all happened. It was a Tuesday. Just another day. Brad was six and had already perplexed almost everyone in his life with his mannerisms, particularly his seeming lack of concern for life. In school, he continually struggled to read and write, just as he struggled to aptly express himself. But then it happened.

Brad and Jim were out running errands when Jim remembered a potentially fun event. A friend had told him that at the local REI, just a few miles from home in Santa Ana, there was an artificial climbing wall and that on Tuesday nights from about 6:00 p.m. until closing, the staff would belay kids up the wall for free. What began in a board room as a way to get foot traffic in the store on the hypothesis that it would drive more sales turned out to be the birth of an American rock-climbing legend. Brad walked in with his Pop, slapped on a pair of rented and oversized shoes along with a full-body harness, and, while climbing for his first time, found the same thing Robert Hooke had under that old piece of cork. It wasn't just discovery, it was revelation. It wasn't just novelty, it was order itself—purpose, even.

Brad climbed that Tuesday evening until the staff could belay him no longer and Jim insisted they get home for dinner where Pamela and his younger sister, Jill, were waiting. But Brad wasn't satisfied. No number of routes that night—or for the remaining course of his life—were ever going to be enough. According to Jim, it was the same on day one as it would be until the end.

By and large, he was hardly challenged by it, at least not physically the way the flock of other kids were. And for the most part, Brad excelled far above the lot of them in both willingness to hang on and in his talent. Jim remembers being pleased, proud as a parent could be, and thoroughly flooded with relief. To see Brad connecting, thriving even, with something new was overwhelming. At last, he was no longer struggling. But where Jim slept on an easy conscience that night, Brad stayed wide awake. He needed more.

A few weeks later, what would've felt like ages to Brad, they returned, this time with Jim's wallet at the ready. They bought Brad his first shoes, harness, chalkbag, and even a set of carabiners. Just as he had before, Brad ran laps around the other kids in attendance, which Jim and Pamela took as an indication that Brad could use a more focused environment. Not long after, they drove a few miles down the freeway to that old gym, Rockreation, in Costa Mesa, and signed him up for a weeklong summer camp.

When Brad walked into the gym, he was immediately taken,

as many are, by the imposing 30-foot-tall and 50-foot-wide lead arch. He was taken by the staff, with their casual, perma-stoned personas, their constant stoke, and their inspiring climbers' vernacular. He was also taken by the shirtless locals and climbing bums who patterned chalkdust across plastic holds and brushed boulder problems with strict intention. He was taken by all of it.

All of six years old, Brad was swept off his feet. In the back break room, where the summer camp kids would gather for their mid-morning snack and midday lunch, a small television set and an old VCR played a series of rock climbing videos on loop. Often, Brad would spend as much time watching these montage reels as he would climbing. Transfixed, he'd soak up every ounce of environmental stimulus, including the floor-to-ceiling painting of To-tock-ah-noo-lah that canvased the entire break room. It was always there, staring back at him.

If we go back to that red school project binder that Pamela dug up and turn the page just after the deep-sea diving testimonial, we see evidence of Brad's first touch to this side of life. Written in chicken scratch is Brad's ode to climbing. He's even got a hand-sketched picture of himself as a stick figure, up on a wall, ropes attached. We all know now just how wide and far Brad would go, but what makes that journal so special is that it marks his moment of transition. Pamela reflected that Brad's marine biology passion would continue for a few years further, but he'd never again be so enamored with the ocean as he was in the years before he found climbing. In that red school binder, Brad showed us the beginning of a series of defining chapters. The first of those would be written upon the tallest peak in the contiguous United States, Tumanguya, also called Mount Whitney.

As goes first outside experiences, few people, let alone kids, make them count the way Brad did. The next summer, at the age of seven, one year after finding climbing, Brad made up his mind to get outside in search of a proper peak. He'd experienced a modicum of outdoor living with the Boy Scouts, but those ventures hadn't gone past a few brief hikes, a handful of miles at best, which was considered a stress test enough for kids of that age group. It would be some time before Pamela and Jim would allow Brad outside for a proper rock climb. So in the meanwhile, Jim considered big hikes—what he would call robust experiences—worthwhile pursuits to hold Brad over. At the least, he could use them to fashion a bit more toughness out of Brad. Still in the middle to lower percentiles for his age group in terms of height and weight curves, Brad was scrawnier than most, though in the mountains he was worth every ounce of salt.

Convincing Pamela that they'd likely just hike a third of the way up the Mount Whitney trail to the Outpost Camp at roughly 10,000 feet, Jim got the green light for the mission. It would be an early summer, high-residual snowpack affair, and Brad couldn't be happier. Jim and Brad spent one night in Lone Pine, getting comfortable, though not getting acclimatized at only 4,000 feet elevation. In the morning—not alpine early, but early enough—they departed the Whitney Portal loop at the trailhead and sauntered up those harshly steep initial miles out of the Portal. For anyone who has been up there, you'd know the landscape by all the striking diversity it offers. For Brad, it was a new world entirely. Coming from the urban sprawl, Brad hadn't seen aspen groves nor those secret pockets of ferns that propagate at the shaded switchbacks and creek crossings. He hadn't seen panels of lichen-covered walls of granite, nor, to his surprise, the blinding patches of alpine snow high above the tree line, which contrasted those rich and buttery blue skies. He was captivated.

Before long they were three and a half miles and 2,000 vertical feet up the trail, at the Outpost Camp some 10,400 feet above sea level. Brad, barely visible from behind the silhouette of his hiking pack, which was the same size as he was, pressed onward, setting the pace. Jim was more than happy to see Brad take the lead, curious to see how he'd respond both to the environment's beauty and its demands. He was also curious to see if Brad would get to a breaking point, and if so, to witness how he'd navigate it on low reserves.

"Let's keep going, Dad."

They did. With a few water breaks, they endured another three miles and 1,600 more feet, vertically, to the footsteps of Trail Camp. Six miles in, past the mythic vista of the Whitney zone overlook, Mirror Lake, and the Trail Side meadows, Brad could've kept on, and surely would have but for the lack of daylight to summit safely. Jim admitted to me that as evening approached, he was knackered, and given they'd gone further than expected, he even made Brad an offer.

"I told him, straight up," Jim laughed from the backyard porch. "I said, 'Hey bud, how about you and me camp here tonight and enjoy some stars. When we wake up tomorrow, we'll head back into town, play the arcades, and get all the pizza you can eat.'"

"Maybe," seven-year-old Brad replied. "But I think I'd rather keep hiking up."

Of course, the next morning, more hiking up was exactly what they did. Brad, the perennial pizza bum—even in his adulthood—had no appetite for carbohydrates or even the arcades. When Jim tells the story, he still looks perplexed, unsure how to categorize it or consolidate the facts. You get the sense that he still wants to decode that operating system, whatever it was, that Brad ran on.

Jim talks a bit like John Long, like a classic old-timer, as he orates his stories, so you can imagine both the oakiness and fullness of his cadence when he laughed as he said, "I mean, what kid, what kind of kid, on this earth, at seven years old, would turn down something as God-given as pizza and the arcade all afternoon? Who does that?"

For most of his bright life, as we see it now, Brad was only ever going in one direction up there. At daybreak, Brad and Jim traipsed ahead during the sunrise and alpenglow, on the shoulder of the ridgeline, with Brad mostly setting the pace. They scurried as quickly as they could up the infamous ninety-nine switchbacks, the stoutest run in the gauntlet to the top, in a fashion that impressed every other hiker on the trail. Just above the Trail Pass, before the junction with the Nüümü Poyo (John Muir Trail), they stopped for water and caloric intake, where Jim noted that things finally began to turn.

"You know, Brad started to struggle, at last," he shared. "With breathing, mostly. He looked over at me with his water bottle at one point and I realized, dammit, this kid is turning blue in the face. There were even a couple of folks next to us who started asking me about it, and they made their opinions on the matter pretty clear. They basically called it child abuse at that point. But I asked the little runt if he wanted to keep going and you don't have to guess what his answer was. I was worried for him, but we pressed on," Jim finished.

Past the Trail Crest and off the leeward side of the mountain, into the Sequoia National Forest they continued. At the base of the final stretch, Jim and Brad passed the iconic Windows, those narrow slot corridors between the spires of the Keeler Needle, Crook's peak, and the neighboring pinnacles—peering down more than 1,000 feet vertically with each outlet on the path. Up there, finally in line of sight with the summit proper, Jim says Brad charged on without any need for support. Jim didn't have to push him, carry him, or even verbally cheer Brad on. He just had to keep up.

Finally, hours after departing, somewhere near midday, a seven-year-old Brad Gobright and his father, Jim, summited the tallest peak in the lower 48. Brad would be the youngest name in that summit registry that season by a long shot. Hell of a lot better than a day at the arcade. According to Jim, Brad was over the moon, and just as blue, glowing through his hypoxic lips, curling his cheeks into that classic grin.

It would take them the remainder of the day and the early part of the evening to make their way back to the trailhead, but they paused the frames up on the summit as long as they needed. They enjoyed the fruits of their labor.

Years later, not long before he passed, Brad would still bring up that trip with his dad during times of reflection. It was a monumental summit, a small window in time where father and son—impossible as it would be in the future—saw eye to eye. Brad was all of three-and-a-half feet tall, Jim roughly 5'9", but as far as they would both call it, years later, they each stood at 14,505'. Brad and Jim would struggle to recapture that kind of unison in adulthood, given the misdirection which lay ahead, but based on that memory alone, they'd always believe it possible.

It is obvious to us now, in retrospect, that this inaugural climb was nature's first touch with Brad; that it set him on a trajectory that would later include some of the boldest, tallest, and fastest ascents in Western history. But what's important for us to better grasp Brad Gobright's bursting heart isn't that we see where that climb would lead him in the future—what's important is that we see where it took him that exact day. What's important is that we see how Brad was taken, raptured by the outside landscape, in a way he hadn't known from life in the lowlands. The imperative onus, on us, is that we see how transfixed he was by whatever lay across the next bend in the trail, or up further into the crest of a rising ridgeline. Just as we need to be the ones able to see how categorically unique it was that he wanted to dwell at elevations and among places that a select few others might only want to visit. Looking at these cornerstones, we can see that for Brad, the absolute truth was that there was a magic world outside the front door, and for whatever it had to show, he wanted to align himself with it.

Much later, when he'd suggest that simply being up on To-tock-ah-noo-lah at sunrise or sunset was among the best things he could do with his time on Earth—you knew it began right there, on Tumanguya. You can also see, by Jim's testament, that being up there did for Brad what all those other efforts at sports, school, and friendships even could not. It allowed him the freedom to be. It shed the pinning self-awareness of his deficits. It gave him a deftness where for so long he'd only had difficulty. Nothing in the social or academic order could have compared, not even close. That first trip was fundamental for all the things it gave him. But if you ask Jim, it was most important because of who it was with and for the togetherness by which it was fashioned. It was the closest thing to pure father and son bonding they'd get for a long while. Up there, Brad and his dad saw eye to eye. Put all those elements together, what it did for him and how it made his folks proud, and of course it turned out the way it did! He was only ever going to go in one direction from there—the foundations were laid.

APPROACH

Once Brad found climbing, save for a short tenure with BMX biking in adolescence, he was transfixed. If climbing was the medicine, or minimally a tonic for all that ailed him, then he saw an ascent up To-tock-ah-noo-lah as the ultimate prescription. The layers of granite packed into that behemoth were a simple matter of spiritual epitome for Brad, as they have been for many others. It is an overused concept, this idea of epitome, by many a mountain climber to explain an attraction to the high spaces for which human language does not suffice. But Brad's climbing, from the very inception, didn't need the metaphor. For its revelation and the connectivity it provided, climbing was his means of deliverance. It was always going to be a tool to make sense of the physical, emotional, and mental sides of life. And to that point, the Big Stone was always going to be his tabernacle. So, spiritual epitome, indeed.

The seeds had long since been planted. They were there in all the videos he watched, in those *Masters of Stone* catalogs that followed Lynn Hill, Dean Potter, and countless others up the most famous rock climb in the world: The Nose. Watching his heroes glide hand-over-hand up the plated slivers of the Pancake Flake on film wasn't Brad's only exposure to the power of that rock. For years, Brad chummed up with nearly all the staff and members of the climbing gym who had their own tales of grand ascents up there, too. And for most of his youth, Brad talked about these climbs and the people who climbed them the way his classmates would talk about Atticus Finch or Holden Caulfield: as legends, icons, archetypes.

Brad's approach to To-tock-ah-noo-lah would take years, perhaps more years than he'd have liked. But then again, that approach went both ways. His wasn't the only journey taken in that dance with destiny. To-tock-ah-noo-lah, carved out by a zillion years of glacial formation and the titanic weave of interconnected earth systems, had also taken some time for its priming. It sat there for God only knows how long, just for the tiniest percentage of vertical explorers to one day, finally, have the tools and the skillset to climb it. The plot does move that way, after all. Though we often think otherwise. Truth is, that stone moved as much toward his life as he did toward it.

As bystanders, it's important to realize that only a few thousand human beings—perhaps even only a few hundred—have ever climbed To-tock-ah-noo-lah, even among the millions who have stood beneath it, or the billions who have lived in human history. Much less common than it might appear, a human climbing upon or standing atop the summit of the mighty To-tock-ah-noo-lah is not as ubiquitous as this digital, internet age would have us believe. The fact that marketing firms and social media algorithms have propagated images of vertical crusaders into our newsfeeds and advertising windows does not mean that it is a feat of common achievement. By the numbers, climbing To-tock-ah-noo-lah might be a short, close second to the number of humans who've been in orbit. Surely, in the years to come, it may even be rarer. So, by dispelling the notion that a human soul ought to ever get used to the idea that we have any business climbing rocks the size of oceans, it's worthwhile for us to understand that every ascent up the Big Stone is something of holy singularity.

Before we even touch the first pitch of The Nose with Brad Gobright, it's important that we approach that rock with respect for all the might and impossibility innate to it. It is necessary we see it the way he saw it, as something incredible, unbelievable. As something that, like him, was against all odds. As we follow Brad in his quest to at first become an "El Cap Climber," and eventually a true master of its realm, we need to keep that awareness, just as he did—that human beings had no business up there in the first place. Mathematically speaking, the odds of a rock like that and a person like him ever turning millions of years of cosmic evolution into a face-to-face meet-up—let alone into something balletic, artistic, transcendent—were only one single hairline above absolute zero. It was downright miraculous, at least ala the Einsteinian, *all of this is a miracle or none of it is,* placeholder, and it stood, right there, just beside the road and right out his window, calling him into communion.

It's my belief that we should keep that frame in mind to fully understand the magic that was on offer up there, just as we would be well-served to keep those odds in mind, too. We'll better feel what Brad felt when we come to the places he came knowing that only the smallest percentage of humans, that fraction within the fraction, ever got there in the first place. Surely, it'll help us through those cold and icy nights sleeping under rocks, which of course he did, year after year. So long as we remember those numbers, so long as we hold the singularity of those experiences, so long as we remember that it wasn't only single events, but entire chapters of Brad's life that were written up there, we can better understand the magic of it all. Just as we'll better feel the magic of its call, and the magic in all the missteps, mistakes, and misadventures that took Brad, often unknowingly, on his unique approach to his crucible of truth.

I believe this is also important because Brad's gargantuan course on this earth is parabolic for our own. Sure, we'll see his journey better if we keep these points in mind. But the real plot underwritten in every story suggests that what is true of the hero's life is also true of our own. Often, as we have with summits on the Big Stone, we find ways to normalize and even deflect the events of our circumstance. We find ways to scroll precisely past the one thing that was the most unlikely of all: our very own lives, with our very own impossibly unlikely plots and people. We, too, are part of a fantastic sequence, after all. Much like with Brad, it was all just as improbable that any of the arrangements of our lives would become what they were—that they would become what they are.

So, before we get fully immersed in Brad's story, I believe we should also submit ourselves to our own. At the least, we may be well-served to hold his story and ours in parallel. If we do, we may find that for every one of his struggles, and, ultimately, his resolutions, we may have overlooked those of our own. Hell, if the goal is to appreciate our lives the way Brad did his, then it may serve us to recall that, like Brad, there is a notion that nobody but us could have possibly had, or been meant for, the experiences in our lives that are specifically ours. The cosmos could've spun out a million more iterations of Brad's DNA like beads on a chromatin string, but there's no way any of them would've been just right, or even remotely made for the life that he came into. The same hand of destiny, or whatever the hell we choose to call it, sliding between the sequences of Brad's life—the good and the bad—pervades ours, too. With all that said, let us look deeper into his full approach to To-tock-ah-noo-lah, because it began long before he may have suspected.

One of the hardest things Brad Gobright had to do in his childhood was to say goodbye to the house that, up until that point, he had spent his entire life in. He was only nine at the time, but that still qualifies as a lifetime. It wasn't just leaving the house that filled him with sadness, though; there was more to it. In fact, like most forms of incomprehensible loss, his pain about it was wrapped up in more of a singular detail. Friends at school, the feel of his bedroom, the muscle memory of it all, the parts that make it feel like home—no big deal. He could let go. But that treehouse. Fuck.

Akin to a five-star climbing route with uniform cracks, no offset, bullet-hard rock, and movement quality that'll make your soul quiver, Brad's treehouse was the stuff of legend. Jim, the landscape architect in his prime, designed and built it by hand, outfitting it with a svelte carpet flooring, interior lighting, and even its own marquee with a mailing address posted to it. Better still, Jim built a vertical climbing wall at the entrance; perhaps the first informal pillar of home training that Brad had access to. Like the hallowed cenacle of Pentecost or the cave of Hira, that treehouse was a sanctuary. Surely, in Brad's eyes, this would not be hyperbolic.

But life moves us without asking our permission. Brad had been struggling in school. Even he knew it. What he didn't know, at least not completely, was the degree to which his parents, chiefly Pamela, were moving heaven and earth to keep him from outright exile in the eyes of the educational system. Pamela was trying and would continue to try all manner of ways to get Brad, now in the third grade, to survive school. Moving houses was just one of many measures in that pursuit. A pursuit that was as old as Brad was.

As mentioned, Brad struggled developmentally. At the suggestion of the pre-school he attended, Pamela and Jim kept him back a year before starting kindergarten, where even at age six, he did not excel. This carried on every year in school, successively, some years being slightly better than others on the merit of certain teachers and their willingness to invest focused time on Brad. But regardless of the teacher, the discord continued in Brad's education. He wouldn't confidently read for years to come, perhaps the most concerning of all his conditions to Pamela.

So in third grade, at nine years old, things came to a crisis point. Private school was no longer an option. In a last-ditch attempt, Pamela had Brad test for a school that specialized in educating youth with dyslexia and other disorders. But to her dismay, even that institution balked at the prospect. They fed Pamela some boilerplate excuses as to why they wouldn't accept Brad as a student, even going so far as to say that his I.Q. was inadmissible relative to their sudden high standards.

In her retelling of it, Pamela eased out a chuckle on the reflection, now years removed. "I mean, you can imagine how distraught I was. I'm there standing at a school for the special students and even they are telling me they can't take my son. What the hell was I supposed to do with that?!"

All the spark she needed for her mom instincts to run on overdrive. Which they did.

In the next year, Pamela would quit working at the office—cutting all the nannies and special tutors out of the equation—and commit to teaching Brad herself while still working independently and full-time from home. They tried it all. There was a phase of biofeedback studies, an attempt at Sylvan Learning systems, classical music before bedtime, therapy—one desperate measure, often at a painfully high price, after another. Jim and Pamela tapped into their retirement and the kids' college savings accounts in full abandon, bending as far as they could, doing whatever they could.

Which takes us back to the moving truck and that sad day when Brad last stepped into his treehouse. He was aware enough at that stage that things were not well. But, in his parents' narrative, he didn't know that they'd literally moved houses just to get into a better school district. It was better that way. But it was also the hard facts. Pamela had done her homework, and for the love of her child, who we would all later come to know and love as a most unique, captivating, danger-prone, but affable climber, she found the family a new home in what she considered a better school district.

Brad took his time to say his goodbyes to that treehouse, in what was surely an outstanding moment of separation. No doubt he took stock of the memories, the way any of us would when reflecting on all the golden frames in a relationship that time, or life, or any other input has pulled apart. Brad would have thought about all the days climbing that training wall. He would have remembered the dramatic, and slightly traumatic, events from the day they taught his grandmother to belay. He would have laughed, with both the pain and comedy not being lost on him as he remembered how, after being taught for more than an hour, she managed to drop Brad from the top of the wall on her very first attempt at belaying. He'd remember all the days he and his sister Jill played Power Rangers up there. He would have recalled the time that the two of them got in deep shit when they were caught spying on the neighbors during what Jill recalled as perhaps their first exposure to sexual intercourse. He'd probably even remember all the days he spent up there as a first-grader, looking for pixie dust during the peak of his Peter Pan obsession.

But the hard facts of life, which Brad already knew about without the help of someone's godforsaken book, persisted. It was time to say goodbye. Just another rough edge on what had become for him an unintelligible journey.

Brad's self-concept suffered gravely in those years. He wasn't just small and marginalized physically, but in his psyche, too. Enough time spent struggling, often failing, had been internalized. All the love in the world can't ward off certain miseries; the kid just had a tough lot. With no clear path or guarantee that these obstacles were ever going to develop from pains into pillars of strength, Jim and Pamela were anguished.

Pamela recalled that while Brad's climbing—especially his first big day out on Tumanguya a year before—was a major confidence builder, it wasn't enough to spring him from the pits. During this transition period between schools, Brad and Pamela sat down for what seemed like just another counseling session with a child psychologist. Something they'd grown accustomed to. But it became an important day, in her recollection, for what it revealed.

The therapist gave Brad a simple sheet of 8x11 copy paper and asked him to draw a picture of the world he knew. Pamela recalls having been amused at first. Drawing was not a forte for Brad, which usually made for a mess on the page. But when the sketch was finished, it wasn't the whim of it or the mess of it that held Pamela and the therapist's attention, it was the interpretation of it. In his best representation of the world he knew, Brad penciled in a slew of grand, overwhelming images—school, other people in his life, the earth itself—and then up in the corner of the page was himself. A tiny, almost hidden stick figure; that was it.

It was at this same time, 1997 on the dial, that Brad also got a habit of illness anxiety, borderline hypochondria. Brad was suddenly convinced that he had cancer. When Pamela's counsel and care weren't enough, and Brad insisted something was amiss deep inside, they went for a series of blood and body system checks. While the resulting bill of clean health, save for the fact that Brad was still in the lower percentiles of growth and development, came as good news, it did not help. Brad was in despair. He was uncomfortable, he was not fitting in, not excelling, not able to gel into the emulsion of life. And not for lack of effort either. Making things more confusing for Brad was the fact that every time he looked over to his younger sister, she seemed to glide where he only sunk. Jill excelled in most places Brad didn't and was already being placed in gifted programs at school. Brad loved her completely, but even those closest to him seemed to enhance the conundrum he knew as daily life. Seeing the resulting sulk, confusion, dejection even, broke both Pamela and Jim. There wasn't an acceptable sense of solution to what was an unacceptable struggle.

It's not lost on me, or his folks, that there are kids in marginalized places whose entire lives are squandered along with billions of others on poor and wasted continents, who grieve and cry for want of basic human rights, lost family members, or the pains of rape and genocide. It's my hope and intent to tell those stories, too, in time. Not only to tell stories, but to take and sustain meaningful action against those plots—an effort I hope will be held in common by all of us. But however atrocious those realities are, this tale is of a different kind. This is the story of a kid who was born to fly, to glide across unfathomable landscapes and up into heights of the human experience that few will ever know. And in his tale, he and his family experienced hardships that do not deserve to be dismissed by comparison with others'. Misery is not a contest.

For most of elementary school, it was a relationship to

the outside branches of life that kept Brad afloat. He lived for the weekends when he could get to the climbing gym or take increasingly long hikes outside. And it was in those years that it became clear, in both spheres, that he was better than most at his age. For once in his life, he was rising above the flock. A fact that sustained him.

Brad's climbing was solely of the indoor variety until he was ten, which wasn't a bother at the time; he was happy with any medium. Thanks to the charity of his Scout leader and family friend, Lynn Call, who had seen his troubles firsthand, Brad was out hiking and camping on a bi-weekly basis. In Scouts, Brad made good friends with a crew of young lads, one of whom was Lynn's son, Roger, who he would remain close with for most of his life. Apart from the leviathan of academics, things did improve on some outward flanks. But where most young Scouts used the badges and skills learned as a competitive metric, often trying to one-up their peers, Brad seemed to latch only to what would enable his climbing. Boy Scout badges were never his competitive quest. His sash and vest remained largely as brown as the tree trunks that Brad spent time climbing upon.

As school continued to be a disaster, Brad was placed on an Individualized Education Plan, a legal document meant to spell out a bespoke course of study for those with difficulties in standard learning environments. He was compliant, as best he could be, never rebelling against the idea of school or learning. To help, Pamela became a 'room mom,' sacrificing even more time in her schedule to be present with him during class. Most days, that meant Brad would leave his peers for hours at a time and transfer to the special education division, where Pamela and others helped. All the best efforts and intentions with her son—a decidedly poignant testimonial of motherly love—never produced the kind of GPA that would allow Pamela to sleep easy. At best, they were treading water. Academics, it turns out, were less a set of steps Brad was going to ascend as they were a simple matter of labors to survive.

Through third and fourth grade, Brad kept on climbing. It was quickly apparent that he wasn't just climbing, he was thriving. Christmas and birthday gift requests, even by the age of nine and ten years old, were exclusive to climbing gear. To see if their son would excel further, Jim and Pamela even signed Brad up for the local JCCA (Junior Competitive Climbing Association) competitions, where, to nobody's surprise, he outclimbed kids twice his age using only half the core tension and footwork. Brad could hang up there for ages.

His petite frame allowed him to use anything as small as a foothold to gain advantage as a handhold, and his uncanny endurance allowed him extended opportunity to sort out his sequencing without ever getting too pumped. For proof of this, you can still find some old clips online, or in the *Inertia* vol. 1 climbing film produced in 1997, when Brad was nine. There's a short segment, his first media highlight, where Brad cruises up the same fifty-foot lead arch that first caught his attention the day that he walked into the gym in Costa Mesa. He flows in his own casual, loose manner across the inverted planes with feet cutting free, hands weaving across one hold to another. Unlabored, Brad floats on the wall the way an Olympic swimmer cuts through water. He always did.

Within a year, Brad had acquired enough points to qualify for nationals, a big deal for most kids. Jim recalled that it wasn't for Brad, though. Even during the flight out to Denver and when stepping into the arena of a proper, amphitheater-sized climbing gym featuring walls double the height of those at his local gym, Brad was largely unmoved by the occasion.

"He just wanted to climb, not compete," Jim said. Later in life, say for The Nose speed record, he'd show much more appetite for it. But even then, you always got the hunch that it was the self-driven variety. His zeal was to better himself and express his greatest potential, only ever competing against his own standards of himself rather than being motivated by besting or standing above another person. A lot of high-performance athletes traverse thousands of miles on foot or up a stone over the course of years for that clarity of motivation. Brad, it seems, never had to.

Brad placed second best in his first appearance at a national-level competition. According to Jim, the kid that got first place looked like a chip off the marble of Michelangelo or a mold cast from some antiquated period going back to Mount Olympus. Shredded to the last muscle fiber, probably climbing in a structured format his entire life, that kid was meant to destroy rocks. You can imagine the surprise when he made it to the final and in walks Brad, this seemingly naïve kid from Orange, five-foot-nothing with bare minimum climbing gear and zero pressure on his shoulders. Even more of a surprise, Brad nearly won. Still, where Jim had wanted to see how Brad's competitive spirit would rise to the occasion, or how it would deal with not winning top rank, he was as surprised as anyone when he saw Brad shrug off the whole experience as just another cool day out climbing.

While Brad was able to shed the weight of competitive pressure in ways that most professionals work a lifetime for, in Pamela's eyes, all of it was important for her son. He was at last learning a modicum of self-confidence. It wasn't just a safe space for Brad anymore—it was a healthy place, a productive space. It was the one direction he could turn when all else fell apart, when he needed the sense of aptitude that the educational system couldn't give him. It was home. And it was important because those struggles were far from over.

When Brad finished fourth grade, he still wasn't competently able to read. Math, history, science, all of it befuddled him. As had been the case for ages, the world seemed simply inaccessible. In the summer before entering fifth grade, eleven-year-old Brad hunkered in with Pamela in hopes to finally surmise the challenge of a lifetime. At the end of her rope, Pamela tried a last-ditch effort when she discovered the Lindamood-Bell design of reading education. Hesitantly, almost without belief that it could possibly work, Brad agreed on the push. It would occupy his summer completely, which also meant no long spells out climbing.

For six hours every day, five days a week, for the entirety of his summer, Brad went to the prescribed classes, with Pamela joining for a large chunk of that same time commitment. Together, the staff taught Brad a new approach to reading and conceptualizing, and they taught Pamela how to continue to teach Brad in the same manner so she'd have the tools necessary to sustain his development after the classes were finished. Unbelievably, something clicked. While he was surely burnt out, having endured nearly twice as much schooling in the form of extracurricular and special education as his peers, Brad made it to fifth grade. At last able to read and comprehend material, Brad may not have cried for this accomplishment, but Pamela did.

While this was a huge leap, it did not absolve all of Brad's challenges. He would again struggle in fifth grade, and he was fortunate that his teacher, Mr. Zuidema, a man who had just done a complete career overhaul to find more meaning in his own life, knew of Brad's struggles enough to invest one-on-one time with him. Mr. Zuidema also loved Brad and his fifth-grade class so much that he went out of his way to become their sixth-grade teacher so that he might be the one to usher the students to the steps of junior high school itself. Pamela felt better for Brad's time with Mr. Zuidema, and his comical, no-frills fourth grade teacher, Mr. Tipple, who gave Pamela deep reassurance one day, telling her that Brad would surely turn out fine in life, that he would likely not remember these days, or his youth altogether as the best time, but that he would be just fine despite it.

Unsurprisingly, Brad's difficulties persisted in junior high, where, if they taught him anything that he could apply later in life, perhaps they taught him how to persevere. Surely it took more endurance, willingness, and effort to just make the mark of graduation each year as it did for him to climb up what were now decently hard grades in the gym. He'd actually been climbing outside a few times, too. The first of which was due to the charity of someone Pamela had first perceived as a good-for-nothing gym rat, Justin Bastien. Justin was only twenty-two years old at that time, working at Rockreation, and had invited Brad for a weekend of climbing at Mt. Wilson, a sport-climbing area just north of Las Vegas and Red Rock Canyon. Insisting to be there to chaperone, Pamela joined and soon discovered that those gym rats, the dirtbags as it were, had some of the kindest souls she'd ever known. They encouraged Brad, included him, invited him, and bolstered him in ways he simply hadn't ever been.

There is a strange, beautiful presence of charity in Brad's early life. Surely it's there upon honest reflection in most of our lives as well. It always seemed like just when the task got too big, when the difficulties ahead seemed somehow impossible, a Scout leader, a friend, a climber, a schoolteacher, someone, anyone, was there just at the right time. Make of it what you will, but Pamela, and most contented folks I know, reflect on those plots of life with a certain gratitude. Our best efforts in life are always needed, but somehow we keep running into the notion that like it or not, we can't do it alone.

Still, junior high was a struggle. Brad lost touch with his close friends from Scouts during that period and focused more on BMX riding than he did on climbing. I think he was aware of how good he was at climbing, and he'd been exposed to the competitive sides of it enough to devolve in a different direction. I think he was always tuned, almost at the level of a default setting, to a pure version of self-expression in what he pursued. He wasn't attracted to an audience, and he didn't climb his best or try his hardest for other people's validation, because for so much of his life he hadn't had that from others anyway. Surprisingly, unlike most who would have come from his condition, Brad didn't have that chip on his shoulder. He got validation from climbing, sure, but it wasn't the validation of others as much as it was one formed within. Something later evidenced by his proclivity to free solo on a regular basis without witness and without having told anyone about it.

For whatever reason, Brad climbed less for those couple of years, choosing his bike, and what Pamela reflects on as an odd bunch of outsiders as friends. She didn't meet most of them, and lifelong relationships never developed from them, but Pamela and Jim were concerned for Brad during this time. He wore the suit of the outcast, something they'd seen for too long already. Before giving in to full-scale parental panic, though, they waited it out. The phase was bound to pass, they thought. After all, the others before it had. Adolescence is such a complex, batshit crazy period in anyone's life, they did their best as parents to trust that it would, indeed, work out with time.

Finally, in 2004, high school came. Pamela and Jim went into it white-knuckled, as full of worry as any parent would be even against their best efforts to let life have its course. As for Brad, we're not entirely sure if he was optimistic going in, but what is certain is that things spiraled quickly. As Pamela and Jim recall, Brad's freshman year was by far the hardest. Perhaps even harder than that third grade year which forced them to move school districts.

After the first semester, Pamela had seen enough and was

within inches of pulling Brad out of school and back into a tailored cut of special-ed. Why she didn't, even she isn't sure. Call it a measure of faith. But Brad was in the weeds. He couldn't keep track of his assignments, had very little order in his backpack or his bedroom, and he wasn't connecting in friendships.

Pamela recalled that it was at this stage that Brad developed that comical panache of his. Much of the quick-witted, unabashed, absurdist humor we all remember as a trademark of his adult life was forged in high school. During that time, when he'd lost touch with most of his older friends and was a rolling stone, he learned that his sense of humor went a long way. He learned that the levity would endear him to others and that it could be used as a tool to distract from his shortcomings. But he wasn't the type for verbal abuse on anyone other than himself. That irresistible kindness of his wouldn't allow it. This meant that often, Brad's humor was purely self-deprecating. He was constantly beating others to the punchline if he thought himself the object or brunt of a good joke. This trait stayed with him until the day he died. I think many of us would agree that it was impressive, brave even, for Brad to present himself and his difficulties with this open candor, with this vulnerability and honesty, even if it was filtered through the scope of comedy.

The other side of me hurts for him, despite how much I can appreciate his methods. Because based on the way he was treated by others, or felt about himself, by the time I met him in 2007, you got the hunch that he always felt 'less than.' Even as he grew up, excelled, and inspired so many of us, it seemed, on a certain level, like Brad always fell back into that persona when there was a camera pointed in his direction. It's obvious to me now that he was so much more than what he presented to most people. It just so happened that the jester was one of the first tools that worked. It endeared him to others, so he kept it. We all do with most of our character traits. We keep them long past the point where they serve us best.

It's important to recognize where Brad's character traits came from, but I wish we could've seen more of him—the deepest parts at a larger scale. Those bits would eventually be shown, but not often and only to a select few. One simply wishes he could've gone through less badgering at a young age, or better still none at all, so as to keep his comedic voice but not so much that he would feel a need to lean on it for so long. That kid was only ever made from light, constitutionally. Just like he only ever had good things to give, and God knows we all could've used more of it.

By the end of that year, his older friendships did circle back around, and slowly his freshman year improved. The combination of an injury while BMX riding and joining the wrestling squad (in the lightest of weight divisions) took him away from the fringes and back into a form of structure. Jim and Pamela recalled that the wrestling team had quite the regional reputation and that the order it provided, combined with the fact Brad needed to keep up satisfactory grades to stay on the team, helped him. By sophomore and junior year, Brad began enforcing some order in his life, completing assignments and taking on one task at a time. On the wrestling mat, Brad quickly proved he had the sturdiest of wills and a deep tenacity for the grind, physically speaking; traits that immediately commanded respect from the jocks. This respect, coupled with the inclusion in a group, did a great deal for his productivity. He never thrived, not in the way he would outdoors, but he grew.

On the wrestling team, Brad forged a dear friendship with Dustin Burd. The two of them shared a love of climbing, were only one year apart in school, and were even closer in age. In the years to come they would forge a brotherhood, often going tit-for-tat in their progression through the grade ranges of hard routes and their journey up ever-taller multi-pitch climbs. Multi-pitch climbs which Brad, at least, always hoped would steer toward To-

tock-ah-noo-lah. It was simply what he burned for the most.

Unfortunately, it was in this same period, over Memorial Day weekend of his sophomore year, that he had the first of what became a standing series of seizures. These would continue his entire life, and would largely remain undisclosed to most of us. His seizures were isolated to sleep alone and never occurred during waking hours. His reluctance to share his condition was understandable, considering how self-aware he was of some of his deficits already. Over several months, Jim and Pamela sought counsel, took him for tests, and eventually followed a prescription given by his physicians on what they had concluded was an epilepsy condition. Brad would need to remain medicated for the rest of his life on antiepileptic drugs—chemicals that affected the same neurotransmitters and ion channels that, in the crosshairs of his learning deficits, already made life harder than it was for most. The aftershocks and resulting brain fog would often last for days. One more lash over the landscape of a thousand.

In 2007, leading into 2008, I knew nothing of Brad's struggles. I'd barely known him for a year, and for most of that time, our conversations never strayed from climbing. We both had goals, and they had little to do with education or reliving the traumas of our past. And superficially, nothing seemed deeply unsettled in the make-up of either of our lives except the need to discover more of ourselves by getting out to nature as habitually as we could.

I was self-centered about much of life, and for the rest of it was mostly just unaware. I wouldn't have had the capacity to relate to Brad's past had he ever reached out for help with it, which it's safe to say he didn't. Probably because Brad was always more invested in the present than he was weighed down by the past. Sure, he was a bit self-aware regarding his troubles, but he didn't feel the need to rehash them. Brad always—whether by choice, skill, dumb luck, or the grace of his higher power—had an unflinching presentness. He was of the now, a trait perhaps as immaculate as his finger power, his deep-seated kindness, and his purity of heart.

But because Brad's presentness did not bring the past along with it, most of us never knew the fires and pains he was born from. Not even a clue. And, given he was still a bit awkward socially, especially around a bunch of pretentious gym rats, Brad didn't fit as well as he would have liked. Not only that, but considering the climbers at the gym fancied themselves champions of technique, Brad's freestyle, lackadaisical, even incompetent footwork was always judged. I'd dig on him from time to time, but I did my level best to keep the criticism constructive and given at a personal level. Others, perhaps, not for callous heart or ill will, made their critiques more public, or at least louder than they needed to—and in front of an audience rather than in private. It wasn't a hazing, but I guarantee that had anybody really known what and where Brad had come from, he would have been treated differently. Unfortunately, he wasn't. Often jokes were made at his expense.

This is poignant because, in its own way, it all built up to that approach on the Big Stone. It was all tied to To-tock-ah-noo-lah for Brad, always was in those days. In 2007, after our trip to Ahwahne together, it was mostly Brad's suggestion that he and I, and our mutual friends, Donny and Matt, climb the Big Stone together. With neither of us having been up a big wall, it was a bit optimistic, rash even, that we somehow decided it would be on the Salathe route. But somehow, that decision stuck.

And so, for the second half of that year, we burned like fire in that gym, concocting all sorts of agendas, few of which were quite as absurd as our "weighted climbing" training regimen. A few days a week, we took actual twenty-five-pound plates from the bench press rack and tossed them into my old Jansport rucksack before setting off on full endurance lead-climbing sets to failure. I am still amazed that neither of us outright blew our tendons apart or killed the belayer when taking whippers with a weighted backpack swinging off our shoulders.

After some time, however, by early spring of 2008, there were some rumblings among the group. Brad had been out a lot that winter and had unfortunately stretched his reputation for climbing in haphazard, often dangerous fashions. On more than a few occasions, his gear placements, which were already suspect, outright failed. Sadly, his anchor rigging wasn't much better. Often, it just came down to a lack of redundancy.

There were also incidents that begat further heckling, such as a time when Brad's partner could not climb past the opening sequence of the well-trodden Left Ski Track on Joshua Tree's Intersection Rock. As luck would have it, a professional crew with an industrial size thirty-foot climbing ladder was on-site testing the failing strength of protective climbing gear the next route over. When Brad saw the ladder, he insisted his partner use it to bypass the lower crux, which he did.

Unfortunately, a tactic like that on Intersection Rock, on a Saturday in peak season, was taken as controversy for some and was borderline blasphemy to the rest. The peanut gallery at the parking lot, the cantankerous old band of rock-jocks who mostly left their bold climbing behind them at least a decade prior, stood up in a riot, believing their scorn as the honest work of men in defense of an ethic. They berated Brad and his partner, and that reprimand continued long after the incident. It was the talk of the climbing gym for a good couple of weeks among the old and crusty, which Brad, in his inimitable brilliance, shrugged off so easily it only incensed people even further. There was a certain lightness, an untouchable mystique that kid kept ahold of, and it drove some men mad. In a lot of ways, Brad just couldn't be touched.

Enchanting as his spirit was in what appeared to be situations of gravitas to most of us, his antics also did him no favors. And even though he was well on his way to redpointing classics in the Park, such as Equinox, an undeniably proud climb, questions of his place on the team continued. Soon, it didn't matter that he had more rope-gunning potential than the rest of us, questions were being asked about whether it was a wise or safe decision to keep him on the team. As I was worse at managing conflict or anything like a confrontation than I was at climbing, I mostly kept quiet for months. But by late spring, a decision was all but certain.

In spring of 2008, our mate Ian Flanders, who later left us all too soon in a BASE accident in the far reaches of Eastern Turkey, came into the scene at Rockreation. While Donny and Matt had known him for some time, he was a new transplant to the area; the little I knew of him at that stage was that for any skill he lacked in free-climbing, he more than made up for in his aid climbing proficiency and by virtue of his outward-facing, pure machismo. Ian had the kind of self-belief that makes legends out of ordinary men. Until you really got into his inner circle, he also had a certain grizzle about him. He was deeply kind and loyal to the bone when it really mattered in life, but that was not the first impression for most, at least not in 2008. Of course, like Brad, it would take me years to learn of Ian's past and the circumstance that accounted for his exterior. Ian was a tough guy on every level and had the frame of a veteran octagon fighter to boot, which, one would imagine, was at least one aspect that was polar opposite to Brad's persona. The two were never going to get on well with one another, at least not in those days.

And so, by some measure of democratic quorum, or happenstance, the day came when Donny and Matt and I had our discussion, ruling out a final verdict on the team roster. By no surprise, Brad came out on the losing end, and even worse, none of us knew how nor even wanted to be the one to break the news to him. Instead, Brad kept on for a good month and half, pushing himself to his limits on the stone.

What we didn't know, not even remotely, was who Brad really was, and why this trip on the Salathe meant the world to him. We hadn't the lightest ember of awareness that he had been coming home to his parents' house in Orange on a nightly basis with updates. Brad was telling his parents, his mom especially, his plans for the route, plans on what leads he was going to take, paired with updates on the team members (none of whom Pamela had met).

We didn't know that Brad was struggling deeply in school, that he was all but ready to quit community college, that he needed a validating experience in life to stand on. We didn't know that every time he went to museums or places of cultural interest with his parents, it pained him, because he couldn't relate to things most people find inspiration from. We didn't know he'd taken so many college tours with his mom, where she'd driven him across the western states hoping he might find a city, town, or community that he could connect with. We didn't know how desperate he was for a sense of place, for a taste of fitting in, for someone in life to hold him up with the unconditional positive regard that every human deserves. We—I—had no idea.

A month later, just six weeks before the trip of a lifetime, our plans came up in conversation at the gym and Ian, certainly the worst person to deliver the news, stood up to deliver the verdict. Ian was not inflammatory and it's not as if he wanted to fight the kid, but in no kind terms did he relay the decision. He told Brad that he was off the team, just like that, as a frank matter of fact; it was not up for discussion. I'm not sure if anybody felt right about it; this was the reason I would later decide for myself that if I was going to do anything of consequence on a wall, the arrangements were never to come at the cost of friendships. But we all chalked it up to tough love or some other bullshit. We didn't have manners, we weren't as kind or honest as we could've been, and I can guarantee you that nobody called Brad later that day to check up on him or share remorse. It's not an attempt to excuse the carelessness we had with his heart. The truth is, we weren't even capable of it. And none of us had a clue.

Brad rushed home that day and burst into tears. For context, Pamela will tell you that Brad was not a crier, period. Kids would often cry when they fell, scraped a knee, or were awakened to pain, sure, and Brad might have had an occasion or two in this vein. But emotional pain, this pain, was different. Pamela had never seen it. The Brad Gobright that none of us knew about, the guy who struggled his entire life, came home that night and sobbed himself to sleep in misery. He stayed in his room for the entire weekend.

Brad hadn't known any heartbreak quite like this. He didn't know what it meant to be gutted, not in climbing. It was, after all, meant to be his safe space. It was where he thrived. It was the only retreat he'd had for years running, apart from the walls of his home and the embrace of his family. And now, at last, life had fucked him sideways here, too. We didn't know any better, but the four of us ripped that kid's heart out that day. We gave Brad a pain that would drive him, eventually, up To-tock-ah-noo-lah, and continue to push him for some time. You could argue it took him to some great and high places, but he would have gotten to all those places on his own, with all the light that he held within. The last thing he needed was our contribution. Knowing all that he had been through now, years down the road, I get it. We did that kid dirty. Served him crow, feathers and all. We took a kid who could float through life in the present moment, lighter than air, and put a chip on his shoulders so heavy it nearly sunk him clean. How he didn't lose the whole of his innocence right then and there, I'll never know.

REALIZATION

April 2008. Brad didn't know what to do next, not at first. Broken for spirit, he'd turn anywhere, including to Pamela, for a couple of heart-wrenching sit-downs on his plight. Hoping, perhaps, that she could walk the coals for him. But as it goes, the most decisive and consequential moments in our lives are only ever born from a willingness to stand face to face with ourselves, naked and true, and face the great void within us with the only tool that ever decoded anything from it: honesty.

Call it the abyss, a come-to-Jesus moment, a realization. There are only so many moments in life where it comes clean, where we cast away all but the essential, and move in the only direction required—inward. That's where the kid was now. Mr. Light-as-a-feather was in deep. But in his depths, he understood one thing only—simply that by hook or crook, his destiny was among the high places. And he would do anything required to dwell just there, eclipsed as often as possible in the kaleidoscopic light that bathes the ageless pillars of the earth.

Without a plan, a safety net, or a dollar to his name, Brad was going to move his entire life toward his purpose. Nothing was guaranteed to him when he made that choice. All he knew was that he was moving toward his truth. And, more by the fibers of his microbiome than by the prescriptions of a book, Brad knew this: if you protect your purpose, it will protect you.

In a rush of insight, Brad took stock of his options. He could wallow in self-pity about not climbing the Salathe, or he could burn everything behind him and force function. So that's precisely what he did. Pained and without a friend for consolation, he looked at his record in school, the past that he had come from, and the future that lay ahead. He didn't want to let his parents down, but he knew his education lay elsewhere. Easing the decision, even Pamela suggested he may just need some time away. Some time, for Pamela, qualified as a few months, maybe a semester at most.

Brad had a further scope in mind, though. He decided that he was going to move to Ahwahne, likely for the rest of his life. That may not have been the way he spelled it out to his family at the time, however. With the help of his mom, Brad filled out his application to the Ahwahnee Hotel, and for the next month he took on as many shifts as he could at the gym. Jim and Pamela made it clear that for his venture, he would have no sponsorship on their end. They told him that they'd love him forever, but they wanted him to know that his journey had to be taken fully by himself—financial consequences included.

This takes us right up to the close of that gas cap on the Arco station off Chapman Ave. Steady at the wheel, like he'd been waiting all his life for it, Brad had the whole of his material existence, including one brand new harness, beside him. Likely he would have spoiled himself for one last meal in Fresno at the In-N-Out Burger, a fast-food chain that in my tenure with him, I never once saw him pass up. I can see him there, completely captivated by the meal in front of him down to the last bite, after which I'd give him no more than five seconds where he might sit in reflection. Just there, at the tip of comprehending the magnitude of that moment and what it spelled out for the course of his life, he'd ponder, but only briefly, before he blinked back to the present, found his keys, and looked up the road with something like satisfaction.

In Yosemite, Brad got busy quickly, investing his time equally in the furthering of three skill sets. For general fitness, he was running free-solo laps on moderates like the Royal Arches, usually before and after work at the Ahwahnee Hotel, which sits just a literal stone's throw from the cliff. For his crack technique, he was committed to rope-soloing most of the classic routes at the Cookie Cliff. And for his strength, he was working circuits of boulders in and around Camp 4. Often, he'd do all three in the same day. Such as it was up on Tumanguya back when he was seven years old, Brad Gobright did not struggle for willpower or stamina. Friendships, perhaps, were all that was lacking.

I kept up with him by text and the occasional phone call, and was inspired when I heard how much progress he was making, especially considering he was already projecting and often sending area classics. Over the summer and the course of the next year, many of these projects would come to fulfillment. But it was just the beginning for Brad. The work shifts at the Ahwahnee Hotel, something he never really digested well, had him beat on occasion, but he was thriving in that Valley. I, for one, was impressed at just how quickly he restructured everything, especially by the gusto with which he did it.

By the beginning of the fall season, Brad was climbing better than he ever had. Time in the Valley and the synchronization of his skills to its unique style and demands were paying dividends. But it was also not without certain scares. Brad had free-soloed miles by that point, but for most people's money, it still didn't look great. Compared to the poise the average climber was exposed to from old footage of John Bachar, or more recently, Alex Honnold, Brad's soloing looked amateur, which for the most part, it was. I've no doubt that he had control up there, but he scared most onlookers in the way he went about it, and, for the simple amount of terrain he was covering, you'd worry it wouldn't take long for him to get into the kind of pickle he was known for on a rope.

On one occasion, Brad nearly got himself killed while rope-soloing out at the Cookie Cliff. At the time, he'd gotten pretty dialed on the Nabisco Wall, a subset panel of the Cookie Cliff famous for having stellar, thin cracks split clean on quality rock. Brad was well capable of climbing any of these pitches individually, but would often tackle them in bunches of laps at the end of the day—sometimes even after having climbed through those aforementioned free-solos and bouldering circuits.

Whatever the regimen was on this day, Brad rappelled in from the top, down to a ledge. When he tried pulling his rope for the next rappel, it jammed into something up at the anchor. After a few minutes of yanking at it without the rope giving way so much as a few inches, he assumed it was lodged hard into a fissure. Hard enough, he figured, to go ahead and climb. Fatigued, Brad climbed the last pitch of the Nabisco wall and, according to him, barely pulled the crux. Like, tip of the fingers, knife's-edge kind of barely. Only when he topped out did he come to find that his rope, which was attached to him by means of his Gri-Gri (belay device), wasn't lodged deep in some crack as he'd expected. Instead, it had tied itself into a fickle coil just around the branches of two small trees. Brad wasn't sure about many things at that stage in life, but, one hundred percent, every time he retold that story, he was certain that rope would've pulled clean off the cliff had he taken the fall on it.

So, with a few strokes of luck and a persistent approach, Brad tallied climbs that only a few decades earlier were the cutting edge of American rockcraft. By the time we caught up in the fall for the annual Facelift event, he was outright making meals of the place.

It was during the Facelift event that September that we had our iconoclastic encounter with one of Europe's best climbers, Sean Villanueva O'Driscoll. The two of them, Brad and Sean, side by side, could not have been more different, even with a supreme knack for sleeping in the soil shared between them. On a day none of us would ever forget, we had a beautiful moment where we learned that more than serving an ethic, Brad had an operating system. And, for all the complications it provided in his youth, that operating system, when taken to the right environment, suddenly seemed to fit. It allowed him to rise above dogma, traditions, even frameworks. Brad's operating system was solely about contact.

After Matt, Donny, Ian, and I had rigged the famed seventy-foot Rostrum highline on a perfect afternoon with nature unfolding in sheets of light beams, a gentle wind, and the camaraderie of a handful of climbing bums, Brad stood up and set himself to climb.

As Brad gathered his gear, Sean, who we had just met—and who had spent hours walking our highline—was there, full of an unshakeable delight. Walking through a series of moving meditations, demonstrating diaphragmatic breathing exercises, you name it, he was on the line doing it. On the rare occasion he wasn't sending the line, Sean would step away, pick up his mountain flute or beautifully play the nylon six-string I'd brought along. It wasn't just that he had uncontainable talent, it was the way he expressed it. At least in our eyes, the guy was more mystic than man. You must understand, back then, for all the context of where we were in our lives—still young and afraid of our own becoming—and for what Sean represented, it was all mind-blowing. Here was a guy demonstrating that you could, in fact, achieve excellence—on a wall, off a wall, when playing a guitar, fuck, even when picking up trash. It didn't matter. Sean made you want to tie your damn shoelaces better, that's how much mystique he had.

We all already knew of his ethic on the wall, too. Sean and his partner, Nico Favresse, were regarded as paragons of class, as ambassadors of a ground-up, no-compromise aesthetic that harkened back to the early days of climbing lore. Never rappelling in from the top, or top-roping, a style that made short-cuts of crucibles, they'd even managed a ground-up, first ascent on To-tock-ah-noo-lah. Categorically, theirs felt like a manifestation of the perfect style. Beholden to the process of learning rather than simply achieving, it was a style that epitomized what we considered to be universal truth: manifesting beauty in this life was ultimately and always about the means and not simply the ends. Alignment to beauty, to the Platonic form of the good, and to an ethic, Sean may as well have been the spirit of Socrates, somehow packed into a Belgian-Celtic frame. Kids like us were all too apt to worship.

But Brad, God bless him, was beyond the rest of us. He didn't know who Sean was, nor the ethic he represented, and I'm sure that even if he did, he wouldn't have done anything different with that information anyway. Brad was unsatisfied with the situation, not because anything was wrong, not because he was cynical, but only because he was Brad. He wasn't interested in learning lessons about living as we were by witnessing Sean live his life. Where we wished for something like osmosis in the presence of the Belgian, Brad understood nothing would come by way of observation alone. Brad was into living his own life. And for that reason, more than watching Sean tie shoelaces with Platonic fervor or walk a highline, Brad wanted to get busy with it. Truth was, one of the best pitches in the Valley, the Alien Finish of The Rostrum, was square under our noses, with nobody on it. It didn't matter to Brad how he would go about climbing it, it only mattered that it got climbed.

It was with that context—Sean the ambassador of a ground-up, no top-rope style, and Brad the unteachable—that it all went down. Brad tossed a line off the top of The Rostrum, setting up the rappel, looked over to the rest of us, Sean included, and invited anyone who might want to join to participate. When he was met with a gallery of blank stares, he simply paused, then looked over to Sean to ask again.

With that childlike smile that we had nearly robbed him of still shining on his face, Brad asked, "Hey man, do you want to rap in here and top-rope the Alien Finish with me? It's supposed to be classic."

"Haha. Nah, man, I'm sure it's a great pitch, indeed," Sean began with his European sailor's accent. "But I'm sorry."

"Sorry for what?" Brad implored.

"Sorry to pass, mate. But that shit's just not in my ethics, man," Sean finished.

Not. In. My. Ethics. Are you kidding?

He didn't say it like an asshole. It wasn't with judgment and was not meant to spur the reaction it received. But the lot of us were so damn mesmerized we couldn't help it. We dropped our jaws. Of course Sean wanted to climb that thing! It's immaculate. But there he was, live and direct, demonstrating to us that some things are so sacred that even the way we approach them matters. I could swear at this point a voice behind me even gasped out a *"Holy shit,"* though I couldn't say who.

It wasn't piety, but dammit it was something. Sean literally could not take to a top-rope any more than a conscientious eater could not take to animal flesh. Brad didn't get it, but the point was he didn't have to. In the best way I can possibly mean this: it wasn't his point to get.

As another voice laughed at Brad for even asking the question, someone else scoffed. In my memory, I just stood there, too mind blown to even react. But our reactions weren't important that day, however unsuitable they were. This moment belonged only to the two of them.

Sean, still stuck in a sincere grin, wished Brad well. And Brad, realizing there was some depth to the moment, paused for as long as he could. But where any one of us regular men might have chosen a number of responses, most likely in some self-centered effort to salvage our ego or keep up appearances, Brad simply returned to his operations in the present. He did not try and defend his position or the impulse within him that lay behind it. He didn't need to. Fundamentally, he did not need to.

Normal folk would need to. An ego, with all its insistence, would need to. And I cannot emphasize enough how special it makes Brad that he did not need to. It was the equivalent of a novice showing up, first chair, to the philharmonic, and strumming bar chords from guitar tabs while the conductor and orchestra insist that only sheet music and Beethoven fit in the concert hall in the first place. You can't fault their craft, but the halls they call home have acoustics, which by design, ask only for music and not for elitism. Oblivious to Sean's ethic entirely, Brad went right ahead and top-roped the Alien Finish under our noses, once again flying into his progressions, actually getting better at climbing while the rest of us were too busy minding the occasion, distracted by the philosophical implication of it all.

Brad was impenetrable and he proved it. In the exact kind of moment that should've written him off, he flew. Against my better judgment, I was reminded that this occasion was, in fact, not the first time I had seen that side of him. Many times before, at many a belay station in my first year of climbing with Brad, I'd been in that same position—looking up at an incomprehensible version of a human who by nature ran only toward the light. Often, the same light that blinded me for its magnitude, Brad chased, and did so as operationally as he breathed.

Up on The Rostrum that day, I took note, on a heart level, and paid heed to the bifold realization within me. I worried deeply for where he might go in this life, due to that particular wandering float he had. I worried he might not always see danger coming. But the other realization was there too. It was an understanding that I was, unwittingly enough, in the presence of something extraordinary, special, one in a million. That I was always going to be inspired by the way he went, to wherever it was that he was going. That was the day I understood the truth I'd struggled to admit for some time: Brad was a most unlikely model, an unheralded, counterintuitive, perfect hero after all.

On The Rostrum that day we also met an all-time paragon in the young Mason Earle. Mason would later become a friend to many of us, and an outright legend for his ridiculous, almost untouchable crack climbing skills, which would only later be outshined by his magnanimity and his superhuman sense of compassion. Mason was the climber nearly everybody wished they could be, and he was also well into his own journey of self-discovery, which was not so unlike Brad's after all. He, too, was on a quest, hoping to find his truest expression on a planet which, up until that point, he hadn't always felt gave him a specific place or purpose.

This meant that he and Brad were destined toward each other. And in the years to come, they would prove it. At that time, though, it meant Brad and the rest of us were awakened, exposed to that "Next Generation." For the rest of us, that meant a quick understanding that for the next decade or so, we'd be the ones on the sidelines, the laymen passionately having our adventures which, while intrepid and standout for the context of our lives, would always and only be sized for our lives. Mason's arc was different—his climbs were going to move needles, not just his own heart rate. It was also clear that of all those among us, the underdog of life himself, Brad, had about the only chance in the group to make his life of such scope. He was the only one among us capable of such a traverse from outcast kid in unspoken oblivion to all-time people's champion.

We laughed at him for how he went about it, but it was precisely that day that we learned that it is unwise to write off what you do not understand. Brad's lights were on, after all, even if by different circuitry than our own. And, in the next week, he managed to climb that Alien roof, on top-rope, with no falls. Soon after, he led it clean. In the years to come, he would memorize that pitch and run laps on it with the ease we employ when navigating our kitchen for a morning cup of coffee. Brad was becoming.

The following week, Brad jumped grade scales entirely when he went from the Alien roof to projecting The Phoenix, one of the most quality, sought-after climbs at that grade in the whole of Ahwahne.

A few weeks later, mid-October, Matt, Brad, and I were in Bear's Ears National Monument, deep in the ancestral lands of the Ute, Zuni, Hopi, Mountain Ute, and Dine peoples, for our first trip on location. While Matt and I were climbing 5.10 classics, seasoned with an occasional 5.11, Brad, on his first day, hiked right up to Air Sweden, arguably the most famous line in the monument at that time—at least one of the hardest and boldest—and proceeded to whip entire elevator shafts in freefall like his life depended on it. I spent two weeks out there learning how to turn my wrist and fingers into a jam or a lock, mostly on top-rope. Brad spent his time learning to fly.

He stayed at the Creek Pasture Campground, overlooking the north and south Six Shooter—or the Bear's Ears as they're better known—which take sunrise and sunset, even moonlight, with such a robust gold and purple glow it often breeds revelation in any onlooker's heart. Always living cheap, Brad loved the desert. There wasn't the concessions industry or tourists and rangers to dodge as in Ahwahne. It was, for the most part, climbers only—a safe space where Brad could float around at night from campfire to campfire, trading warmth for tall tales—a practice of storytelling he would also soon master.

In the winter of 2008, Brad returned south and stayed in Joshua Tree, perhaps his favorite stomping grounds, to cut his teeth further. He mostly stayed at the Pit, a defunct climber's campground which has since been removed, just outside of the Park. Days were spent largely free-soloing, especially in Echo Tee, a small section near the Barker Dam, where Brad ran successive laps on its moderate face and crack climbs, typified by its best route, Big Moe. Brad learned to be comfortable in that grey space between a highball boulder and a proper free-solo, often running circuits in the Hidden Valley Campground, including numerous routes up the iconic Intersection Rock, a preferred sunset experience.

During this period, Brad would occasionally check in on the home front with a brief text message or short phone call. Many nights Pamela worried, as mothers do, where her son was and if he was taken care of. Neither she nor Jim knew anything about his soloing at the time, and they wouldn't for a few years to come. All they knew was that he was a work in progress, and that his path, for however meandering it was, was for the first time in a long while making him deeply happy. They got a closer look as 2008 turned to 2009 and Brad, without much of a plan, stopped by the house between road trips. I'm sure in his mind it was only meant to last a few days, but whatever money he'd saved while working at the Ahwahnee Hotel had dried up.

That winter, Brad took as many trips as he could—often on shorter scales, like single days or occasional weekends—and he signed up for more of those belay shifts to squirrel away a few bucks. He and Dustin Burd, his good friend from high school, climbed in Joshua Tree often, where they'd solo tit-for-tat with one another in a microcosm of the old Bachar/Long heyday. Brad spent time with anyone who could hold a rope, too. He added up days at the graffiti-laden Riverside rock quarry, perhaps the top candidate on the shortlist for the world's least inspired climbing locations, with any partner he could find. He also managed days out at Tahquitz and Suicide Rocks, just beside the sleepy town of Idyllwild. Brad dug his teeth into all of it, linking routes, exhausting partners, and taking whippers as he had on my watch the day that we first climbed The Vampire, about a year prior.

At home, however, things were not well. It would be a long while before Brad could spend significant periods of time in Orange County, let alone at home, without feeling the friction of the life he was born into. His course, the climber's life especially, also rubbed his folks the wrong way. Naturally, they feared for his direction when he came home that winter, turning that brief weekend stay into a month-long squat. All he could talk about was his climbing plans as opposed to his life plans, which concerned them, especially when Pamela and Jim learned that their son, the boy they'd raised to be kind and well-mannered, was out pinching food just to keep the traveling roadshow going.

Sometime in early February, Brad's lack of work ethic dug into his parents. He was, after all, twenty going on twenty-one. Some of the classmates he'd gone to school with, family friends even, were within a year of graduation from university already. Brad, of course, wasn't. He also hadn't had a job since the seasonal work at the Ahwahnee Hotel ended back in October. Because of that, tension on the home front was high. Being in the same room as his folks was impossible at length, because eventually questions like, *What did you do today?* turn naturally toward, *And what are you going to do tomorrow?* Add up enough tomorrows and you're looking at riddling out the plan for the future, something everybody in Brad's life was trying to decode.

It came as no surprise when his parents provided an ultimatum. If Brad was going to stay home, he needed to work full time and pay rent, or be fully registered at school. Also, his car, which was on its last legs, was going to need attention. Jim even offered to teach Brad how to fix it. Feeling pressure, perhaps even backed into a corner, Brad saw it all as a threat to his climbing. Because of this, things got worse at home. Brad was irritable, outright rude to his dad especially. They argued, rubbed shoulders, tried and failed to bond over car repairs, and eventually, Brad walked out. Insisting he'd be fine, Brad took the sixty dollars he had to his name and left the house.

After a two-week stay in the parking lot of the climbing gym—something many of us have done when our luck was down, showering in the men's room and heating meals by microwave—a repentant Brad came home with his head down. His parents, God bless them, knowing he'd missed the registration window for the spring semester and that he was no closer to landing a full-time job, took him back anyway. Within a few weeks, Brad had locked down a part-time gig at a local golf course as a dishwasher and busser, where he worked for the next couple of months. I can only imagine the spite he would have held for the rich and domesticated, the business folks, with their degrees and bank accounts, one banquet shift after another. Brad knew himself enough to recognize that even he was capable of a certain hate, and it wasn't something he enjoyed seeing in himself. He needed to get free.

By March, Brad had helped convince Dustin, who was himself seeking a radical life change, that Orange County was not the place to be. They would set out, as they had often done, together on a road trip and then eventually make their way back to the Ahwahne, where they'd both get a job for that loathed Delaware North Company. Dustin was as good of a friend as he had at that point, but the relationship was not without its complexities.

Dustin was an exceptional climber with a smooth, flexible, almost effortless grace on the wall—a contrast to Brad, whose rigidity relied most on muscle and grunt. Where Dustin was a natural mover, Brad was a natural fighter. And the polemics didn't stop there. In Brad's eyes, Dustin didn't care enough about going to his limits, or push at them enough, especially for all the grace and talent he had on the wall. For Dustin, Brad cared too much, and about one element only. He loved that Brad was the most stoked kid in the building, but he wanted a friendship more than just a partnership. He wanted someone to talk deeper with. The fact that Brad didn't avail his emotions often frustrated Dustin. Dustin also felt, at least on his end, a sense of one-upmanship in their relationship. A vague, underlying tone, which, real or imagined, never sat well. Because of that, over the years he detached often, and in so doing took extended periods to explore other outlets, education included. As with any kids, certain substances may have been a part of that exploration, too. Brad, though, had little patience for that process. He saw it as Dustin throwing pearls to swine. Dustin's lack of dedication, as Brad saw it, drove him mad.

On the competitiveness, I don't believe Brad was ever the type to draw primarily from that vein for his own motivations. But I could see him purposely outperforming Dustin from time to time, if for no other reason than to motivate Dustin to put down his schoolbooks, or his other vices, and tie back into a line.

Some of the best moments those kids ever had were together; some of the most infuriating ones were too. In the years to come, they'd swing between the highs and the lows. Only rarely, on a few blue moons, would their energies line up, but when they did, they yielded legendary days out. Spring of 2009, perhaps, was one of those small windows.

After climbing the Rainbow Wall, a gold-standard multi-pitch in Red Rock Canyon, Nevada, they set out for a month-long road trip toward Zion and Bear's Ears National Monument. In Zion, they tested their metal on a free-climbing attempt of the Moonlight Buttress and quickly learned that it was, indeed, a real ass-kicker. Free-climbing, ascending with just hands and feet for all upward progress, rather than with the aid of equipment to pull up on, is seen as the gold standard. In free-climbing, the climber still uses ropes and equipment to provide safety in case of a fall, but the climber does not use that equipment to aid in upward progress. No regrets between them, they agreed; going in over your head was how the hard folks were fashioned. It was how Brad was always fashioned. Most climbers only have the ego and the physical pain threshold to push like that, to take a beatdown a few times a year at best. Brad made it a part of his daily metabolism. Ass-kicking himself back to the ground was a manner of being, not something he saved up for.

By the time Brad and Dustin made their way to Bear's Ears, they were on a tear. I was out there for a few weeks on my own journey and watched with great attention as Brad nearly sent his project, Air Sweden. It would take him another year, but that wasn't the important part. Brad was climbing with a new and truly contagious sense of belief. The kind of belief that goes just as far, if not further, than the hours you put in doing fingerboard sessions. Out in the desert, the boys were catching fire.

A month later, in June of 2009, I was in Ahwahne (Yosemite) for a few days, waiting out a storm with a few friends hoping to jump on The Nose. Brad was back in the Village, working again at the Ahwahnee Hotel, and out of his forthcoming kindness he offered us a place to stay. At the time, he was sharing a small employee cabin with a quick-in, quick-out, West Indian roommate, who somehow never stayed home. With the extra bed and floor space available, Brad invited us in just before the rain came.

Having just free-climbed the Astroman, a legendary litmus test in the progression toward To-tock-ah-noo-lah, Brad's luster was visible. He had every reason to boast about his recent climbing accomplishments, but he didn't. Not that night. Instead, we spent the evening talking about something deeper: beauty. Maybe it was for the rain, or the closed quarters; truth is, I don't care what brought it on. I was just happy to see him let his guard down. That night, Brad opened up in ways that I would only see first-hand a precious few times.

After dinner, and just after sundown, he brought out his laptop and put on *Forrest Gump*. I didn't know it until right then, but it was a story that he related to intimately. He kept that movie close over the years, but I don't think the reason he did so was because of the easy parallels he or anybody else could draw between himself and the protagonist's noble fool archetype. Brad's struggles were different, and though he and Forrest Gump always had a profound presentness in what society would call inopportune or pressing moments, they were not perfect parallels. Brad related to that character not for his nobility or his foolishness. He related to the character because he saw a common link in what they were chasing.

It was all there in one of the final scenes. Near the end of the film—when Gump is entertaining a grand recollection about the stars in the Vietnamese sky, the million sparkles of sunset glistening over the water in the bayou, the perfect reflections of two skies over an alpine lake, and the union of heaven to earth in the violet sunrise of an Indigenous desert—I remember seeing Brad holding back tears. Transfixed, softened to the brow, it overwhelmed him because it all looked so much like the life he had been living. Here was someone else who, in a life defined by trials and tribulations, was always guided by the light. It wasn't the archetype of the character; it was the beauty the character found in nature, in each of the crucibles of his life. That's where the movie touched him. It validated the multitudes of quiet, even hidden moments of revelation that lay out there, inextinguishably, just for him. Works of wonder, always around the bend, softly wooing him despite life's disarray.

By summer, Brad was climbing even higher, farther, and better, both with Dustin and with his newfound Colorado companion, Scott Bennett. Scott and Brad would end up tied to a rope for an uncountable number of missions, incessantly pressing one another for high adventure, big linkups, and speed climbs, which they exercised with a tooth-crunching, deeply blue-collar voracity. Scott and Brad would hone each other for years to come as iron sharpens iron. Scott was also one of the first people Brad met who was living the dirtbag profile to its most exquisite degree. Perhaps just the kind of enabler he needed.

According to the boys, it was during this time, circa 2009, that Brad's gumption for dereliction grew. He seemed to progressively care less about material order in his life on many levels. When Brad overran the engine of his old Honda Civic, blowing out the pistons and unable to spot a repair, he sold it for scraps on the dollar to a local mechanic in Oakhurst, and then hitchhiked back to work at the Awhahnee Hotel, one hundred and fifty dollars the richer. In his mind, it was one less construct to worry about.

The simpler the better. Especially considering he already had employee housing and it was only a five-minute approach to world-class climbing.

Scott was on a similar path as Brad. Spending on the dime and sleeping even cheaper, Scott camped out of his car, the only vehicle they needed to get around in the Valley. It was also with Scott that Brad excelled in his understudy of the unwritten climber's tradition—food foraging leftovers at the Lodge buffet. But just as Brad was not naturally gifted at mathematics or speaking in tongues, he was also not gifted in swiping food. His practice at it, like his safety measures when climbing, would need some amendment, especially considering that on more than one occasion, his sticky fingers landed him in the hot seat. Brad was becoming elite by climbing, sure, but his skillsets did not transfer in the application of being discreet while pinching food.

Still, Scott and Brad were a formidable duet, and they were fast becoming good friends. It wasn't just sure passage up hard and dangerous climbs Scott was capable of—as a caring, loyal friend and a kind spirit, he was plenty good for emotional support, too. I remember Brad telling me about his recent climbs when I visited Ahwahne again for a friend's wedding that same season. He didn't brag, but damn, he sure was elated.

A month later, Scott and Brad climbed the Regular Norwest Face of Tis-sa-ack (Half Dome), a Valley climber's tradition, and perhaps the final step in the progression toward To-tock-ah-noo-lah, following The Rostrum and Astroman, in a mere ten hours. With a 2,100-foot face, after a calf-bursting approach up to the base, that pace put them at about 1,000 feet vertical every five hours. If they added 1,000 feet more and kept that pace, they'd be looking at summiting To-tock-ah-noo-lah in a matter of fifteen hours. It was all finally happening; Brad was only a few steps away. Just one year and one month since moving to Ahwahne, after having been dropped off the team and sent reeling into one of the lower points in his life, Brad Gobright was on the cusp of his definition of greatness.

In the middle of summer, Brad got a second iteration of a used, crappy Honda Civic and took to the road, climbing at the lesser populated Sierra alpine and high-country locales, The Needles, Tuolumne Meadows, and The Incredible Hulk. Due to a recent snafu at the Ahwahnee Hotel, his now-former place of employment, Brad was on a leave. He didn't know it then, but the Ahwahnee Hotel would not take him back for a third, fourth, or any other season. He'd already worked his last shift. Much like his youth, however, Brad's time was not wasted.

Riding the high of having climbed Tis-sa-ack successfully, free-climbing all but a few crux moves on his first attempt, Brad hustled. In Tuolumne meadows, he ran laps on 5.12 single-pitch routes with Dustin Burd, while on "rest days" he free-soloed the classic Tenaya Peak, Matthes Crest, and Cathedral Peak loop. Moving fast and free in the alpine country was an inspiration for Brad, where he could sink into that long view and tap in on flow state. Out there, under such a captivating landscape—feet on forest floor and hands on hallowed rock—the climbing didn't have to be at his limit, it simply had to be non-stop. Often, from dawn 'til dusk, it was.

At The Incredible Hulk, he and Scott Bennet climbed the all-time-classic moderate route Positive Vibrations, easily onsight (free of falls, first try, without any information on the climbing sequences or the gear placements), which was then followed up by nearly sending the far steeper and stouter Venturi Effect, just to its right, a week later. The Venturi Effect, first established by Brad and Scott's heroes, Peter Croft and Dave Nettle, had been on Brad's list for some time. In a recently rediscovered journal entry that I wrote on a piece of scratch paper from 2007, there's even a note of the Venturi Effect on my naive and overzealous "to-do" list. Next to it, only one asterisk modifies the text, which says, *Brad's idea, not mine.* Flush with consecutive rounds of 5.12, delicate and powerful endurance climbing at 12,000 ft elevation, it was a proper test for Scott and Brad. For its altitude, its high demand, and its ego-deflating cruxes, it's not a climb that many rush into.

With the rate Brad was churning out next-level, all-day endurance and grade marathons, it's easy to just start listing them off without pause—as things that were supposed to be there or supposed to have happened. But these are all the types of routes that many among us may dedicate years toward without any success. This was the year that Brad traversed from just an all-around good climber—the kind that will get up a handful of big routes and hard grades in their lifetimes—to a masterful one.

After The Incredible Hulk, Brad moved on to The Needles in the Sequoia National Forest, with local pirate and raconteur, Darshan Awhluwalia, a Southern California transplant. There, on the Warlock needle, a 1,100-foot spire of golden, lichen-spattered granite, Brad onsighted the crown jewel, the king line of the range, the Romantic Warrior. Sustained 5.12 climbing through crack, face, and delicate angles—the kind of nuanced movement Brad would've been heckled for butchering just a few years prior—became a canvas for him to exercise his craft upon. Through this raging series of climbs in the spring and summer of 2009, Brad put the final strokes on the canvas. More than ever, Brad was ready to stand face-to-face with the most famous rock climb in the world, The Nose of To-tock-ah-noo-lah.

In mid-September, Brad came back to Ahwahne with his

technique, endurance, and energy as tightened up as possible. He was climbing fast, he was climbing clean, he was alight, and everything in its right place. All he needed was a partner. A partner he found by mining the local campgrounds, where he met a fellow named Russell Facente. No surprise for Brad, at least the Brad of 2009, the partnership was simply an order of shared aim—getting up To-tock-ah-noo-lah. And for that purpose, their partnership mostly picked up at the base of the first pitch and left off not much further than the final tree at the summit. This first trip up To-tock-ah-noo-lah would not be a matter of deep friendship, though all things would come in time.

Brad's first literal run up the Big Stone was more a function of climbing than it was a function of friendship, a fact that does not minimize the excellence they marshaled in that single push. Not only were Brad and Russ climbing The Nose, but they were aiming to do it in a single day. Some of us hear of such feats so regularly that we don't even bat an eye. But be not calloused by the regularity with which these types of climbs occur. Ascending that rock in a single push, in a single day, is a monumental display of wits, competence, and mastery.

Together, Russell, having had more experience, and Brad, providing the speed of youth, climbed The Nose in fourteen and a half hours. Exactly thirty minutes quicker than expected based on Brad's pace with Scott when they climbed Tis-sa-ack just a couple of months prior. Beginning the climb at dawn, near 5 a.m., they swapped leads in blocks, with Brad taking most of the lower and middle free-climbing leads. Russell, craftier in his aid-climbing technique, led the more complex pitches. In spots such as the Great Roof, perhaps the most iconic pitch of the route, Russell ran out his lead in style (going considerable distance without placing protection), just so that Brad would have a quicker, easier job following in second position. They both went boldly in their respective leads up the wall, and together they topped out the climb of a lifetime just in the embers of sunset.

The dream Brad Gobright had carried since he was a dwarf-sized seven-year-old was complete. Every first achievement up on that wall is almighty for the fortunate climbers stuck in the thick of it, and perhaps Brad's was no more so than the next. But surely on its context, not just where it was born from, but where he was yet to go, that day was one for the highlight reel—a crystallized timestamp on his path of becoming. In the face of years' worth, an entire childhood's worth of desperate toil and unending misfit, Brad Gobright found the special, irreplaceable sense of belonging at last. He found *place*. There it was, all along, in the high spaces he'd been overtaken by as a child. It was among the grandeur of nature, in the oceans of granite that were not all so unlike the oceans and sea life that stole his attention for so long as a make-believe deep-sea diver. It was in the intricate, mesmeric detail, in one grain of quartz and mineral, one pitch at a time.

After having been made fun of, heckled, scorned, and kicked off teams and friendship circles, after having been told for so much of his life that whatever the task may be, he simply was not doing it right, Brad Gobright championed his own course. He found the light within himself and demanded it burst forward. He became.

SOLO

Brad closed a chapter when he climbed To-tock-ooh-no-lah. In front of him now stood the improbable traverse he would take from dark horse to legend. Of course, that was never his goal. His thoughts would have been more immediate, like where and what he would climb next or what he was going to do for cash now that the Ahwahnee Hotel had him on the blacklist. Still, it's my belief that he would have recognized the freedom before him, and aside from simply enjoying the present moment, he may have even asked himself what on earth he should do with it.

What lay ahead wasn't going to be easy. It would not be an elegant life, nor come without a cost. But paradox is the mark of most fascinating lives. He stood often on both the cusp of brilliance and the edges of disaster. What lay ahead, his course in the coming years, was an intricate series of peaks and valleys on his irreversible path.

Brad followed a cycle that many climbers have, for generations, ventured—revolving North, South, East, and West, by latitude and season. For Brad, everything revolved around the big stuff during spring and fall in Ahwahne. Between those peak seasons, though, he was on the circuit. Boulder, Rifle, Reno, Estes Park, Ten Sleep, Salt Lake, Index, Bend, Bishop, Saint George, Summerlin, everywhere in between, these are all pit stops, or sometimes even long-term life stops on the climber's path. They are the places we come to call home. They are also where we intersect with others on a shared path. The wayward life does more than connect us to landscapes alone; it brings us together with our fellows.

But the road can be a devil in disguise, too. If there is anything a person is running from, the road will not free them from it. If something is amiss within, there ain't no climb, no place, and there sure as shit ain't nobody that can free a person from the bondage of their own self. Take the cycle one too many times, you'll be chasing only shadows. At the end of the day, if life needs to teach you a lesson, no geographic runaway plan will stop the inevitable. And for my money, that's what Brad was up against next—the inevitable.

In the coming years, Brad was going to blitz the stone like a bat out of hell. He would literally make history. But he was also going to run a few other cycles out there. In time, even for Brad, all the glory of the climber's life would have to face a certain brand of truth and consequence. He'd find that even in abject poverty, there can be gluttony. And when it came to relationships, to engagements with other humans that finally had some stakes hanging in the balance, much was to be learned—especially with love. And sometimes, in the quiet of it all, on those rare occasions when staring at the stars or the opulent bursts of sunrise and sunset wasn't enough, he'd even have to face remnant questions about whether he was or was not proud of the guy in the mirror. Realization might have been the theme of the day when he made his longtime dream of standing atop To-tock-ah-noo-lah come true, but real life, the main course, was only just beginning.

November 2009. Brad started off the rest of his life on a tear. After autumn in Ahwahne, he was back on the road to the Bear's Ears National Monument with the revolving crew of Mason Earle, Scott Bennett, and Dustin Burd. Singular goals in mind, Brad was quickly back on his project, Air Sweden, the notorious extension of the Sweden-Ringle route, which compresses (movement likened to squeezing a refrigerator with a bear hug) up a heinous arete block at a dizzying runout above proper small gear. He'd been romanced by the climb since he'd seen videos of it a few years earlier, and, after putting in the requisite work for it in the fall of 2008 and spring of 2009, he was ready. Brad sent Air Sweden, living the life of his heroes before him and ticking one of his first 5.13 climbs in the process. The first of what would become hundreds more in his life.

He was settling in perfectly during these months, especially with Mason Earle, who would later describe Brad as "the little brother I never had." Brad's relationship with Mason and the other boys was often highlighted by moments of camaraderie and climbing. Occasionally, according to some, a touch of rivalry or one-upmanship pervaded, but only in brief. Bragging rights were always second chair to the joy of self-discovery. Brad, being big on practical jokes, would often find ways to ruffle somebody's feathers, usually a sign he felt safe enough to be himself. At night, he and the boys would chase adventure in the form of gigantic fires and tall tales, while feasting on cheap pastries and pantry goods such as canned beans and rice. They would eat whatever they could find, whether it be at the supermarket or in plain sight.

One somewhat legendary evening, the boys came across a pile of roadkill—a fallow deer that had been struck by a car. Not wanting it to go to waste, Mason quickly knifed up and separated the hindquarters, skinned it and carved away the tendinous fascia, then put the meat of it in their oversized camp pot for a long simmer with a little *mirepoix*, potatoes, and boxed wine. They may not have been Michelin-level critics, but to the boys, that meal, at least on taste, was better than Thanksgiving dinner, which would arrive just a few days later. As Scott recounted, though, turkey day was pretty damn standout too.

"It was a proper rager, as I recall," he said. As if deep frying an entire turkey and partying with the locals wasn't enough, after the meal, at the behest of a fair amount of cheap swill, Mason, Brad, and Scott took turns scooping the solidified greaseball remains from the frier and hurling them into the community campfire. It wasn't so much "fireworks on the fourth" as it was mortar shells in the trenches, but it got more laughs and scares than any other entertainment that evening. Locally, their campfires—and they themselves—became infamous in short order.

It was the good life on daily repeat; free food, often at that charity of others, and constant entertainment by the campfire, often in the form of more gas explosions. Couple that with the sounds of banjo and guitar of which Mason was a master and the company of rock-weary, kindred spirits, what more could a band of young men ask for? Women? No way, not in those days. These early cycles did not have Brad, or any of the others, left wanting for anything but the red desert and its rock that lay before them.

On a highlight day in December, Brad, Mason, and the first voice of climbing radio, the legendary Chris Kalous, ran train on a regional classic, Winner Takes All, out in the distant Disappointment Cliffs of Bear's Ears National Monument. In consecutive order, they each sent the 5.13 (-) route, first go. Brad, going last in the train, had perhaps the most pressure to achieve, and as Mason and Chris recalled, was already exhausted from multiple days on without rest. Brad's fingers were painted red, chock-full of gobies (pressure ulcers), cuts, and blisters, bloodied and torn to the tips—an excruciating hand to play on a finger-crack. Often, it's not for a lack of friction, but for pure pain threshold that many of us let go at a certain point out there. But not Brad. His monstrous appetite, his brutal capacity for pain—surely a tuning his dad had long ago helped him with—was precisely what got him up that wall.

The three of them stood out there, no other soul in sight, in the vast lands of the ancient desert, spoiled rotten with the goods. As often happens after such a magnanimous high, they bailed on the roped-climbing altogether and went down off the bluffs, into the lowlands of the canyon floor, scurrying around boulders at whim, keeping things light, free, childlike. The real kind of enlightenment.

In February 2010, I caught up with Brad in Red Rocks, just outside of Las Vegas, and I got that sense that his recent ascents were fashioning something of a gem within him; that he was well on his way to a different order than the rest of us. Celebrity, or even some accolade for his course, was still going to be years away, so it wasn't obvious on first impression. But I could see the fire in his eyes, and I understood right then that he was making that traverse toward some measure of excellence. More importantly, I could see how that fire related to his inner tuning. It was the most honest way he could have been living.

We sat together on the floor of a Motel 6 bedroom, a room which we'd managed to share between six other climbers for the sake of cost, while Brad pulled out his laptop again. It wasn't Forrest Gump running across America this time, but a highlight reel of Brad doing his own version. Brad had simply seen too much beauty out there on the road, between highways and deserts, between the high places he called home, and he wanted to share it. There were shots from The Needles, from Payahuunadü (the Eastern Sierra basin), from the great indigenous sandstone deserts near Moab, and of course, shots from Ahwahne. Many of them, surprisingly, had nothing to do with climbing at all. Often, his camera was just as focused on a spot of lichen as it was on a single set of bloody fingers plugging into a crack climb. He knew I was into climbing for the beauty of it more than the accomplishment, and he couldn't keep those photos to himself for the sheer revelation they'd given him. It was a touching slideshow, personally curated, of all the places life had taken him. Places he and I had often talked about in our first year of climbing together.

After his one-on-one slideshow, we joined the gang for dinner at a local buffet. Brad, of course, didn't eat with us for its moderate cost, although he did spoil himself to a five-dollar In-N-Out Burger meal on the way. Based on how full he was of satisfaction that evening, he didn't need to eat much anyway.

Earlier that day, near sundown, when the gang was all busted up from a full day of climbing, Brad set himself to perform one of his first free-solo climbs with an audience. Of course, that made most in the group cringe when it was happening, as nobody had witnessed an act with the potential for such exacting, mortal consequence. Some of us had been in car accidents, lost loved ones to disease, or seen death on the streets in developing nations, sure. We were familiar with the possibility of death by dire circumstance, as something at the edge of the human condition. But it's another thing entirely when somebody walks toward it, when someone willingly marries the potent finality of death with the balletic weavings of art right before your eyes. It's not that anybody expected Brad to fall, but things happen. He easily could have, and that idea alone forced those who were present to acknowledge that potential death. Most people do not have an operating system that allows them to free-solo, which is why they don't. But concerningly, many of us don't even have an operating system to witness it. Rather than ask what experience the soloist may be having, we think only of worst-case scenarios, and our limited curiosity and empathy in turn limit our ability to observe. Unphased by the concern of the audience, much like that day he top-roped up on The Rostrum, Brad climbed it anyway, sans-rope, for his own reasons. While it was happening, most everybody in attendance looked away, also for their own reasons. Proper 5.11, Brad took the Yak Crack straight to the anchors without a hitch.

I'm not entirely sure why he chose that climb in front of everyone, as he was always more of a solitary soloist by type. But, for whatever reason, he did. Perhaps it was just the fact that he knew he could, and, as some mountaineers have said, *because it was there*. As with much of his climbing at that time, it wasn't with the greatest poise. But once again, where many saw the inevitability of something like calamity, just one move away from the young man, I saw a human being shining above me, where all others stood below. It was, all said and done, just one more of the many blasphemous, heroic images I had of him taking on light in a way nobody else could.

What it did show, what everyone saw with or without their eyes open, was that Brad was beginning to take his free-soloing to a new level. Where he might end up, nobody really knew.

A month later, Brad took an impromptu trip to Payahuunadü, the Eastern Sierras, with a few new friends he had met while staying in the dirt at Joshua Tree. One friend in particular, Kevin Mohler, would soon become a mainstay in Brad's upcoming years. Kevin was perhaps the only person more dirtbag than Brad. And for that reason, along with his easy-going, relaxed aura, he became a good friend and even better travel partner.

Kevin was on a break from society, and, as they do for many, it lasted longer than planned. Coming out of the mold after his four years in university and stumbling into a broken economic system with the financial crisis of 2008, he traded a predictable path for an unknown direction. By the time he met Brad in Joshua Tree, that direction had taken Kevin to a life almost completely free of material possessions. Where Brad had the most beat-up car in the parking lot at a climbing crag for years running, Kevin didn't even own one. Where Brad would swipe leftover food from the tabletops of buffets and dining establishments, Kevin would be willing to go one step further: a full dumpster dive. As it was said at one point by one of their peers, "All the climbers had a little bit of the homeless in their make-up; Kevin, though, was more like a homeless that just happened to have a little bit of climber." New to the rockcraft, Kevin was also Brad's first understudy.

Together they made a habit of climbing boulders without crashpads and climbing on ropes without much gear. Day in and day out. Especially Brad. According to Kevin, during that spring season, Brad only took two actual rest days. That meant that between March and April, Brad climbed fifty-eight of sixty days on. The young man could not help himself.

A month later, Brad emptied most of what remained in his wallet on his gas tank, driving for his first trip to what would eventually become a second home: Boulder, Colorado. There, Brad climbed primarily with Scott Bennett, whom he had met the previous year and with whom he had already climbed Tis-sa-ack. Being brief by his standards, staying just a few weeks, Brad mostly sampled the Front Range's inexhaustible acreage of vertical rock. He would come back soon enough, though, and make a life's work of the routes in Eldorado and Boulder Canyons. But the Valley was calling.

In May of 2010, Brad returned to Ahwahne with a mission. Together with Mason Earle, he had eyes on a new line up To-tock-ah-noo-lah—a direct start set plumb beneath the famous heart formation. To get reoriented, as the granite in Ahwahne has its own *terroir*, Brad took another lap on The Nose, this time in just eight and a half hours. He'd nearly cut his time in half, which deserves a certain pause, because making that much improvement on just a second go was completely unheard of. If his first personal ascent of The Nose represented a next-level aptitude, this second ascent was a statement of exponential growth. One does not just climb The Nose of To-tock-ah-noo-lah with such abandon. People toil up there. There's such a minute percentage of those who do it in a day, let alone under ten hours.

Brad's success on The Nose was not soon to be mirrored on the Heart Route, however. Beginning in May of 2010, Brad and Mason took on this grandiose project, which would eventually have five 5.13 pitches and a slew of sustained 5.11–5.12 climbing, piecemeal at best. For their first season, reconnaissance work and equipping the route was the name of the game. During more than a week spent at base camp, on their portaledge (a hanging sleeping cot) a few hundred feet off the deck, Mason and Brad drove bolts into the stone by hand, fixed anchors, and plotted a map of their dream climb. But between unseasonable wet spells, they'd only ever get as far as nailing down a few consecutive pitches at a time.

Never one to be sullied for too long, Brad managed to scratch his itch in other ways. With Scott Bennett, he did his first pass on the Salathe Wall, the climb he'd been booted from a few years prior, in his trademark ass-kicking style. Brad free-climbed most of the route, except for a few of the hardest pitches, in just 10.5 hours. The idea that Brad could free-climb even large swaths of the Salathe, at that stage, was an exceptional testament to both his fitness and endurance.

As if that wasn't enough, Brad and Scott Bennett jumped on The Nose immediately after summiting, going for Brad's first multi-route link-up on To-tock-ah-noo-lah in an attempt to top-out the monolith twice, by separate routes, in the same day. Ambitious as he'd ever been simply couldn't cut it after just four pitches up

The Nose. Brad was broken, physically, from his mighty efforts on the Salathe. He retreated to the meadow where he ate pizza and swashed a round of King Cobras with the band of locals that he was now calling friends. A week later, for his twenty-second birthday, Brad went back to The Nose for another "lap" with Scott Bennett and completed it in a whopping six-and-a-half hours. The pace of progress was unjustifiably remarkable, borderline absurd.

The road trip that Brad called his lifestyle had been going for two years by the summer of 2010, and while his climbing life had never been better, other fronts hadn't improved. First, his job. After a few incidents in the Valley, Brad had been blacklisted from working for the Delaware North Company, or so he figured, considering he couldn't seem to get back on respectable terms at the Awhahnee Hotel. It wasn't just the incidents in the Valley, such as being cited for riding in the back of my open-cab pick-up truck, that bit back at him either. Brad made a habit of pushing the boundaries in his tenure at the Ahwahnee Hotel while on the clock, too. Whether by climbing in his work outfit while on break, or by eating food from the guest's rooms while housekeeping, none of it endeared him to the powers that be.

That spring was tough on Brad, like sandpaper on an open wound. Weather had been unusually wet and cold, which meant not only more days frustrated, not climbing, but more nights shivering, too. In June, his second iteration Honda Civic was broken into by a local bear, causing damage he didn't have money to repair. For years his parents warned him about a break-in, especially considering he always kept his climbing gear in the car, uncovered and exposed. Usually, Brad would just shrug it off along with all the other social norms that seemingly never stuck with him.

"Don't worry about it, Mom," he'd say. "It doesn't matter where I park. My car is always the worst one around, which means nobody will ever break into it."

Having taken my own junkyard pick-up truck for more than 250,000 miles of hard living, I related to his sentiment—beater cars were practically never targets, and therefore, rarely locked. The only problem was, in an Ahwahne bear's eyes, you look right past exteriors and the combustion chambers when putting a valuation on a set of wheels; it's all about the processed meats or the simple sugars inside the car. Something Brad was never short on. Yet the poor guy never saw it coming.

After the break-in, a cardboard filler and some duct tape would be the make-shift window for a long time to come. It was something he could laugh about around the right bunch of like-minded climbers, say, at a bonfire in Camp 4, but his circumstance bit back at him on the odd occasion he slept in the car rather than in the boulder fields. It wasn't as amusing, or comically inglorious, when buckets of rain soaked in during every storm.

Beyond that, the nights were cold—like, Baltic cold. By June 27, just eleven days after his magical birthday on The Nose, Brad posted a rant on his social media page giving some clue to his despair. Broke, even by his standards, tired of dodging rangers and sleeping with one eye open, desperate to find work, and sick of the tourists, Brad was unwound. Not only that, but from my conversations with him that summer, it seemed like these woes were just symptomatic of greater, deeper dissatisfaction. Not climbing due to weather and not working due to his unemployability left him without an anchor. He'd been to the mountain top, but that couldn't keep him from the certain valleys below.

Hoping to find work, Brad moved back to Orange County for the tail end of summer, a move that must have felt like a step in the wrong direction. While there, he paid $180 a month at the generosity of an acquaintance to rent a small living space in the city of Irvine, not far from the climbing gym where he intended to pick up shifts. Brad worked a handful of youth summer camps— the same ones that he had once attended in his elementary school days—and belayed kids during their ever-revolving birthday parties on the weekends. All of it was miles removed from the high spaces he craved. But at least he was warm.

By autumn he was back in Ahwahne, ravenous in appetite but short of accomplishments. Within a week of sleeping in the boulder fields, he'd gotten a nasty bout of poison oak, dodged rangers, and been caught stealing food from the leftovers of a tourist's pizza box at the Curry Village deck. Adding to the turmoil, the weather fell into a maddening cycle of melting hot days followed by brief, monsoon-like wet spells. The temperate windows between the two were seemingly never long enough to make gains on the Heart Route project with Mason or anything else he had his eyes on. Brad was riddled by life that fall.

Brad questioned much about his course at that stage. He kept a tension, not so obvious to all but familiar enough if you knew where to look. Often, friends like Kevin and Dustin noted little things in almost any situation could annoy him. Whether it be a constant noise in the background of a conversation, or a long line at a grocery store, when it came to the small, daily stuff, anything out of tune could drive Brad mad. If you asked about the undercurrent, as some of us did on occasion, it usually didn't take long for something to spill out.

"You know," Brad said to me once, while shopping at a supermarket after climbing, "sometimes it's just this big mess of not wanting to work all the time, which is what you have to do on minimum wage. But then if you don't, you're always worrying about money. I'm climbing a bunch, but I don't really know what I'm doing with it all. I mean, it doesn't always make sense."

Usually, he'd put away the vulnerability and laugh it off as best he could.

"I guess I'm just going to keep eating ice cream and I'm sure I'll forget about it," he mused, a pint of Kroger ice cream and canned fruit in hand at the checkout stand. "That should work. I mean, it usually does."

Sweet tooth aside, Brad would often turn to his favorite stories. He could feign a jester, a storyteller, even a Luddite or a cynic most days of the week. But ninety percent of the time is not one hundred percent of the time. There were moments where those jokes about his misgivings on the modern world or ow absurd his life was were only a frail front to the pain. It was in those darker moments that Brad needed support, perhaps, escape. While he wasn't at the age to sink into his subconscious submarine anymore, he did have certain habits he could return to.

For one, Brad always found solace in tales of hope. Brad had a penchant for watching the *Lord of the Rings* films, and, more often, reading the books, as they'd always given him a great sense of direction. Maybe that was because underneath it all—behind all the warring factions, great battles, and haunted pasts—it all came down to a couple of pint-sized, unlikely heroes, who, in a world flush with magic, revelation, and high consequence, carried a burden that no others could simply by taking one step at a time. Or maybe it was because Brad remembered that long before he could independently read for himself, his mom had read the entire series to him. First novel to last, front to back, when Brad was in elementary school—right about the same era they moved houses—Pamela and Brad spent countless nights together, reading books, captivated by the grandeur of Tolkien's magical world. I think he gave himself permission to sink right into those stories, and those homesick memories, the emotional equivalent of comfort food, because sometimes even Brad Gobright had to admit that the weight of life was, in fact, a juggernaut. It was not all whim, delight, and unbearable lightness, after all. Not always.

In addition to the *Lord of the Rings* novels, Brad also found guidance from an unlikely source: Steve Jobs. On November 21, 2010, Brad posted one of his favorite speeches on social media, the 2005 Steve Jobs commencement address to the graduating class of Stanford. A speech that spells out the absolute necessity to follow your heart, to dream big, to go boldly in spite of, and especially when in, adverse circumstance. It's an ode to living completely, being honest to your ambitions, to trusting the work of the long and unseen road. Over the years, since I had known him, Brad always said it was something he kept coming back to. It was the equivalent of a trail cairn, one he would turn to especially when it got cold and lonesome out there in the emotional landscape of his heart.

In the winter of 2010 and 2011, Brad worked part-time in Southern California and climbed full-time. Stuck in one location, still paying rent, he managed to eke out a series of mini road trips, which would usually last 1–3 weeks. With a new sense of discipline, he was making tremendous gains with his climbing, too. He began to train proper rather than simply exercise. Hangboard workouts, core workouts, long spells calibrating power, then endurance, then a little of both before he'd reset the cycle. He was getting out to the usual spots, Joshua Tree the most often, but he'd also take whatever he could get, which often meant sport climbing out in the wasteland of used needles and graffiti-spattered boulders at the Riverside rock quarry, in the inland empire.

By spring, he was back in Ahwahne, spending time with the revolving circuit of characters who called it home. On most occasions, this meant hanging out at the SAR (search and rescue) sites with the veteran cast of Valley locals. It also meant swinging from campfire to campfire at night, waxing tall tales of adventure to itinerant campers, usually accompanied by Kevin Mohler, his sidekick and hype man, or with Mason Earle, whose reputation and musical skills walked well ahead of him.

Brad built relationships with many of the locals, perhaps none as pure as the friendship he forged with the To-tock-ah-noo-lah fixture, Mr. El Cap himself, Tom Evans. Tom was and is a veteran of life and of the military service who had come to the Valley three decades earlier in his own vision quest as a climber. After a few major turns in life, he found himself spending nearly every climbing season for the past two decades at the El Cap Bridge, telephoto lens and tripod at the ready, unwittingly becoming a living pillar of Yosemite's climbing culture. A lauded raconteur, scribe, and elder statesman of the rock tribe, Tom Evans had a heart of gold, a lot like Brad. And it was Tom who would look forward to seeing Brad in the Valley the most, often saving a seat for him at the Yosemite Lodge Café in the mornings and evenings, where he would hope to hear a recap of Brad's daily adventures. Their bond became like that of a father and son.

Brad also began climbing with Southern California local hotshot and roadster, Bronson Hovnanian. Bronson and Brad got on with much of a big and little brother dynamic, which at times would pull them apart as firmly as it kept them together. They'd bicker, tease one another, and push boundaries in their relationship, which created the occasional rift. But generally, those rifts were short-lived, and, as with any relationship, they would learn over the years how to have patience with the other.

For the most part, Brad was plugged in, but usually not enough to show all sides of himself to everyone. Many of these friends wouldn't ever know about his childhood struggles or his ongoing epilepsy management. But they were friends enough, faces he could rely on, people to laugh with. A tribe to hold on to while life kept moving.

Brad kept in touch with his childhood friends infrequently but enough that whenever he did catch up with them, he couldn't help but compare the roads they were on to his scattered path. By now that core group of mates from Boy Scouts were all at the cusp of graduating from those fancy institutions of higher education. Some were even in the workforce already and not far from planning weddings, too. While he was out on the high and lonesome path, Brad, like many of us on the road, kept that awareness of his peers' direction in contrast to his own. I'm not sure if that awareness compelled him to seek accomplishment any harder in terms of his craft or in his lifestyle, but I know he wasn't blind to life happening in other ways for other people. And again, for a few seasons running, there had been some difficult times.

The spring of 2011 was not all that Brad would have wanted. Though he had been making short work of projects at the single pitch level, Brad was not mirroring that proficiency on the big stuff. Weather hadn't lined up for To-tock-ah-noo-lah, which meant that his projects on both the Freerider route—his newest goal on the Big Stone—and the Heart Route weren't moving. Feeling desperate for accomplishment, possibly even influenced by the slow buildup of comparison, Brad buckled. It wasn't so much that he slipped; in my eyes, it was the aggregate of all his inner unsettledness getting the better of him. Because of that, he lost the poise to decipher a good climbing decision from a bad one. On an obnoxiously hot day, soon after Mason and Brad had called it quits on the Heart Route for the season, Brad walked up to the iconic Columbia Boulder in Camp 4, home to the most famous boulder problem in the world, Midnight Lightning, and made a regrettably poor pass at it.

By that time, Brad had Midnight Lightning wired, perhaps a little too well. Because of that, in his haste on that day in late June, he zipped up the boulder without his chalk bag or a condition check. There, Brad came face-to-face with the infamous *mantle*, the top-out, finishing move on the boulder. It's the kind of press-out move that a person does when climbing out of a swimming pool without a handrail, the moment where their triceps and feet are at the same level on the rim. Only it's miles different, because on Midnight Lighting, what the climber is grabbing is much smaller. Add in the fact that the climber's feet are fifteen feet off the deck with a rocky landing beneath them, and that mantle move is suddenly a hell of a lot more committing than hopping out of the deep end of the pool. It's a move that stifles many competent climbers, even on a good day, which, with the heat, poor friction, and Brad's greasy palms considered, it was not. Without a crashpad below him, from fifteen feet off the deck, Brad slipped and fell directly onto the uneven rock slab at the base, breaking his foot on impact.

The next day, as Brad sat at the Yosemite Village Cafeteria, local nurse, climber, and inspirational figure, Libby Sauter, who worked on the SAR team, was in earshot. She gave Brad's wounds the once-over. Obvious upon a casual inspection, Libby confirmed the broken foot without any need for a medical-grade scan. Giving what painkillers and splinting she could, she told Brad he'd best get to a hospital for a full look. That might sound obvious, but it took some convincing on her part, as Brad wasn't sure of his insurance status and didn't seem to mind spending another night sleeping on it. With the help of Kevin Mohler, Brad got to the local hospital for some formal triage and casting.

Brokenhearted for such an unproductive spring in the Valley, Brad sulked in disappointment. He'd been told he would need at least six weeks off his foot and off the walls, a time away from rockcraft that he'd never had to endure. Unsure where to look or go next, those questions he had been fermenting on about life and purpose were never so unpleasant to face as when he was forced to look at them after being put down by an injury. Not ready to go quietly to the indoors, Brad went instead on another road trip, true to himself even in the struggle.

The Sḵwx̱wú7mesh Úxwumixw, or Squamish Nation, has become a haven for climbers during summer in the past forty years. Striking landscapes closer in scale to the distant Scandinavian fjord lands than to anything American fill the sea and sky with compelling texture, contrast, and topographic relief. Beauty abounds in this area of British Columbia, as does a rich indigenous backbone and a lifetime's worth of rock to scale. For that reason, Squamish attracts many climbers with its distinct aquamarine and mystic allure, just as it did Brad. So, with a medical cast more clunky than his car and a bank account more broken than his foot, Brad hit the road with his friend and perpetual stowaway, Kevin Mohler. They were Canada-bound, chasing the winds of change.

International travel, for Brad, had not always been his escape, nor a scenario where he'd been most inspired. The summer of his sophomore year in high school, after barely passing his math final and advancing into his junior year, Brad's parents took him and Jill to Italy and Switzerland on holiday. Industrious as always, his folks pinched pennies for the trip by hard work and savings. Brad, however, didn't see it that way, and only went begrudgingly. An intrigue with modern art would come later in his life, but at that stage, no art or edifice stood a chance on the young man. Even in the halls of the great Uffizi Museum, in front of *The Birth of Venus* and many a Sandro Botticelli work, Brad was empty for emotion. You couldn't pull a heartstring in him. The usual romance one feels in Florence, with the cobblestone streets and living history of Roman architecture all around, was entirely lost on him. Burnt out on the museum tours, he spent a couple of days in his hotel room during the Italian portion of the trip, playing video games while Rome, with its quaint charm, viticulture, sambuca, espressos, agnolotti, and fascinating byways kept on.

But boy, if you could have seen his eyes light up the first time he spotted the Matterhorn. If you could have seen him stomp soil into the earth with every step he took when they hiked up it. Nature had his heart in ways the art world simply didn't. That's where Brad switched on. It was always for the revelation of the natural condition, more than the human condition, that Brad stirred awake. As with much of life, though, seeds are planted by way of exposure. Travel, whether by climbing or by Fodor's, does change people. I think all of it prepped him for the man he would become, and, years on, Brad would turn a corner on his opinions. He would later find out he just needed to fall in love with an artist and arrive at a place in his life where what he was expressing on a wall was more than an unchecked, inborn fervor. No doubt, when Brad, at last, lived more of life away from the walls, he came to appreciate much more of the vast human expression. But, in 2011, with a broken foot and an itch for the rock that went deeper than the itch inside his cast, he wasn't quite there yet.

When Brad drove into Canada, up that Sea-to-Sky corridor for the first time, and looked across the Howe Sound, with the might of the Stawamus Chief and the picturesque bedding of the town of Squamish beneath it, it stole his heart. Instant switch. Broken foot, bank account, life plan—all of it, irrelevant. This was the kind of travel experience he'd always craved. Because of that, Brad would spend the next two months in Squamish climbing his brains kaput, all on the mighty budget of sixty U.S. dollars. That is literally one dollar per day for two months. He would simply do whatever it took. Camping illegally beside the Squamish River, foraging food, taking handouts by the charity of others, Brad would chase revelation down to its last ray of light, something most of us had a hard time appreciating, perhaps for our own lack of sight in the first place.

What most people couldn't see was the light he was chasing. Busied by the chaos of his lifestyle as it appeared outside-in, few had the equanimity to see his internal quest. It didn't matter what love a person had for the kid, whether it was that old Boy Scout friend—now with a degree and an ordered life—or the parent who had raised him to earn his keep and respect the rules. It's almost as if the closer they were, the worse it looked. He had a broken foot and a busted car with a cardboard window, which kept the entirety of his material existence and his net worth not-so-secure. He lived in a forest because he could not, or would not, pay for camping. He and a band of friends caught fish from the river as often as they purchased food from the supermarket. On top of that, he made a habit of going to the local Sikh temples to shamelessly take advantage of the free homeless meals they gave away. He knew little of the world around him and even less of his direction other than to never turn a corner if it did not feel gut-level true to himself. He wasn't employable, and he made a habit of petty theft. He often climbed without a rope, and, by all appearances, he could not give a damn about God and country. A position in life that perhaps only Steve Jobs, his holiness the Dalai Lama, and Christ himself would've seen as perfectly on course.

However big of a mess his life was becoming, Brad's time in Squamish was the getaway he needed. Heading back toward Ahwahne in September, he even wrote a short post declaring that Squamish was one of the most beautiful places he'd ever seen. Cast-free and with a now-mended foot, Brad took three weeks to climb in the Oregonian high plains, at the birthplace of American sport climbing, Smith Rock, on his way back south. Quickly, he was on area classics, working routes in the Aggro Gulley, which hosts a collection of steep 5.13–5.14s, as well as routes on the lauded Monkey Face.

Long passed were the days where he'd be happy to squeeze out a single difficult pitch on a trip. By now Brad was climbing well and strong enough that few climbers from his older days would have recognized his evolving prowess. On occasion, he might still botch a sequence or two, but in large measure, he had evolved to something akin to a deft, precise rock dancer. Most important, after years of flailing on what most humans would call proper hard grades, Brad was developing that innate sense of confidence within them. Just believing that you belong in those thin slivers of high-performance in the first place is often key to succeeding within them.

Just as he did with climbing, out on the road Brad focused on the beauty that surrounded him. During one of the last days of his trip, after a week's worth of smoke from local wildfires had pooled into a stagnant haze over the sky, a summer monsoon swept in and stole Brad's heart with its magic. Up on the West Cave of the Monkey Face formation, a stand-alone pillar that looks down at the Crooked River and the lush green agriculture fields that lead toward the town of Terrebonne, Brad took in a view for the ages. The rain clouds cleared over a damp, glistening earth below, and past the horizon of everlasting forests and the strato-volcanoes we call the Three Sisters and Mount Bachelor, the sun cast a series of hallowed beams across the horizon. Clear blue sky opened anew.

Painted in a dazzling gold, that shimmering cleanse of light— the kind that cuts through all space and baffles our senses with the contrast and hope it provides—caused Brad to stand in awe. He snapped a single, impeccably timed photo for the memory banks, overwhelmed. Revelation in hand, it was all the affirmation he needed. It was moments like that, he later told me, that kept him going. It's what kept him on course.

A month later, after having returned to Ahwahne for the annual Facelift event, Brad was in peak form. Confident and plugged-in, he pondered a monumental move. Free-soloing—something he had always done but had not necessarily been known for—suddenly held his attention at much larger scope. In the Valley, historically, there is a process one follows in free-soloing at a serious level, and it passes through The Rostrum.

Though he hadn't soloed anything so tall or demanding, at an internal level, Brad was ready. *But why?* one might ask. Rationale is something you ask for from an architect, perhaps, from one who designs by trade. But it is not the lot of the free-soloist. Experience is the stead they keep, meaning one does not free-solo so much for a purpose or a reason as much as for an experience. That is because there is a demand of presentness, an insistence on being more than rational, which pervades the soloing space, which makes it a thing to be done more than a thing to be understood. Brad, with all his quirks, with his deep focus that was always diagnosed as absentmindedness, was nearly flawlessly designed to occupy this very kind of space. With his evolved, borderline craftsman-level climbing skills now in the forge, he had the ability of body as much as the gifting of mind. Not that it mattered to him, but if Brad was going to free-solo The Rostrum, he'd be in the realm of the elites.

On Halloween, October 31, 2011, Brad took the alternate path down to the base of The Rostrum, walking beside the crystalline, emerald pockets of the lower Merced River. Shoes laced, chalk at ready, under the dozens of gorgeous green maples, Brad breezed up the first pitch. An initial crux comes in the opening thirty feet of the second pitch, where, by most climbers' sequencing, you spend a few body lengths of movement attached to the wall by only the last digits of your fingers and the butter knife surface area of the sides of your feet. It can't be more than one percent of your integumentary system and musculoskeletal sheath that are keeping you and your body from the perils below, but with that said, it is a truly righteous place to be. As he later explained, that part was a personal favorite.

Atop the third pitch, at the car-sized ledge which provides both rest and the option for escape, Brad debated what he had done, and, in a moment of reason, even questioned if he should go further. He could, after all, just walk right off that ledge and scramble to a small climber's trail on the ridge. It was a means to safety and had he stopped right there, he shared, it still would've been a day to remember. But the north face of The Rostrum and Brad had a long history, and more of it yet to make. And he was enjoying it. Like, completely, full of delight, with massive satisfaction.

After nearly twenty minutes at most, Brad was under the final headwall, a classic wide pitch that stumps many a first-time climber for its blue-collar composition. Nearly 1,000 feet off the deck, elated for the dream that was unfolding into reality, one locker move after the next, he nearly burst with excitement when cresting the final yards to the top. And, in what he described as a "brilliant shiner of a blue sky" mixed with clouds and sunrays, Brad topped out and was somewhat surprised to see a small gathering at the summit. Halloween, after all, beckons a good party as much as any of the holidays. And there, at the top of The Rostrum, a slew of friends and Valley locals had gathered to walk the highlines, play their gypsy tunes, and dance upon the earth. According to resident big wall fixture Mash Alexander, who was the first to see Brad turn the lip at the top, Brad smiled like a teenager—with that awkward, trying-to-sell-it face—and then got clever. At the precise moment that Mash realized Brad was not wearing a harness, jaw dropped in awe, Brad looked down to where his harness should have been, then quickly made a gunslinger pose and shot a joke from the make-believe gun at his hip.

"You know what they say on Halloween," Brad said with a laugh, "sometimes you just need a scary good time!"

Baffled by Brad's anomalous ways, Mash gave Brad an inspired hug and welcomed him into the circle. In a highlight reel frame that lasted until twilight, they sat up there, alight, drinking beer like it was a birthright, celebrating Brad's further coming of age. It was a day for the books, the kind that constitutes the legendary among us.

When glorifying Brad's character and his climbing, it should be noted that not all people are called to such feats, nor should they be. Ropeless climbing is absolute in its consequences, and it should not be glorified or celebrated as an act unto itself. We are not better off for having gambled on death, surely not if we have only done so to say that we have. The whole point of the rockcraft, as I see it, is to find our own edge in life—something we each get to define for ourselves—and then to learn the internal and external skills needed to operate competently within that space. We are there to learn of the challenging, the unseen, the unfamiliar—learning which, ideally, affects how we relate to others in our orbit. In the face of the wildest expression of movement a human being can muster—that of free-soloing—many of us will be encouraged to remember this: there are as many edges to walk, to learn of our condition, as there are people to walk them. The ultimate edge, that free, harrowing air that blows beneath the soloist's feet, I can assure you, is not a necessary component to the great learning of the outside life. It is an extraordinary, at times brilliant piece of the human experience, but it is not for all. The fact that any human can have this solo experience does not mean that everyone should. In Brad's life, for his arc, it is something to remember. That day especially, it was even something to celebrate. It still is. But in the air of the mountains, every man, woman, and all other expression among us most know their own lines. How we shall celebrate Brad's quest, his art, and his soloing as it relates to his character is in no way meant to parallel anyone else's journey. To suggest that any of Brad's feats, topically, would do for you what they did for him would be an operational and logical fallacy.

But, boy, did he kick some ass up there.

FORGE

The climber's paradise of Bear's Ears National Monument, surrounded by the ancient lands of the Dine, Zuni, Hopi, Ute, Uintah, and Ouray tribes, always held a special place in Brad's heart. At the tail end of 2011, after his autumn in Ahwahne, Brad returned for one of his many cyclical trips. A good November out there, among the auburn canyons and the everlasting petroglyphed walls, can rival any place of the natural order for its might to move the human spirit. The desert at the onset of winter, with its wild weather patterns, its sheer sharpness of texture, and the weight of its vast emptiness upon your senses, is of another world. Here, beauty comes in many colors, but especially when it's following some kind of deep, mercurial storm—revelation truly is all about the light. The kind of light that can cut through any darkness. The kind of light that can woo and reawaken even the most fractured and brittle heart.

For my money, touching base with that beauty was as much a foundation to Brad's movements across the continent as was anything else. Climbing was his means to truth by ascetic suffering, a process he followed by virtue of wedging his fingers into oblivion, often separating nail beds from cuticles in the fissures of rugged cracks and by forcing situations of desperate groveling and runout climbing. But that was only one side of the equation. The aesthetic path, his Beauty Way, that was the counterpoint—it was his other quest for the light, one he found by following the earth and its seasons. He may have been living in squalor, stuck to the dirt nine days out of ten, eating processed pastries and fast food, but that only amplifies the point. As the parable says, he was living on more than bread alone.

While out there that November, Brad had a standout moment when he established his very own first "first ascent." In the climbing world, that means you're the first person ever to climb a certain route. It means that it's never been done before. It's historic, and it's a rare thing to pursue, as most climbers choose to venture up already existing routes. It's also special because only the first ascensionist has the experience of taking it from the stage of a working idea to an actual part of reality made manifest. Once a climb has been done, generally it's easier for others to repeat. That's because climbing, like many things, is more mental than it is physical. And in that realm, it's simply harder to do that which has never been done than to do that which has. Because of that, establishing a first ascent, especially in the harder grades, requires an air of deep, intuitive connection to the craft. You've got to be at least partially a visionary.

Up on the Sabbatical Wall, an alluring outcrop above the Beef Basin Road, Brad and Scott Bennett toiled with a couple of locals, looking to score routes off the beaten path. While Brad was never the type to seek out being the first in a top-dog context, he was drawn to the route by some compulsion, perhaps for its high-quality, finishing headwall. Elated for the opportunity, Brad struggled through the difficulties in just a few short sessions and became the first to complete what would become a robust 5.13 (-)

climb.

Brad's first ascent was most memorable for him not because it would stamp his name in a future guidebook but because it happened so organically. All of his heroes in climbing had been the type to put up first ascents, and now, as a byproduct of simple devotion to his craft and his decision to live his life on the road, he suddenly found himself doing the same.

The climb would not be an instant classic, however, as it had sections of loose and dirty rock, but tradition dictated that as the first person to climb it, it was his charge to name it. While most of the routes at the Sabbatical Wall were titled on the theme of childbirth or pregnancy—with names like Immaculate Conception, Shotgun Wedding, even Stem Cell—Brad went in a more general—and I believe sentimental—direction. Brad named his route simply Mother. Sure, it fit the bill on the maternal or gestational theme, but I have no doubt that Brad was saying something more with his choice of title. This was his primary first ascent, his first chance to leave a note for the rest of us in the history books. And with that awareness, and the awareness of everything he had been through in life, his thoughts moved to the person who had been his chief advocate. It was an ode to Pamela, his rock, his anchor, his mom. Somewhere, back home, as he was flying high and Pamela waited with bated breath for the next update, Brad was out there just the same, thinking of her. An image I choose for its foundational beauty.

For all the glory Brad found from the transient life in 2011, though, he still carried much of the same inner tension. Pamela and Jim worried from home as their son flew with the wind, anxiously awaiting news which only came infrequently at best. On occasion, Brad would call, telling of a new climb, a first ascent, or a giant link-up he had done, talking of high feats and a burgeoning community of friends. The kind of news that made their hearts soar with pride. Stories which they told to friends and family at church as much as at the dinner table. Inspired, they rode the mighty and vicarious coattails of their son. Other snippets, though, the rough and tumble sections where he wrote back about a near-death incident, about financial, relationship, or even health problems, stole whatever faith they had in his process. For as many of those proud, reflective mornings Pamela and Jim had at the coffee table, burning bright with inspiration, there were always the equivalent nights spent pining in fear and bewilderment.

Relationships, particularly of the intimate order, had baffled Brad his entire life. And, while for many years he wouldn't have considered commitments beyond climbing, those years had passed. Brad was not simply an aloof, absentminded anomaly of life. As a climber, he did have tunings that would confound most of us; he had a certain detachment of existential fear that many are weighed down by when on the sharp end. But that was not true of him entirely. Brad was not a fool for life, however much he struggled for concepts that others might take for granted. He was a human being, of course, a person longing for connection to more than rocks alone, to more than the court of jesters and raconteurs that filled the campfire circles by night. Brad longed for love.

In February of 2012, Brad had an awakening. He had been in Boulder for a few weeks, and for nights on end had been sleeping in his beater, second iteration Honda Civic—the one that had the busted window. Without a free place to stay or a means to pay for one, he often parked his car near the hills of Chautauqua Park, where he would run free-solo laps at the famed Flatirons each morning. But the bitter, biting cold, at times down to -10 degrees Fahrenheit, was not something he could overcome. Those nights, long as winter in the north, were desolate places for him to consider his path. With so many houses aglow in the nearby neighborhoods, their chimneys smoking, Brad was forced to ponder more than he cared to.

Brad shared that one morning, as he had parked just beside an elementary school, he woke up to a batch of children walking past him, laughing, talking, carrying on with their lives in warm coats, with their backpacks on and sack lunches in hand, as only children do. Suddenly awoken emotionally, Brad froze in awe. Something, perhaps either the tenderness and undeniable innocence of it, or the way it was all framed by the sharpest beams of morning light, bankrupted him on the spot.

His eyes flooded with tears that he only kept off his cheeks out of a desire not to blink. He couldn't miss one second, let alone look away, even if he wasn't sure why. Perhaps the emotional breakdown was onset by the week of artic cold, all alone. But regardless of the cause, Brad saw an epiphany in those children that was as powerful as any ray of light he'd seen in the high spaces of the outside life. There was a preciousness in it that he had not expected, a revelation nested in something so basic, so every day, that he longed for it. Alone in that car with frosted windows and the fog of his erratic breath, Brad wept. Emotionally undone, overwhelmed by the contrast these school children showed him to his life, he surrendered any pretense and let the floods of tears free.

Brad wanted more—more than the rocks and campfire stories, more than what the photo albums that he'd gone out of his way to show me from his laptop could give. A week later, in a post online, Brad shared that his life "really couldn't be any more unromantic." That was followed a week later by another post where he simply said, "Boulder is great, but for the past few months I've been feeling kinda aimless."

Of course, Pamela had a sense of where his heart was. Even as others commented online, urging Brad to pour himself further into climbing and assuring him that romance and all its trappings were the quest of fools, Pamela knew her son was unfulfilled. Because of that, she despaired.

Brad went in the only direction available, or at least the only direction familiar, and kept climbing. By the end of the month, he had scored every route on the Rincon Wall at Eldorado Canyon—a stout collection of historic and dangerous trad-climbs—under his tally. Most of the routes, apart from being hard as nails, were established by his heroes. A fact that would have made him feel at least partially on course. The routes were also reputed for the headspace they required, as they were not only hard but had hard consequences. While Brad managed fear in a manner better than most, he was not absolved from it. He knew when danger was close, and he understood that he was courting it. This is an interesting fact to bear in mind, because whether he was driven simply to be his best or by the emptiness he may have been running from, this would become among his boldest seasons on a rope.

By spring, Brad had taken a couple of trips to the infamous Black Canyon of the Gunnison—where even climbers known for having strong metal quiver and shake with fear—and he was in full project mode. The Hallucinogen Wall, a visionary free-climb stacked hand over fist with runout, 5.12 climbing and a single 5.13 pitch, had his attention for some time. He'd spent multiple sessions hanging off the line alone, mini-tractioning the route (a top-rope style, akin to a self-belay). But this time, with local badass, climber, and heroine, Madeline Sorkin, he'd come to send it proper. Brad and Madeline both excelled in the hazardous terrain, climbing on the razor's edge of balletic performance in the face of hard consequence. Madeline, who established the first female free-ascent of the Hallucinogen Wall, would become a mainstay in Brad's life as a friend, and, more importantly, a mentor. Because of her understanding and compassionate character, she was one of the few he would truly open up to.

Moving quickly to Ahwahne for the spring, Brad shifted back into a climbing version of despair as his projects stacked up above him without any success. In another brief post online, he shared his disillusionment—surely enhanced by his sleeping arrangements in the boulder fields—and summed the entire season up as simply, "unmotivating."

Back on desolation's road, he looked north for a change of scenery. It seemed almost as if every time Brad had a moment of internal strife, he went further into his craft and further down the road. When his operating system was overrun, when he felt the weight of life around him, he pushed even deeper into his primary function. Brad gave himself to the outside life the way poets give their livers to the page. But the danger and the pace of it all was catching up to him, and just a month later in Squamish, the show would come to a stop for his second drastic injury.

On a nondescript day, Brad went outside and repeated a handful of boulder problems, as per usual, without the crashpad. Largely, he did not make it a habit to jump on climbs he had a chance of falling from. But for whatever reason, perhaps influenced by the sum of his recent dismay, or perhaps because the season in Ahwahne had been so wet and rained out—as had his first few weeks in Squamish—Brad jumped on a rock in poor conditions and got himself in a pickle.

Just as he had pitched off the top of Midnight Lightning a year earlier, Brad took a dive off the upper section of a boulder, landed offset on his right ankle amongst the uneven hazards below, and crunched bone to earth like a mortar to pestle. It took less than a heartbeat, a blink of an eye, and the seizing of his breath for Brad to realize he'd just fucked himself proper. He was alone for that one, so there was no telling the flood of emotions he felt or how long they would have taken hold of him. But in some time and with great pain, Brad hobbled on his non-injured lower limb back to the forested campground at the base of the Stawamus Chief. Defeated, he found phone reception, swallowed any pride, and called the anchor, Mom.

It was the middle of July and his entire summer season in Squamish was circling the toilet bowl. Bear in mind he had spent half of the previous summer in a cast, and, having been washed out by weather in Ahwahne during the recent spring, he'd arrived at Squamish short on patience and ready to rage. Now with his foot swollen to the size of a baby watermelon, however, he found acceptance a virtue lacking in practice.

A day later his sister, Jill, who had been watching her brother's escapades over the years with a certain pride, flew in at the Vancouver airport. On break between semesters at UCLA, Jill had been charged with caretaking and transport by Pamela and Jim. They knew Brad's ankle was in pieces, they simply didn't know how many. Unwilling to gamble with a major healthcare bill, they wanted him home for convalescence.

Jill was always the adventurous type, too. The type to go anywhere and learn of any peoples for the fantastic human experience it provided. An attitude that tallied her more than a handful of pages stamped in her passport. She had even visited Brad in one of his first seasons in Ahwahne and had insisted he take her up to the base of To-tock-ah-noo-lah for the famous alcove swing. Launching hundreds of feet into free air by means of a pendulum rope swing, she showed that guts were not exclusive to the men in the Gobright clan. And she would do the same to get Brad home. After Jill arrived from the airport by bus, they quickly broke down Brad's tent, gathered his personal effects, and swiftly blasted south. Jill put foot to floor, cruise-controlling at the pace of a bullet train, which did her no favors in the eyes of the Oregon State Trooper a few hours down the road. She was a hellion on the highway, according to all in the family.

Jill recounted that, on the way home, while suffering in the air condition-less heat of Brad's car, they recovered much of the space between them. They laughed, cried, listened to music—nearly detonating Brad's already fuzzy speaker to the likes of Modest Mouse and other angst-heavy melodies—and bonded as they hadn't in years. Brad, of course, worried for what lay ahead, sure that his old man was going to grind him down with insistence for a life plan all summer long. Jill, the adoring sister, did her best to remind him that regardless of his current aimlessness, he should be proud of all the things he'd done thus far. That more than anything, it would all work out, of course. She even suggested to Brad that he and his dad may not have been all that dissimilar, a reason they so often butted heads. It was a hard message for Brad to hear.

No doubt Brad wanted a fuller life, but the question was, would he search for it or simply maintain his status quo? To be young and coming of age is an inglorious affair, after all. The notion of integration, of living life and finding answers on all sides of the equation is by default a threat to the norm. At least in my experience, questions of life at that age riddle the senses, because solutions often look only as either/or rather than yes/ and. Accounts from his mom and sister agree to his growing desperation, but was he able or ready to share that with others? Who knows how many talks could've been had, how many conversations died just on the tip of his unsure tongue. Wrestling with those themes mostly on his own, season in, season out without a true mentor that he could see as understanding his take on life, Brad was at times maddeningly brain-bound. Once home, Brad sulked immediately in the confines of his room, where apart from trips to the galley and the head, he remained for the first week.

Push came to shove over the next eight weeks as Brad

recovered in Orange County. For all he'd done and all the places he'd been, something about home still took the wind out of him. I suspect it wasn't home as much as the homeland. It was what it represented. To some degree, home still carried the unresolved fragments of a challenging past, and in Brad's eyes at the time, home also meant a bubble. It represented the other path, the great flock of humankind who played the game, who set to task, who chose security and no longer sought the extraordinary out of life. Of course, climbing rocks is not the only way to find the extraordinary of life, nor is it even necessary to. But living beyond comfort is. And, while I'm no expert on the human condition, I can see how it would have looked from his eyes. Being home pained him.

Maybe it was as simple as that sense of disconnect, on instances like weekend mornings when his parents would take joy from sitting at home with a cup of coffee and somehow seem to long for absolutely nothing more than to stare out the window and enjoy the next sip. Maybe it was those simple, hallmark moments, the ones that are completely on repeat in homes not just in America, but all over the world. Maybe he knew there was absolutely nothing wrong with any of it, but for some reason he couldn't wrap his finger around, he knew there wasn't anything right about it, either. Maybe it was the strange isolation at the realization that their comforts were not his comforts.

With Brad, you never really knew unless you're one of the lucky few. Who knows, it could've just been as simple as having a busted ankle. But my hunch, especially when you hear it from his mother, is that there was a whole galaxy swirling behind his blue eyes. According to Pamela, that pain lasted all summer. Tethering between acceptance and anger, there was as much forward progress as there was despair. Some days, the closest Brad got to any form of exercise was by way of the remote control or video game console. The fact that his hands never got on a keyboard to bullet point a resume was not lost on his parents, either.

"If he was going to use his thumbs all day on a computer," his dad said, "he may as well use them to get a job."

Brad struggled, as anyone would. The civilized life is a sharp about-face for someone who has made the falcons' perch their home for years on end. Taking comfort in the absurd, as he would see it, Brad watched the entire catalog of *The Office* more than once over that summer. Relating to the comical reckoning it gave to the nine-to-five existence, it comforted him.

Homelife that summer was a low point for Brad. He struggled to see it all as the high-water mark that his mom did. After all, for Pamela and even Jim, their wayward son was finally home. Brad's lens was different, though. And when, as would naturally happen, Pamela and Jim asked of his course going forward, Brad was unable to parse the care behind their concerns. It's not as if they wanted to take the wild out of their young son. They didn't want to see him domesticated, but they did see past the next bend in the road on the arc of life, and they hoped he could too.

Those days—those conversations—pained Brad the most. Not because he wanted to escape them, nor because he thought, deep down, that his parents didn't have his best interest in mind. I think Brad hated those talks because, like many of us at various stages of our lives, he didn't have any answers. Even more, because he was injured, he didn't have access to the kinds of experiences that he thought would deliver him answers. He knew even then that there was no magic sentence he could utter at the dinner table that would make his parents suddenly assured about his course. The whole thing—his security, their security about him—all of it hinged on experiences he didn't have and a perspective that he both wanted and was afraid to evolve. At the end of the day, 2012-Brad-Gobright did not have the answers that he, more than anyone, would have longed for. Hell, if he was anything like the rest of us, he probably even hoped they would've come by simple devotion to the outside life. That was the fallacy many of us made all along, thinking our noble climbs would confer such noble lives. It's a sad day when any poor soul realizes that no number of pitches will fill the void, or even teach them precisely how to fill it.

Brad had spent his entire life knowing that his deepest tuning called him to the high planes. Objectively, no bullshit, he was born to climb. To be on lead, way up, gunning hard over small gear, in deep with a commitment factor that'll scare most people into a fetal curl, and to navigate that space without losing his cool, that was Brad's sweet spot. More than most, by psychology especially, he was made for that.

The problem was that he hadn't ever expected there to be so much more to navigate or integrate beyond what he was best at. Brad's fantastic abilities for presentness gave him a specific, magical view of life. He taught the magic of the present moment to those in his orbit the same way Siddhartha Gautama taught of the lotus flower, without words and in ways only a select few comprehend. But the present moment alone does not give you purpose. And perhaps, the greatest challenge for Brad that summer wasn't so much that he didn't have any rocks to pull on as that apart from those rocks, he didn't yet have a clear purpose to stand on.

By the end of October, Brad was as healed as he was going to be, and, after having consolidated the last six weeks of his homestay into a full-blown fingerboard and pull-up regimen, he was arguably stronger than ever. He spent most of the fall "looking" for work, or so he told his folks, while girding his fitness for his next few seasons of climbing. By winter, he was back in Boulder, about as far away from home as he could fashion at that time. Prophets, they say, never get on well in their own lands anyway.

In the spring, Brad climbed most with Scott Bennett, who, at that point, had become his trusted friend. Motivated for a strong showing in Ahwahne that year, Brad was linking big days of successive, hard pitches, usually taking laps at local crags on nearly a dozen 5.12, and a handful of 5.13 pitches, per day. The collective sum of his and Scott's efforts paid in full soon after, on a whirlwind trip to Zion National Park.

Before Scott arrived, flying in at Las Vegas, Brad put in a reconnaissance free-climbing lap on the Moonlight Buttress with his recent big wall contemporary and friend, Madeline Sorkin. Moonlight Buttress, an immaculate, varnished 1,200-foot pillar of sandstone that juts out from the flanks of its neighboring rock formation, is a historic masterpiece for the rock-climbing tribe. First climbed by pioneer alpinists and icons, Jeff Lowe and Mike Weis, in 1971, then later free-climbed by the equally legendary duo of Peter Croft and Johnny Woodward in 1992, the Moonlight Buttress focuses on a singular, finger's-width crack system that runs plumb top to near bottom with unrelenting 5.12 climbing.

Years earlier, in 2009, Brad and his old friend and climbing partner, Dustin Burd, had attempted to climb it, knowing it was one of those stopping points on the path toward big wall mastery. But young and unqualified at the time, they were roadblocked at the first crux pitch, an enduring 5.12 (+) corner that carries on for well over 150 feet of incessant demand. Where Brad struggled to even get past the first fifteen feet of it years before, this time he sailed. He and Madeline free-climbed the route in a single day, an exceptional standard by any measure. But that was only the beginning.

A few days later, after picking up Scott from Las Vegas, Brad returned. This time, the boys put their metal, and their appetite, to the test on a major linkup. In nineteen hours alone, they free-climbed four classic routes: Sheer Lunacy, Moonlight Buttress, Monkey Finger, and Shune's Buttress, all in a single push. Each one of these climbs is standard grade 5, meaning, the long and hard type of route that most competent parties need an entire day to surmise. Most mortals would toil to climb and find great soreness from having ticked any individual one of those routes. The notion of four at once, for the average among us, is baseline absurd. Each of the routes except for Shune's Buttress was consistent in difficulty with multiple pitches of 5.12, or 5.12 (+) climbing. Shune's, at 5.11 (+), was the "easier" fare. It was a standout day, one which Scott later remembered with great clarity years down the road from atop the pulpit of the St. John's Lutheran Church in Orange, at Brad's memorial.

Later in spring, Brad was back in Ahwahne, eager to try the newest and hardest line this side of the continental divide—Father Time. Established on Middle Cathedral, just opposite the meadow to To-tock-ah-noo-lah, by the understated, multi-generational legend and alpine specialist, Mikey Schaefer, Father Time was—is—Schaefer's opus contribution to the Valley. Reputed for the handful of years it took just to establish the route in a ground-up, old-school style and for the mastery level of both grizzly fitness and technical prowess it required, Father Time was an old school ass-whooping wrapped up in a new free-climbing era. The list of those lining up to sign their names into the catalog of it was incredibly few. But to no surprise, near the tip of the spear, there was Brad. It wouldn't happen that season, but his success on Father Time would come.

By summer, Brad again traveled up to Squamish, his favorite change of environment, where he dominated nearly every piece of granite that he put his hands to. Ever on the kick for a good speed climb, Brad teamed up with local native and once-in-a-generation alpinist, Marc Andre Leclerc, on multiple occasions, to set the record on the Grand Wall, Squamish's iconic, centerpiece route up the Chief. Still pinching other people's pennies, having not worked all year, Brad and his old mate Kevin Mohler kept with the habit of standing in line for the free homeless meals at the Sikh Temple, in shameless fashion.

One day, memorably, they climbed the Freeway Wall, an 11-pitch route, before the lunch at the Sikh Temple, then rested during the afternoon at the Visitor Center Café for its free Wi-Fi. At dusk they went back, doubling down on Sikh charity for a free dinner of chana masala, with just enough time to take another lap up the Grand Wall, which happened in less than two hours.

For all the hard, often above-5.13 climbing that Brad was doing, perhaps his highlight that season, as he told it to me, was the night he climbed the Grand Wall without the headlamp, under the light of a full moon. Getting a climb so wired that he could navigate it in the dark, in the coolness and intimate cloak of night, is where he found the magic.

This easy, freewheeling life was the sweet spot for guys like Brad and Kevin. One can imagine it's hard to have too much tension when things are clicking on all cylinders like that. But life wasn't all wine and roses. Wherever Brad went, his loneliness went with him. Kevin recalled that regarding romance, Brad had tried to talk to some women, but was often left flummoxed by the uncomfortable approach required, let alone by the actual commitment itself. He didn't talk about it much, but Brad still wanted more from life.

Upon the start of fall, after having spent another season in Ahwahne, Brad took the cycle back into the indigenous deserts, mostly around Bear's Ears National Monument. There he climbed with a revolving cast of friends, ticking multiple 5.13 projects in short order with the same tenacity and forward style he was by then well known for. Ridiculously strong, but not purely a strength climber, Brad had learned at least some of the nuance required at high-level climbing, though he was admittedly not the best at slowing things down for the sake of clarity up there. It was not in his nature to pause when pressed against the mat.

While part of Brad's mental strength was his internal Jiu-jitsu—that unique ability he had to slip under and away from the gravity of a heady lead or its consequences—most of his climbing was characterized by his unrelenting forward progress. Never the type to think or stay too long in one place on any given lead, Brad executed his climbs by his ability to go further into the red zone than most can or are willing to go.

According to friends, though, even with his improvements, Brad was still good for the occasional shitshow. Often, he'd forget to bring the right gear or sometimes forget to place it. But he made it out of those pickles as often as he stumbled into them, always reminding the friends or onlookers around him that when it came to the dangerous side of the line, Brad just had a way of dealing with it that many of us didn't. He could stand right up to The Nose of danger and somehow still execute. Face to face with bitter consequence, Brad's resolve never buckled. Nor did his self-belief. At least not on a rock climb.

In the lowlands, though, Brad was not the same man. He had his doubts, and he lamented many of his mistakes. According to Mason, Brad regretted that he'd been fired from his job at the Ahwahnee Hotel. He was not proud of all disciplinary actions that came upon him. He also wasn't proud that he'd been stealing food and small merchandise long past the point where it still served him. And while none of us worried that Brad was gunning in a deeply criminal direction, for the things he was doing, we did worry for the consequences. A fraction of which came to him shortly after.

In 2013, during one of those interstitial periods on the road, Brad ran in the wrong direction with the law. Alone for a week in the desert, Brad was killing time while waiting for friends to arrive. Wandering the Moab area one day, Brad, without great tact, walked into a general store and played his usual hand, stealing a few energy bars. While I'm sure he knew that stealing was flat-out inappropriate and wrong, like many of us, he would have had ample justification at the moment. Figuring it was just another easy pinch, Brad beelined for the exit. It didn't, however, go as expected. It was with great surprise and even greater dismay when Brad got to the exit doors, only to find the manager blocking his escape route. The poor bastard was busted.

At last, facing a modicum of his karma, Brad was lucky to get away with a simple misdemeanor from the local trooper who the manager had called in. Had he a different color skin or been a little further down on his luck, Brad could've spent a least a night in the county bin. However fortunate he was, Brad did not see a silver lining. Minimally, he was ashamed.

With no levity to lighten his wings about it, he conceded, this was not a simple misfire. It was not on the level of the cute misadventure or the self-deprecating exploit that he would normally wax and get a laugh from while at a campfire. This was a low point. It was him, alone, out there in the in-between spaces, without friends or a rock to climb, feeling a lot like he didn't fit so well into life. Not an unfamiliar perspective considering the early chapters of his youth.

Knowing of the wrath to come, Brad called his mom first, rather than his dad, and explained his position. Pamela, whose chief identity and pride are in being a mother, was not easy on Brad. Her heart broke that the young boy she had raised to have a work ethic and morals was out there living off the rails. She didn't care how well he was climbing. Her message was clear. First things first, goddammit, *how can you be proud of what you're doing up there if it comes at the cost of who you are everywhere else?*

Understanding the degree to which his actions were breaking

his mother's heart was not a highlight of Brad's big life on the road. It was not an easy fix, either. Another climb, at another grade, to another high place under another ray of heavenly light was not the antidote. Brad would need to move in other directions.

A few months later, worse for the wear and with his head low, Brad asked his mom to help him sort out the results of his legal offense. Getting on the phone with the criminal justice system was the type of thing that overwhelmed him, and he knew it. So did Pamela. But she also knew that if he didn't respond to the charges presented, his situation would worsen.

So with that motherly instinct to protect her kid firing, Pamela sat on the phone line for her son. The secretary on the other end of the line was not empathic, though, and even gave Pamela a lecture about why her adult son ought to be able to square these accounts for himself.

"No grown man," the secretary berated Pamela, "should be having their mother deal with the trouble they made for themselves."

A point to which Pamela conceded.

All said and done, Pamela arranged a community service program for her son that would keep the crime off his permanent record. "I mean, he can't afford to have a stain on the application for all those jobs he isn't searching for," she later joked.

At the time, though, there was nothing up for laughs. Pamela made it clear to Brad that by his actions, at cost of this "dream" he was after, hearts were being broken.

Pamela wasn't the only one though; Brad was broken, too.

From those lonesome moments watching school children while homeless in Boulder, to his breakdown after his run-in with the law, it was written all over him. In a striking conversation one night, in need of a shoulder to cry on, Brad got honest and told his mom all of his greatest fears. He told her how he worried for the things in life that he might never have. The kinds of things that climbing alone would not enable. He told her he was concerned, that he struggled, that he felt less-than in certain situations still. He told her he had never known the joys nor the toils of love. He'd never stayed up all night looking into someone's eyes, held hands, or opened his heart to another with full abandon. He told her he hadn't found a true sense of purpose, that he was following his heart the way Steve Jobs and all the greats had told him to, but that he couldn't see where it was going, nor why he'd been made to follow such an obscure direction in the first place. He told her that he was afraid more often than it seemed, usually off the wall. And, above all, he told her that he felt alone.

Brad carried these burdens with him out there in the great wide open. He didn't show it much, understandably. Perhaps he didn't feel that others would get it. Perhaps it was part of the herd instinct in a life where he'd already been so left out for so long. But he struggled, a fact not often seen while he was busy flying into the highest echelons of performance climbing.

On one occasion that same year, Brad was driving out to the Bear's Ears National Monument from quite a distance. Fatigued, worn down by more than just the drive itself, Brad stammered into a rest stop to sleep off the night. Hours later, near the faintest light of dawn, Brad woke up a few hundred meters away from his car, in the bush. How long had he been out? He didn't know. But it was freezing, below zero, and Brad was nearly hypothermic. He later came to the conclusion that it must have been an extreme case of his epileptic night seizures, and that somewhere in the mis-juggled frames of his life, he hadn't taken his medications. This wasn't the result of forgetting them for just a single day, either. Likely it had been weeks, a further sign that on a fundamental level, he was struggling.

And so, toeing the line up, down, around again, Brad closed

out 2013 divided. The exquisite frames of his life were running side by side with the alienation he quietly kept in his most private moments. The glory of natural light from his high climbs was contrasted by the darkness of his inner confusion. On the path, but without clear sight of it. Living on both sides of the beam, exactly where we find our deepest human experience. He was right there, in the thick of it.

On November 27, 2013, while out climbing with a friend, Brad posted a photo he took of a most immaculate piece of daybreak, when the North Six Shooter, also known as the Bear's Ear, momentarily pushed out from the thicket of a winter storm. Snow-brushed, dusted at the tips which were painted white over its auburn sandstone roots, this lone desert tower rose above the carpet of clouds, out of the darkness and into only the faintest hint of light; weathered, poised, beautiful. Not so unlike Brad.

He had thousands of moments like that, spread across the continent in the litany of his thousands of pitches climbed. He had light like you can't imagine, colors for days—all of it— positioned right next to the empty nights in a lonely tent, or in his car, or during the few weeks that he spent back in Orange County at the end of that year on community service, picking up trash in a homeland he still rather hated.

Back in Bear's Ears National Monument, a week after posting that snow-capped photo of the North Six Shooter, the lurid, charcoal clouds finally cracked. Much as they had in Smith Rock, a year before, light rays from the center of our solar system blasted the horizon of sandstone walls, varnished in sherry and burgundy, with photons brighter than the fires of a space rocket at liftoff. Hiking off the cliff bands and into the golden haze of wild grass and brush at ground level, Brad and his climbing partner were moved to tears, because there, at the edge of the civilized world, at the end of such a tidal orbit around the sun, everything in nature still screamed the undeniable truth of life: revelation is eternal. Darkness and light, pain and pleasure, epiphany and mystery, it was all in the forge.

ANCHOR

For all the confusion that preceded it, Brad's next chapter came almost completely out of the blue. Brad Gobright, the young man who at this point was known around most western U.S. campfires by virtue of his maniacal climbing prowess and his quizzical persona, at last found love in 2014. Cue the Minnie Riperton and the chirping melodies of springtime in bloom, because out of nowhere, at least in the eyes of his folks, Brad found a special somebody.

As a newcomer to romance, one of the most beautiful parts of this relationship was the chance it gave Brad's kindness to fully show itself. It's always possible to demonstrate care in climbing partnerships, but love is another expression entirely. It is a sustained matter of not just will, but heart. It is about gentleness as much as it is about vulnerability, something Brad and his climbing partners often missed while connecting during twenty-plus hours of climbing up thousands of vertical feet. Precisely what he had been longing for. This was an opportunity to learn of someone completely, to love them fully, to commit toward their wellbeing unconditionally—it was an entire landscape of untouched terrain. New skills, at least different ones, would surely be needed.

In their time together, Brad would show that kindness and consideration were qualities he carried in spades. Because he didn't know the rules or the way things worked, in the context of having not dated or lived by any libidinous decree, he moved softly, slowly. In some ways, that lack of wherewithal to the dating world made him the perfect blank canvas for it. He wasn't playing a game or a field. He didn't have an agenda and he was not after sexual conquest; he was after connection. He always asked if he was navigating the relationship respectfully, if he was availing himself enough, and if he could do better, whether that be in showing care through his deeds or in affirming his partner by his words. He hadn't experienced any cat-and-mouse, hadn't been damaged by a past trauma of love, and didn't know any other way to operate apart from presenting himself unabashedly. He was transparent almost to a fault. While many people had seen shades of his inner softness and purity of heart, it was in relationships like this that Brad bloomed brightest.

From what we can gather, Brad and his first love—who for privacy and personal respect will remain anonymous—met in climbing circles as early as 2013. She was close in age to Brad, not only by calendar year but also in the age of discovery, of learning of herself. Creative, artistic, very well put together in ways Brad had often struggled to be, she'd recently flirted with the road trip as a place to find her own direction in life. She was a Southern California transplant, ethnically grounded with a love of family and, offering easy chemistry at the time, she was a climber. Not only was she a climber, she was a newly smitten climber. She hadn't been at it long, not compared to most of the locals in Ahwahne, but she had fallen for a life outside, and she'd fallen hard.

In late 2013 and early 2014, in shared circles, they met and slowly came into an acquaintance before a modicum of attraction arrived. Whatever confidence Brad had garnered in the past six years of life on the road and from his climbing experience was quickly washed away in the face of this new landscape. Because of that, Brad was not the smooth criminal and heartbreaker that old papa Jim had been in his heydays at the Red Onion. Brad was quiet around her, shy more than anything, to the point of undeniable awkwardness—but then again, weren't most of us?

Soon, though, they connected. Brad learned how to have a conversation and not trip over his tongue in the process, which was admittedly difficult. In the light of his eyes, she had the look of a queen and a heart of gold. So, words as a would-be suitor came in small doses. That kept up for long enough for her to realize that Brad was far more than the bumbling wallflower she'd first encountered. With baby blue eyes and a most unique charm, Brad was an adorable catch. Curious about this eccentric, bright suitor, she soon fell under the spell of Brad's smile. Brad had vivaciousness, a zeal, and it was just as new to her as any of her traits were to him. And, each time they spoke, she couldn't miss his unfathomably pure heart which sat beneath and orchestrated each of his best traits. Brad Gobright, for all his quirks and difficulties, was a gem, which isn't to say he was perfect. Lord knows he was only beginning to round the bend in his path of becoming. But if, as climbing icon John Long once said, "a genius is a person most like themselves," truest to their spirit despite all the brokenness life throws at them, then Brad was an original. Perhaps even the archetype. Which meant that his girlfriend, a brilliant mind in her own right, had surely met more than a muse; she'd met an equal.

Love is many things, if not at the least a new lens. For the first time in his adult life, apart from the unflinching love of family, here was a person who was choosing to love him completely, a concept that blew his lid. Here was somebody who was not interested in comparing him to another climber or another lover the way we often do, but who was willing to take a wholehearted adventure into the wildlands of love. Someone who wanted him, no conditions or filters applied. The gift of that, outside of every other blessing this relationship would grant them, would be of such enormity that it cannot possibly be overstated. Brad, like any of us, would have forever thought himself apart from, rather than a part of, when it came to gelling into the world around him. He'd simply always been an outsider.

But to be loved, fully accepted by another, that's the kind of gift that gives a person wings. Mutual love gives the kind of assurance and steadiness of character that people pay attention to. The kind of comfortability that can keep a person fully at ease, even as the marquee guest in front of a packed theatre at a movie premiere, without their heart skipping a beat. Because, years down the road, that's precisely the comfort that Brad had acquired.

In the words of the 2013 Pulitzer Prize winner and *New York Times* writer, John Branch, on stage at the Castro theater and Reel Rock film premiere in 2019, you got the notion that "Brad could entertain a theater full of people, showing up the likes of Honnold and Caldwell, and be not changed one bit." But it wasn't solely for his climbing accolades and his Nose speed record that Brad was unaffected by fame—it was for the experience of having been loved by a single person at full acceptance. Because of that, no fickle crowd or passing pleasures of stardom ever had a chance to change Brad's essence. He'd already found the freedom and security he needed, from having been loved and from having given it in return.

While love was on the books, financial stability was decidedly not. Brad spent the first few months of 2014 living in Southern California in an inglorious space he found to save as much money as he could—a closet. For the scraps he earned on minimum wage, totaling two hundred dollars a month, Brad managed to rent the actual closet space of a walk-in pantry from a band of stoners living commune-style in a rented house in Orange County. Neither his sleeping quarters nor the perma-stoned lifestyle the tenants kept made any improvements on Brad's attitude about the county he grew up in.

Short on parking spots in a dodgy neighborhood, he'd leave his car down the block when coming home from work each night, where he'd walk into a perpetual cloud of reefer byproduct at the front door. Holding his breath with intolerance, he'd then head past the barren kitchen and into a spartan corner of the closet where diaphragmatic breathing and a pair of headphones to block out the noise were his means to chase an elusive cycle of REM sleep. If it weren't for the rangers, the bugs, and the cold, he'd have probably been better off staying in the boulder fields of Ahwahne. Civilization, at least that version of it, never seemed all too civilized at all.

Brad simply could not reconcile how to buy in on a life that seemed, in his eyes, to sacrifice all contact with the natural, revelation-based world for the spiritual equivalent of empty calories, endless mind or mood-altering chemical filler, and everlasting commercial entertainment. He could eat empty calories—those millions of pastries and cheap donuts—to sustain his contact with the natural world, but he could not work that process in reverse. While many live integrated, quality lives within the matrix, it is, unfortunately, the trend of the human condition not to. He couldn't help but see it as this dualistic either/or. And in that framing, as with the way he approached much of his life, Brad was only ever going to go in one direction—not toward, but further from the bell curve.

For the purposes of savings, though, the housing situation served its function, and by April, Brad was off to visit Boulder once again. He had wanted to spend the season in Ahwahne, working for the Delaware North Company and spending time with his girlfriend, but for the third year running, Brad found himself stonewalled after the interview process. While his girlfriend got a job at the Yosemite Mountain Shop for the summer, Brad sailed off to Colorado with high hopes in mind to tick a few remaining projects in the area. Brad also took that season away from Ahwahne, not just because he didn't feel welcome, but because he knew that to round out his skills he needed to climb in new spaces.

With his focus ever on To-tock-ah-noo-lah, he went the way of the warrior, training by a series of labors in a distant land. That summer, Brad teamed up with local native and climbing community stalwart, Jesse Huey, to climb at Long's Peak—topping out above 14,000 feet on the famed north face, which climbers know better as The Diamond. Brad also soloed his now-regular routine of pitches in Eldorado Canyon, which he usually tackled after work but before his nighttime gym session. Newly employed at the Saint Julien Hotel, the poshest plot of land in Boulder, he was also back in the service industry. At work, he got on well with the management team, and for the lifestyle it afforded him it did not leave the bitter aftertaste that his time at the Ahwahnee Hotel had. He had a place to stay that wasn't a closet, and he could even afford a gym membership.

That summer was also the first notable period where he pursued the harrowing craft of speed climbing. No matter how it's sliced, the risks one is committed to while on a modern speed ascent are among the highest in the sport. It is a realm of overt, exponential danger. Almost exclusively climbed simultaneously with minimal gear placements, speed climbing has served some of the worst injuries and deaths to the climbing community in recent memory. But Brad, with his particular focus points, with that levity and never-let-go constitution, was among the best fit for such climbing. And his old pal Scott Bennett, who by now had climbed the world over in places like Patagonia and the Himalayas, was a most apt counterpart.

Together that summer, Brad and Scott made a habit of rehearsal climbs on the Naked Edge each morning to inspect the route conditions and practice movements before tackling an evening speed-pass at it. A climb that once defined a generation for its grit and commitment had been whittled down to the afternoon musings of two monkeys who could cycle it from the bridge at the base of the canyon to the entire length of the route, down the cliff band descent, and back to the start again in less time than it takes to watch a sitcom.

Brad's speed climbing, sport-climbing, multi-pitch, and even his gym climbing continued in a flurry as summer quickly turned to fall. By October, when he quit his job at the St. Julien Hotel for a move back west, he and Scott had taken the Naked Edge record below the inconceivable twenty-five-minute mark, clocking in at 24:57.

Brad's first spring and fall not in Ahwahne were meant to fashion him further, and by all appearances, they had. Being a step-aside year, designed to invest in the long play, it gave him more time to train in the world-class local gyms, which also paid dividends. Ultimately though, Brad left Boulder that fall not only for climbing, but for a new direction. He'd been flirting with taking up a steadier, passion-related occupation in the form of mountain guiding. In Joshua Tree that November, Brad was due for an official AMGA (American Mountain Guides Association) weekend training course.

On the way, Brad stopped in Moab, the heartland of western desert climbing, to spend a week with his girlfriend for the first time in months. Together they climbed up the infamous, brilliant Wingate Sandstone towers around Castle Valley, enjoying vistas of the La Sal mountains which stood covered in snow just a few miles away.

In Joshua Tree a week later, Brad happily reconnected to his roots. Near sundown, the caramel-colored sunbeams radiated over the eponymous trees, which cast alien shadows as the landscape morphed from a bright, rugged desert into a violet, twilight setting, a land of a thousand silhouettes. But even while connected to those highlight-reel frames, Brad struggled for engagement on that trip. His plans to inherit the industry standard, tools of the trade, fell flat against a stricter rubric than he was prepared for. To Brad's surprise, the practical rigging and rope safety skills, such as self-rescue, and the theoretical components of the Mountain Guide course were taught, and tested, in an academic format. A format that took Brad straight back to high school. Losing confidence quickly, Brad did not finish the course—a striking blow to his sense of direction at the time.

However, given that Joshua Tree is close to Orange County and the holidays were in full swing, Brad came back to the roost. He returned home that winter to recover the time lost with family and to seek advice from his guiding light—mom. His relationship with his girlfriend was still new, and flourishing, but already he could sense that going forward with it would require some tact, and as with any relationship, some compromise. At the least, he would need guidance, and who better to share his concerns with than his original anchor, mom.

Pamela encouraged Brad to focus on the importance of his romantic partner, which, as far as she could tell, was more than just a passing whim. In fact, Pamela and Jill later admitted that the first thing they did after hearing about his new girlfriend was an online investigation through social media. As Pamela put it, they outright stalked her; most families just call it due diligence. What Pamela and Jill discovered was that not only was Brad's new bird someone they wholeheartedly approved of, but also that she and Brad were quite the fit for one another. All signs in the affirmative, Pamela encouraged Brad to keep up his dream of climbing so long as he kept working, and to take on the adventure of life with this sweet new girl who, during the recent holidays, they had met.

After a month living back home, with Brad and his partner each staying at their respective parents' houses, they took their first habitat adventure together and moved to Las Vegas. It was, after all, a climber's paradise. And in the city of sin, the blank spots in Brad's resume were no demerit. He was as employable as anybody. By February, a month after moving, Brad secured a job at the Red Rock Casino, just a ten-minute drive to the endless playground of the Calico Basin and only thirty minutes to the base of the Black Velvet Canyon.

The giant vertical shields of the Black Velvet Canyon, home to some of the longest routes in the range, were a fixture for Brad's soloing craft. Often, over the seasons, he would drive out after work and climb in an hour what most parties tackle in an entire day. Routes like Epinephrine, one of America's most blue-collar, multi-pitch 5.9s, were among his favorites. He could breeze through 2,000 feet of vertical gain in a whistle. But he hadn't only come to the desert to climb its tallest offerings—the Vegas area is home to one of the densest scatterings of elite level climbs this side of the Atlantic. There are more 5.14 routes in this desert zone, per capita, than there are three-star Michelin chefs in San Sebastian or Tokyo.

By mid-March, only a couple months after having moved to the desert, Brad topped out his second 5.14, a climb called F-Dude at the Virgin River Gorge, in the I-15 corridor between Mesquite and St. George. His first had come a year prior while in Boulder on the notorious line, China Doll. These would be just the first markers in a series of performance high points in 2015, a list of climbs so impressive that the aggregate of them would lead fellow climber and writer, Chris Weidner, to call Brad 2015's "Breakout Climber of the Year."

In April, Brad was running on all cylinders. He was also running in some elite circles of the climbing tribe. Still, it was at least a little surprising to most when Brad teamed up with alpine ambassador and climbing icon Hayden Kennedy for a weekend in Red Rock. Hayden, Piolet D'Or winner and three years wiser from his controversial, heroic ascent of Cerre Torre in Patagonia—where he and partner Jason Kruk famously chopped Maestri's Compressor Route—was among the most adept, tactful, and elegant of climbers on the planet. Deeply focused, rhythmic, high-commitment, and heralding, his climbing was more art than lone physical discipline. He was also, and more importantly, among the most grounded, kind, humble, and sincere spirits that anyone could meet, period. I'd had the luxury to share a rope and passing conversation with him a handful of times, years prior, at various crags between Mexico and Ahwahne, and have never met someone who was such a complete package as Hayden was. He had the talent that only the gods can gift, combined with the tools and awareness in his climbing that the talented so often miss. He had a rockcraft that was among the highest order, and yet a humanity that was even higher.

Hayden and Brad, each on their own stage of self-discovery, had met the previous year by means of a seasonal Christmas-light hanging job, owned and managed by Brad's alpine partner, Jesse Huey. It was precisely the kind of specialized, well-paying, itinerant work that young climbers dream of. Earning an honest buck is one thing, but for many climbers, at least the ones enchained to the road trip, there's a certain satisfaction in knowing that what you did for the wealthy elites, in some way, propelled you just a little further. That your freedom was underwritten by their spoils. Hayden and Brad shared many sentiments on society, and even more on climbing, which endeared them easily to one another.

Together, with Brad's grit, raw power, and impenetrable bravado, and Hayden's even keel, they charged up the remote Buffalo Wall and climbed a modern classic, Crystal Dawn, in a ground-up push. While Brad struggled to free it onsight, he knew immediately that a sustained climb like Crystal Dawn, with its successive 5.12 pitches and its crux 5.13 (+) segment, was well within his abilities. Just two weeks after his first attempt with Hayden, Brad returned with local climber, Josh Janes, and scored each pitch clean from bottom to top.

Years earlier, a climb like Crystal Dawn would have been a multi-season project; so would following the likes of Hayden and going tit-for-tat while swapping leads. It was all further evidence that Brad had ascended into a different sphere. It wasn't just that Brad was climbing well, it was his new sense of place, his comfort in the zones of high-performance, and the high-performers that came with it. That was the part that awestruck us onlookers the most. It was the fact that somehow, over the years, while driving full speed at goals that most of us thought impossible, he'd actually made it.

By swinging for the fences, and often missing, Brad made a habit of defeat. But what most of us would internalize as grand failures, he discovered to be trade secrets. This was precisely a part of that inscrutable, foolish wisdom he manifested. Full abandon, with all its inglorious missteps, was the path. Unless you were born from some privileged lineage or were given an ungodly hand of talents, if you wanted to traverse into the realm of greatness in this life, you must be willing to fall as a manner of being. Of course, greatness for Brad had nothing to do with accolade or recognition either; rather, it was simply to dream and to chase the unachievable, which is to say, to follow his heart.

Brad showed us that impossible dreams were the only safe dreams to have—anything less risked not living at all. And falling, that wasn't failing after all. Falling was how you became. It was the key. Brad knew this from action alone, from living true to his tuning. A knowledge that endowed him with a growth mindset years before it was *de rigueur*. Even better, he didn't have to articulate it. It wasn't a philosophy to be read in a book; it was a function of him serving his highest orders. Climb, period. Not climb and only fall sometimes. Not climb to chase grades. Not climb when you've had the right food and sleep and training window. Climb. Follow the heart, get on what calls you, and climb. The rest will be found in action, more than analysis. The kid was an existential lightbulb. Only in 2015 did some of us start to realize just how plugged in he'd been all along.

Over the years, what this approach gave him was unflinching self-esteem. It gave him respect as well, hence his growing access to an elite inner circle. And, combined with that new self-assurance, the gift of giving and receiving love, he was unstoppable. By the end of May, Brad free-climbed what he thought would be another multi-season project. Desert Solitaire, an old aid-climbing route and new free-climbing classic, stacked with the sustained 5.12 climbing and a stopper 5.13 crux pitch, went into Brad's resume without the fight he had expected.

Not only was Brad breaking through new thresholds in peer groups and climbing communities alike, but he was also in-frame while doing it. Brad came into the focus of a few key industry photographers that year. The exposure those photos gave the world to his character was, perhaps, more important than the exposure it gave him to would-be sponsors.

2015 was when most folks, at least those not in his circle of friends or those he'd grown up with, finally came to meet Brad

Gobright. Classic to Brad's spirit, these increasing pulses of notoriety did little, if anything, to sway him from the simple delights of life. He still worked, and still ran his program of climbing outside and training indoors, often accomplishing all three in the same day. He still came home each night in his beater car, still got flummoxed by the little things of life, and still took joy from many of them as well. He still ate whatever he could afford. Perhaps the only thing he wasn't doing any longer was putting those troublesome sticky fingers to task. He was no longer in the habit of stealing. He still climbed moderate routes with the same zest as he did the hardest ones. He still climbed with his girlfriend, often on routes far below his capability, and he still loved it. But it wasn't just the climbing that drew them together. Just coming home from work and spending time with her and their dog gave Brad a roundedness, a satisfaction about life like never before. He couldn't be happier.

By June, the couple decided to head back to Ahwahne. Brad's partner once again found a job in the Valley at the local Mountain Shop, which meant another season for her to be inspired by the grandeur of its humongous walls and the vastness of its climbing community. She, after all, was only a few years into it and still burned with wonder and inspiration for all the places her commitment to this way of life had taken her. Being in Ahwahne meant being around her favorite people and places. Happy for what this move represented for her, Brad also knew what it meant for him. For the first season in ages, he'd have a place to lay his head. She was granted employee housing, and that meant—unofficially of course—that Brad had it, too. As far as he was concerned, unfettered sleep was better than an entire park without the tourists.

Inspired by the recent ascent of Tommy Caldwell and his partner Kevin Jorgeson's seven-year project on the Dawn Wall, Brad and Mason Earle reconvened to settle the score. The fact that Brad had taken an entire year away from the Valley honing his craft left him burning with desire. Not just for their Heart Route project, but for all of it. The young man was ready to rage.

Within the first two weeks in the Valley, Brad took advantage of his short weather windows, dodging the torrential spring rain floods to climb both the Regular Northwest Face of Tis-se-ack (Half Dome) at a blistering pace, rope-solo, and the classic, Astroman. On rainy days he and the gang, usually comprised of Mason, Kevin Mohler, local transplant James Lucas, and even Mr. Free Solo himself, Alex Honnold, would run laps on hard climbs at the overhung amphitheater climbers call the Jailhouse Crag, an hour down the road.

On June 2, 2015, to the surprise of everybody but Brad, he finally free-climbed To-tock-ah-noo-lah via the Freerider route in a blasphemous fifteen-hour push. The surprising part was less what he had done, but *how*. Very few among the elite tackle that route or any route on To-tock-ah-noo-lah as a free-climb, in a single push, in a single day. Remember, free-climbing as a style is different than the usual aid-and-mixed-climbing approach. When most parties climb big walls, they free-climb (execute every move with their own hands and feet while using a rope and protective gear as a means only to arrest a potential fall) what they can, up until the terrain gets difficult, and then aid climb (actively pulling on the rope and gear to aid in the upward ascent) the rest. It's damn hard work enough just to clog up a big wall in the old-school aid style; it's light years different when you get to big wall free-climbing.

For the execution and demand required, when most folks do climb the Big Stone free, they do so piecemeal. Often, out of need for at least one full rest day, it becomes a multiday affair, which is usually a tall enough order on its own. Because of that, the unspoken rule of thumb up there is that anybody who is attempting to do a route in a day has first done that same route in a multiday, traditional style. Climbing it in a day, all free, before having climbed it on a multi-day ascent is literally doing it out of order. It's tantamount to some poor kid trying to muscle through a hundred pull-ups in a single, unbroken push before having ever done them by way of separate sets. You just don't do it like that. The fact that Brad did it from soil to summit in a fifteen-hour push, as his first free-climb on that wall, is all-time spectacular. He was simply on fire, which meant, with the benefit of a good weather window, the time had come for the Heart Route.

The Heart Route on El Capitan was a line first envisioned by Mason, who perhaps had the greatest perspective on the whole process, having truly seen it from start to finish. Once upon a time, while climbing the nearby Golden Gate in 2009, the Heart Route was but a passing thought in his consciousness—a thought which, for no known reason at the time, he kept hold of. That was its beginning, the smallest seed of an open and yearning mind. Years later, with all the life he and Brad had traversed between them, it was so much more. How the cards and planets aligned that spring of 2015 is still, by his account, a great mystery, especially considering where both his life and Brad's had been and where it would take them in the coming years.

Mason was born and raised on the east coast, and only a few years before meeting myself and Brad on The Rostrum in 2008, had moved out west. At first, that was to Durango, Colorado, for that old try at higher education. Quickly, though, his true directions came to light. Feeling like he never really fit into a place in life, much like Brad, he too followed his inner calling. Mason's heart sought adventure, rapture, and beauty. It also sought climbing. It didn't matter that he had immaculate talents for music and string instruments, Mason felt most himself with his fingers plugged into the earth. Because of that, in a matter of one semester, he went from college student to college dropout, and even sooner, to Ahwahne. That's where he met Brad and I on The Rostrum, as well as the full community he'd orient his life around for the next decade. It's where he first climbed a big wall, which he soon made a habit of, and it's where he made friendships that would last a lifetime. Friendships like his and Brad's. Ultimately, the Heart Route project symbolized the culmination of that most precious friendship with Brad, who he still considered his brother.

It was also the apex of Brad's coming of age. From the first pitch off the ground until the summit proper, Mason remembered that it was that year, 2015, that Brad burned on an entirely new level. The collective sum of those wayward years in the forge, the now yearlong relationship to his girlfriend and the confidence it gave him, fashioned what in Mason's eyes was a sharper iteration of Brad. It was a ratified man. No longer prone to flop in a panic or create some legendary junk show on lead, Brad was operating on a premiere cadence. With his usual—and uncanny—levity floating him past high-consequence situations, but with the addition of an undeniable craft in his movement, Brad's climbing was a revelation.

"That Heart Route was a remarkable first ascent for us both," Mason reflected years later. "But more than that, for me, the real joy of that climb was the moment I realized that Brad Gobright had graduated. We hadn't climbed together for a few seasons at that point, you know. But man, had he come up."

For years, apart from the many pitches of nails-hard 5.13 climbing, the duo had been stonewalled by a single, nearly ten-foot alabaster sheet of granite a few hundred feet off the ground. A dynamic, full jumping move they later titled The Dubstep—the only solution they could come up with to surmise this chasm—was going to be where this route would live or die. At least one of them would have to successfully jump that gap and get their hands on the marginal holds at the other side of it, and they'd need to do so with enough strength and control to keep their bodies from swinging wildly out from and eventually off of the wall they clung to. As history and genetics would have it, Mason found success on the move before Brad. By merit of his great coordination and his longer frame, Mason bridged the gap, and in doing so, opened a pathway for them both. Unfortunately, in doing so, Mason also injured his shoulder. A costly trade that would bring added trial to the upper pitches. Brad was unable to pull off the wild move and instead had to use the rope to swing him past it, but as first ascents go, all systems were still a green light. For the project to be established as a viable free-climbing route, the only requirement was that one of them do it.

After sending the Dubstep, the first ascent was fully up for grabs, a fact that excited the locals for its consequence. New routes do not happen often up on the Big Stone. Soon it wasn't just good old Tom Evans, the To-tock-ah-noo-lah photographer and resident historian, who was on the scoop down in the meadow; many others gathered to witness. And, from day one, with Mason and Brad already on the wall, the cinematic specialists and big wall veterans, Ben Ditto and Cheyne Lempe, were in position. Having ascended fixed lines on a nearby route, Ben and Cheyne had rigged their perch beside Mason and Brad to document the historic plight. It wasn't getting as much press as the Dawn Wall, but there was fanfare and excitement all the same.

The company could not have been better for Brad, especially when, halfway up the route and on a restful afternoon, he celebrated his twenty-seventh birthday. Together on a couple of portaledges, the boys gloated in their position and took an afternoon to hoot from the high camp down to the monkeys onlooking from the Valley below. They'd been on the wall for a few days by that point, sleeping on the hanging cots at night, which is usually a point of some discomfort among climbers. But considering how close they now stood to the full realization of their dreams, Mason recalled, they could've stayed up there for another month. Pitch after pitch, mostly that blend of consecutive 5.12–5.13s, things were falling into place.

On one of the final hard pitches, a harrowing 5.13 arete which climbs out of the heart formation and links it to the upper section of the Huber Brother's Golden Gate, Brad took the lead. Mason, with his injured shoulder, felt his limitations overwhelming him. In fact, he recalled, if it had come down to him having to lead that pitch rather than Brad, it may not have happened at all. He was destroyed. But where Mason had carried them through The Dubstep, Brad was now in position to carry them to the top. There, climbing out of the closeted Heart Formation and into the light of day, 1,800 feet off the deck on a relentless and heady 5.13 pitch, Mason recalled that Brad Gobright glowed as never before. Mastery-level climbing, full-on tactile brilliance, and impeccable footwork in motion, Brad danced over the sheets of granite the way Alaphilippe dances on the bike pedals.

"That was the moment, for sure," Mason shared, aglow. "That's when I put my head down and tipped my hat. The way Brad summoned his technique on that pitch. Damn! It was obvious. The student had become a master. No doubt about it."

Brad took that pitch clean to the top, no falls, setting the line for Mason to follow. Barely, at the tip of despair, Mason was able to climb through his injuries and send the pitch without falling. Above them, where the route links up with Golden Gate, remained two distinct 5.12 (+)/13 (-) crux pitches and nearly a thousand feet of rugged, 5.11 climbing.

The next day, a threadbare Mason managed to follow Brad, who could've gone on another 1,000 feet if needed, to the top.

The journey of five years and ten Ahwahne seasons had been completed. Together, atop the mighty To-tock-ah-noo-lah, Brad and Mason paused for a gargantuan embrace. They'd just established a new free-climbing pathway for the history books. Better still, they'd established it to live to the mark of their dreams. Six days, five nights, thousands of feet, and one almighty V10 Dubstep-dyno the better, Mason and Brad had climbed the Free Heart Route.

In total, the Free Heart Route packed nine pitches of 5.13 climbing, a short handful of 5.12s, and twelve pitches of gritty, full-value 5.11 climbing, including one 5.11 R/X (severely dangerous) pitch above the Heart Formation before it links with Golden Gate. The notion of how rare a first ascent up there is was not lost on Mason. All variations included, there are more than a hundred routes up To-tock-ah-noo-lah. Of those, there are little more than a dozen established free-climbing pathways. It is rare space, indeed. And, of those free-climbing routes, only a handful of names make up the list of those who have made the historic, first free-ascent.

Tommy Caldwell and the Huber Brothers, with all their skill and might, took most of the spoils over the preceding two decades, leaving precious few paths for the intrepid climbers of this current generation to plunder. A fact that led Mason to appreciate their climb with a finer lining. It also struck him that of the billions of humans out there, only that fraction of a fraction ever gets the opportunity to climb at all. It is, by nature, a situation of spoils. Narrow that margin down to those who try climbing To-tock-ah-noo-lah, a dismal percentage, then narrow it further to those who manage to summit it. Even fewer. Take that yield and then consider how many humans successfully free-climb it, and lastly consider how many humans get the privilege of establishing a first ascent in so doing, and you've arrived at near singularity. Gobsmacked by the undeniable gift of such a unique human experience on this marvelous planet, Mason could not contain himself.

There at the top of the world, Mason basked in the afternoon sunbeams. And soon, he was also soaked by the spray of the celebratory King Cobras that the crew had shaken and shot off like cannon fodder at him and Brad. With malt liquor lining his brow, covered in the wash of celebratory suds, Mason thought not only of his fortune among the few, but the unlikely path which took him there in the first place. He thought back to his own big move away from college, and all the years he'd spent climbing with his unlikely friend, Brad.

So, when it came to the Heart Route, when it came down to that blue-eyed goofball and master in the making, Brad, who stood just beside him, Mason understood both the inevitability and the impossibility of it. How exactly the troubled elements of their childhoods or the inner tunings that had led each of them to an individual rockcraft ever landed in such an arrangement was beyond him. Mason thought back to those early years, running around the desert with Brad from 2009 to 2011. He thought about how hard people were on him. He remembered, almost painfully, how ostensibly uncool and awkward Brad had been once upon a time. He thought about all the moments he stood up for Brad, how he had protected him from the untimely laughs of others. He thought about that struggling kid who had somehow become his huckleberry friend.

Were it not for that nineteen-day Dawn Wall ascent by Kevin and Tommy, he and Brad would not have had that drive to seek their own epic journey to completion. The truth is, it was fundamental to their success. In fact, all of Tommy's first ascents were. His climbs in the last two decades showed everybody what was possible. And Tommy's first ascents—not just the Dawn Wall but nearly all of them—were only possible from the fires of life he'd been forced to walk through. Had Tommy not famously been abducted by a militia of radicalized soldiers in Kyrgyzstan years earlier in the heart of the Kara-Su Valley, those ascents could have been equally compromised. Had those nameless, remote soldiers never been radicalized in the first place, had the whole wheel of events on modern continental Asia not spun at all, those soldiers wouldn't have Kalashnikovs in their hands, nor would they have abducted Tommy for geopolitical protest; which means Tommy doesn't make his harrowing escape or burn with a fire under his ass after the fact, which means the Dawn Wall may not have had a suitor willing to suffer seven long years of toil. And that means Mason wouldn't be up there showered by sunbeams and cheap swill.

Looking over at Brad, Mason was overwhelmed by a perspective he could barely hold. Like a giant, warbling bubble—mystical in its shape but fragile to the touch—this full, unlikely web of sequences dazzled his consciousness. Whatever it was, it was undeniable. How else can one decode the fullness of the present moment and the totality of pieces that composed it into harmony, but by feeling, by shade, and by shape? Greater men have called it revelation. Others, Zen. Whatever the term for it, it was humbling. That Mason had his old mate and newly-minted climbing ace, Brad, there with him put a smile into his heart that could not help but shine outward.

"Incredible stuff up there," Mason offered in reflection. "But one of the best parts, to this day, was having a front-row seat on Brad. That kid just took off from that climb and never looked back. It just made me so damn happy for him. Everybody rooted for Brad to make it, not just on the Heart Route, but on his entire path."

It was no lie. Brad was beloved across state lines. Some still carried worries about his penchant for danger, but that was a different conversation than simply loving the guy. With his quiet humility, his goofiness, and his inimitable spirit, Brad had endeared himself to everyone: the locals, the search and rescue crews, and of course, Tom Evans, who kept a seat open for him the following day at the Village Café, excited to hear a first-hand account of their historic climb.

After the Heart Route, Brad continued blasting forward, but that doesn't mean that he never looked back. The present was where Brad lived more often than most, but he was happy to stop on occasion and ponder all the places he'd been. He, too, once confessed to me how wild it all was that his life was suddenly so rounded, so full. How fortunate he felt and, around his lady, how often he felt that way.

One fine afternoon, shortly after his ascent of the Heart Route, Brad and his girlfriend sat on the summit of the Manure Pile Buttress—a cliff that looks much better than it sounds—with an ease that money simply cannot buy. With the entirety of Ahwahne from Glacier point to Tis-se-ack spread before them, they considered the richness of their life—their fortune to call so many wild spaces home. Hearts full, they owned that plot of granite and basked in it the way the old guard of Robbins and Chouinard did. As nobles to splendors. As children to the earth. And that's where Brad had his revelation, founded on a simple, conscious gratitude. Brad buzzed with delight up there, tapping into that deep, inner agreement to and satisfaction with all that lay before his wide eyes.

He thought of his course over the years, of the unknowable outcome that was planted in the totality of his wayward adventures, which so far had led him to that exact time and place, with that woman he so loved. He thought about how privileged even his hardships had been, for what they had finally fashioned. He considered not only his past, but his partner's past, and her family's past, too. He laid under that sky, goosebumps and all, realizing just how spoiled he was to be the one and only human on Earth, right there, on that rock, with that view, in love with that exact woman, his head gently pillowed upon her lap. How on earth had life ever become such a majestic tapestry? How fortunate he was, after all, for having crawled out of that submarine and put himself on the sharp end all those years ago.

By the end of June, Brad had moved back to Colorado with the intent to slingshot his momentum onto the Front Range. His girlfriend, still working at the Yosemite Mountain Shop, stayed behind while Brad jumped headstrong into his next project: his first feature film. On the heels of his recent success in Ahwahne, his now good friend, Cedar Wright, insisted they document him precisely in his moment of bloom. As far as Cedar was concerned, Brad represented not only the rise of a dark horse, but the last of a dying breed.

It wasn't the loss of the traditional dirtbag alone that Wright mourned; in some ways it was the loss of the simple climber. Wright understood that climbing's history was not all golden, even throughout its golden eras. He knew that it carried a legacy of Western, white privilege and that it left other cultures and genders behind. That was not the nostalgia he was out to recapture. He was thrilled to see climbing's culture move in the direction of equal participation and representation. But somewhere in the pulse of it all, over the course of Wright's climbing tenure, he lamented that we'd mostly traded savagery for security.

Cedar wanted to show that, while growing our conscience in correspondence with the growing number of climbers is a good thing, you need not marry heaven, earth, and every single planetary and humanitarian cause together in some woke, quasi-conscious weave every time you went outside. As important as all those things are, it was equally important that people remember that climbing is about climbing. Which is to say, it is about the wildness of the human spirit. Its historical strength is that it invites us to live in the hemisphere of the unknown, the unsure. It calls us not only to the wild, but at times, and for the sake of some inner growth, it also calls us toward the unsafe. Because, just as love, everything worth a damn in the human condition, ultimately, is.

Enter Brad. As a climber, he fit Wright's mold perfectly, which was not to suggest he had only one dimension to offer. In fact, more than any other time in his life, Brad was demonstrating incredible capability. Learning that he could move beyond the clumsy, intellectually challenged narrative of his youth, he was growing exponentially. A growth that came by voraciously digging through a catalog of audiobooks, by engaging in new and expansive relationships with others, and even by learning the principles of physics, a course of study he self-directed.

But more than a thinker, Brad was always a doer. He could take interest in many things, but unlike many of us, he never got lost in the plane of the intellectual. He was never the type to live only by the rational mind alone. Above all, Brad lived by the heart. That orientation meant that he was always, invariably, going to chase down visceral experiences. He was always going to live life to the lees. This insistence on adventure climbing—on living the real life, not the imagined one—was precisely what Cedar wanted to capture. It was the premise that you do not need to have your shit impeccably ordered to do great deeds; you just need to do them. So, after that gigantic spring season in Ahwahne, Brad returned home to Boulder that summer to work on the film that would change his life: *Safety Third*.

In October, as would happen on a quarterly basis, Pamela insisted on visiting Brad for a check-in. She had already followed him to Ahwahne, Las Vegas, and a handful of other destinations. Now, for the first time, she touched down in Colorado. Following her own wild heart on the premise that she would always meet her son wherever he was—be that a dusty campground or a pitiful apartment—she'd later hold each of these trips as precious memories, as timestamps on the highlight reel. These trips were revelatory for her and always softened her heart.

With each new town, with every new gang of faces, she was clued in just that little bit more to the magic of the community her son was connecting to. She loved climbers, particularly for their connection to nature, for the way they looked after one another, and, even though she'd prefer more of them to be tuned in to a deeper purpose, she loved that they lived simple lives, that they did not get lost in the superficial tinsel of the modern world.

Over a week, Pamela and Brad took hikes in Eldorado Canyon, visited the charming town of Estes Park and its nearby lakes, toured the Denver art museums, and even did nightly family meals with his roommates. Pamela loved it.

"You know, it was like a sitcom. Like *Friends*, but on steroids. There were almost a dozen of them living in that four-bedroom house, and even a few were living in their vans in the driveway. All these wonderful people and characters, all in a similar stage of life, just passing in and out all day. There was so much good energy. And they all loved Brad," Pamela shared.

The realization that her son fit, that people adored him, that he was connected to and even celebrated by others, settled her maternal instincts. Moreover, it filled her heart. She was elated that he'd found his way into such good company.

However much Pamela loved the cast of characters in that housing unit, Brad insisted his mother not stay in such squalor. Pulling a few strings with his local hookup at the St. Julien

Hotel, the aforementioned poshest place in Boulder, Pamela was blindsided with surprise when Brad got her a room, fully comped. According to Pamela, for the course of her stay, they treated her like royalty.

That was not the first or last time she'd come to learn of her son by the respect he commanded. At one of his future film screenings and slideshows, which was full capacity, she'd been ushered to the front without even asking. The people who'd waited hours to keep their seats quite literally stood up in a flash and graciously insisted that Brad Gobright's mom sit in their seats. Another time, at the food deck at Curry Village in Ahwahne, an employee comped her entire meal, without Brad even being there.

"No mother of Brad Gobright should be paying for a meal in this place," the custodian said with a smile.

It blew her away.

But more than the ceremonious or the splendid affectations that came her way on that trip, what brightened her bulb the most was watching how Brad connected to his partner. Still working at Ahwahne for the season, his lady was one month away from coming to Boulder to live with Brad for the winter, but that did not hamper their connection.

According to Pamela, more than anything, she could see that her son was a changed man. He was smitten, and not only that; he was alert, in touch, communicative. Not a moment went by when he wasn't talking about his partner, or if not talking about her, then calling, or at the least, texting her. Even though they'd been together for a little over a year, Pamela still hadn't seen them that often. Nor had she seen her son so fully enamored as he was even while his partner was in another state. Boarding the flight back to Southern California, it wasn't the beautiful places Brad had taken her that Pamela held closest, nor was it the cast of roommates and friends she had met—it was the sure, lasting joy, the knowledge that her son was in the arms of another. It was the fact that he was so grounded by giving and receiving fundamental love. A change of fortune so very welcomed, especially when Pamela considered the conversations she and Brad had shared regarding his fears of never finding love at all, only two short years prior.

2015 was, by all measures, the best year yet for Brad Gobright. He even declared as much by the end of it. He was climbing better than ever, and doing so in nearly all disciplines: speed, big-wall, sport, even free-solo. More importantly, he'd been granted an entirely new operating system by virtue of that special, loving relationship with his partner. His already wonderful life, with his climbing, new sponsorships, and the feature film in production, was put into overflow when his girlfriend moved from Ahwahne to Boulder that November.

Incredibly, despite how spread thin these commitments could have made him, Brad still excelled. Every relationship needs attention in this life, no matter how busy we get; a fact not lost on him or his significant other. Somehow, they both managed to foster that and grow it in the middle of this newfound, frenetic pulse of attention. I'm certain there were days when he would have wanted to climb at the crag or the gym more, but chose not to for the balance he sought from life. Which means he must have discovered that truth that many among us well know—that if you give your attention rightly to the things that matter most, everything else will, and does, line up.

In the same season that he and his partner lived in that adorable commune with a dozen others, Brad ticked his next 5.14 project, Cheating Reality, on the iconic Devil's Thumb up in the hills of Boulder. Additionally, at 5.13d, he sent the 1996 Tommy Caldwell test piece, Third Millennium, at the Monastery in Estes Park.

Shortly thereafter, Brad also called Cedar Wright and Taylor

Keating, telling them that he was ready to put his already extreme solo of the Daub-Griffith—a wildly tenuous arete-climb in Eldorado Canyon—to shame. After a month of on-again, off-again work at mastering his sequences, Brad was ready to climb the unthinkably desperate Eldorado Canyon hero's line, Hairstyles and Attitudes, without a rope. A climb so demanding, so low percentage, so fully committed at its crux that, once in the thick of it, it would quite literally offer Brad only one of two end results. He'd either end up at the top or fall instantaneously out of Wright's frame, down to the bone collector. There was no down climbing, and therefore, no margin for error.

And so, after a week in contemplation, Brad came to peace and readiness. The first time he'd attempted the solo, a week prior, he climbed up to the crux, and, overwhelmed by the nerves and consequence of the occasion, buckled in execution. At perhaps the last possible exit point before the mark of no return, Brad reset course and climbed down and off the route. Safety, it seemed, even for an outrageous ball of stoke like Brad, was not third after all.

I understand that it was a lot of self-preservation up there, when push came to shove, but there was also more to it. A climber only makes it through the soloing world safely by measure of their operating system's tuning. The fact that Brad couldn't always articulate his choices verbally the way some might prefer is not to suggest he didn't have the internal process. He showed us, right there, he had a system running checks every time he pushed upward.

That day never made the final cut. Which is a shame because Brad showed us, as the noble often do, that the real stroke of mastery is as much in knowing when to hold as when to fire. But at last, after that hike off the cliff and a week's worth of contemplation, a process that most of us also never got clued into for the feature film, Brad came back as settled as operationally possible. I mean, it is Brad we're focusing on, not a Tibetan monk. There would always be an immeasurable stoke flying co-pilot to any equanimity with that kid.

All the readiness in the world was no guarantee for safe passage, however. Brad had a hell of a run at Hairstyles, and not exactly in the right direction. It was the kind of batshit, near-death moment nobody runs on repeat.

In a now-famous, gut-dropping sequence that Wright filmed, Brad came within micrometers of death during his solo. In the thick of the proper crux—where he would not be able to escape by down-climbing—Brad's operating system kinked for processing. He skipped a beat. A move he had done at least fifty times running by rote memory went haywire when his primary, left foot buckled for tension just as he needed it most. His right hand, pressing to a hold that sloped just gently to his right, subsequently took on more of his weight, which caused an immediate imbalance. In the time it took for a synapse to relay across the entirety of Brad's myelinated nerve network, heaven and earth stood still. Without his left foot actively pulling him toward center, the force of his right hand pulled him in the wrong direction, both away from the hold his left hand was aiming for, and—because his foot lost the engagement to his hamstring and hip—also away from the wall.

What exactly caused the error? Surely it wasn't a lack of ability. Was it nerves? A lapse of focus or the absence of a single deep breath? Possibly. More important than the cause, in this case, was the response. The fact that Brad was able to check his skid, reapply upward force, and reach the next hold still amazes anyone who watches the footage. Somehow, with the force of life suddenly awoken in each parcel of the mitochondrial network, Brad latched the hold above him, dispelled the impulse for complete sympathetic takeover, and put together a composed sequence that got him not only to the top of the next move, but also to the bottom of his next breath.

Eventually settled, with Cedar struggling to hold the camera still beside him, Brad found his way to the top of the formation. It was a free solo for the ages. Likely one that would never go repeated, too. Hairstyles and Attitudes, an Eldorado classic, had taken Brad to the edge of his existence.

It didn't just take Brad to the brink; it took Cedar there too. Remember, Brad was more than the focus of Wright's film alone; he was his friend. He was the kid who looked up to Wright as a mentor. He was the kid who would come over and play with Wright and his partner Nellie's absurdly cute little pug, Gus. And that person, that friend, had nearly just died.

Wright struggled for what the loss would have meant, especially if it happened while he held the camera. One more reason, among many, why he put his best efforts into that film. Sure, Brad probably would have soloed Hairstyles anyway, but for all he risked out there, Cedar felt the obligation to make the best film possible. The better it turned out, the better and more secure Gobright's future path would be. A path Wright hoped would not imitate anything near the events he'd witnessed that day.

With Cedar's help, Brad secured new sponsorships in 2015, and, that same November, Brad also received his first national-level press when writer Devon O'Neil and *Outside Magazine* ran a piece on Brad simply titled, *Brad Gobright is the Next Great Soloist*. In the article, O'Neil spelled out the progressions Brad had recently made in his climbing. Specifically, O'Neil mentioned how standout Brad's climbing in 2015 had been, and he introduced armchair athletes across America to a kind, wide-eyed antihero that few could root against. O'Neil also made the inevitable comparisons to the great Alex Honnold, who apart from being perhaps the most crafted of professional climbers, was and still is the most well-known. Because of that, Brad had landed square on the center of most people's map of notable adventure athletes.

Adding to the notoriety, Cedar Wright wrote a feature story of his own for *Climbing Magazine*, titled *Ode to the Dark Horse*, for the December 2015 publication. Brad, landing two features in less than a month, soared in popularity almost overnight, at least in the climbing world. But, to nobody's surprise, that accolade wouldn't change him a bit.

Hearing news that he'd made the magazines, Brad walked himself into the nearest bookstore on Pearl Street in downtown Boulder. Magazine in hand, Brad sat in a corner just beside the aisle, read the work, and then texted Cedar a sincere thank you. After finishing the piece, Brad stood up, put the magazine back on the shelf, snapped a picture of it, and then posted that picture to social media. In his post, Brad noted the article, thanked his sponsors and all involved, spoke about how stoked he was to be in print, and then gave the world an ironic new hashtag. Comically, imperfectly misspelling his own punchline, Brad simply wrote #toexpensivetobuy.

The kid could not have been made any better were there a million more iterations of him. How could you not love the blue out of his eyeballs or the shit out of his grin?

Brad Gobright was the happiest he'd ever been in 2015. His life, for all the perplexities it had once presented him, had come together into the kind of weave most of us dream of. The permutations, his mosaic of exterior details, were less important to him than the inner fount they sprang from. It wasn't just that he'd climbed better than ever, or that he'd finally come into a modicum of financial security by way of his new sponsorships. It was simpler, purer than that. It was love. Something from which the rest of his life blossomed.

Those of a more skeptical slant might say it was his insane

finger strength that accounted for those first 5.14s he climbed. Some will say it was his comprehensive, relentless training regimens, both indoors and outdoors, that took him up the Heart Route. Others will insist it was his innate tenacity that pushed him past his near-death pulse on Hairstyles. And each of those may well be true for the line item they correspond to. He was getting returns from all the groundwork he laid for years, alone. But the bloom of it all, and all at the same time—that was a different accounting altogether.

That ingenious splendor, that burst of light and glory he'd tapped into, holistically, for those twelve months on his twenty-seventh orbit around the sun: that was love. That was caring for someone and seeing the world anew. It was being accepted, regarded, taken completely for who he was. It was the gift of belonging. Everybody who knew him well or for a long time knew it, too. He hadn't just found a partner in his girlfriend. Brad Gobright, forever the unmoored, had at last found an anchor. Something he, and every one of us, were the better for.

RECOVERY

January 27, 2016. Face-deep in the opening moves of the Boulder Canyon test piece, Viceroy, Brad came ass-to-ground when hurtling against more of the inevitable in his path. Choosing to lead the notorious, nails-hard route by skipping the bolts and placing his own gear, Brad charged out the gates too psyched for his own good. With a storm rolling into town and the film production on a timeline, Brad made the call to jump on the route against his better judgment. That masterful practice of pausing that he'd demonstrated on Hairstyles a few months earlier fell backseat to his inert, unchecked enthusiasm. His rationale: there wouldn't be many days left to film before things went into post-production, and he had been riding such an enormous swell of momentum anyway. As goes worst-case scenarios, he wouldn't have thought beyond the possibility of simply not sending.

Choosing a traditional style, Brad tied in, leaving the quickdraws behind and taking only a handful of small cams (the requisite pieces needed when foregoing the safety of the bolts). Quickly, he made it just fifteen feet off the deck while protected only by a single marginal cam. At the first desperate pull, a move so powerful it tested the breaking point of his legendary finger strength, Brad buckled. Set up in haste, he pulled with his hands more than he pushed with his feet. Between the minuscule, single millimeter-sized edge his right foot was posted to and the cold temperature of the rock—numbing the feeling out of his nerves— he reached for the next upward hold more than he drove at it by pushing his feet. Half a second later, life changed.

Brad fell. At light speed, nonetheless. Too quick for anything but desperate observation, he pummeled toward the ground, yanking that lone camming device out of the wall in a shitshow neither he nor his belayer could readily avoid. A millisecond later, upon his percussive smash back to Earth, gravity compressed his spine so hard it squeezed the osteoblasts out of two vertebrae and hammered his left ankle into rubble. Air taken from his diaphragm, he seized with a whole-body contraction for a second longer until, when registration at last occurred from receptor to brain stem, he erupted with a single, searing expletive. "*FUCK!*"

For the next thirty minutes, Brad rolled and spasmed uncontrollably, grateful only in the knowledge that one could not possibly be paralyzed and simultaneously be in so much pain. At the hospital an hour later, the emergency staff triaged him to a modicum of comfort, where, with great regret, he called his mom, his boss, his girlfriend, and Cedar. It wouldn't be his last injury, but for all the groundswell he'd come into 2016 riding, it was disastrous.

Reminded of his injuries in Ahwahne and Squamish in 2011 and 2012, Pamela fought off her anxiety by starting a prayer chain with her network of friends and loved ones. Meanwhile, Brad's partner, shining as the caretaker she'd always been, visited him immediately at the hospital for a much-needed boost of morale. Within days she'd rally the peer group and community at large, organizing an impromptu get-well-soon fiesta. She'd buy him a video game console to pass the time, and help him with everything from cooking food to rides to the climbing gym, where he could train by hanging on the campus board. She'd stand behind him even when he could barely stand up himself. Supported as he'd never been in his previous injuries, Brad made an internal resolution: he'd come back even stronger.

It's not that his parents weren't also caring during injuries past; they were saints. But this was a different time. He was a professional climber now, which meant that his recovery had an ordination about it. It had a direction; a world apart from his injuries in Squamish four years earlier.

Back then, an injury meant time to think about his lifestyle and how he might find some means of self-sufficiency. It meant he had to go home because he had nowhere else to stay. It meant stress and fracture in the delicate relationships between him and his parents, between their desire to care for him but also see him care for his future—a future which in 2012 did not seem to foretell a climbing career. But that was then.

Because of that, this injury, though more severe on paper, was less a low point for him emotionally. Rather, it was a springboard. Mentally, Brad carried a resolve that most of us hadn't seen in his previous injuries. He knew what he was capable of and he knew the path to return to it. This isn't to suggest that road was easy, or even remotely pleasurable. But by the time Pamela came to see him for a survey of his injuries and his recovery in February, a month after his fall, she could see things were different on this go-round.

"I just couldn't believe the way she took care of him," Pamela shared. "I came up there ready to play nurse and clean house and just help them put their lives in order. But she'd already done it. She had it all covered. It was so reassuring as a mother to know that at last, Brad had someone."

But it wasn't only his partner. Pamela recalled that on the night they went out to Golden, Colorado, to a local gym for a slide show Brad was presenting, the community did as much for his recovery as the members of his household.

Brad was always good with a crowd. With that tension-melting, self-deprecating nonchalance and his easy, non-philosophical view on things, he'd marry the impossibility of his accomplishments with the absurdity that percolated within them. He knew how to genuinely, nakedly show himself as himself. And that, apart from his monumental climbs, inspired most. On that night at the climbing gym, Pamela recalled that Brad had a comfort, a lightness, up on stage that she hadn't seen before. He was completely plugged in, secure. Orthotic back brace and all.

Knowing he inspired others inspired Brad, you could see it. It kept him from that dangerous wake of despair that many can fall into following a big injury or life setback. Ultimately, that connection to the community, those slideshows, the validation of it all, kept him away from the darker sides of his injury. Two vertebral compression fractures and a busted ankle are never going to be a pleasant experience, but for what they offered, Brad found the fulcrum.

All systems of support considered, nobody saw Brad rebounding so high or so fast on the heels of that back-breaker. Ten weeks and hundreds of minutes of hang-boarding in a back brace later, Brad came back to Viceroy, the scene of the accident, and climbed better than he had all winter. He did, for the sake of safety, clip the bolts this go-round, rather than plug his own gear. But the actual climbing itself, those stern moves that take both the finger composition and the body power elite to the gods of Olympus, they succumbed. Brad climbed well—better, in fact—than he had when he injured himself. With that, it was decided to green-light his course forward. He wasn't going to rage right away, and it would be a few months before he felt confident enough to whip large on gear, per *modus operandi*, but it wouldn't be long.

Two weeks later, on April 29, 2016, Brad was 2,500 feet above the Ahwahne floor, on the A5-traverse pitch of Golden Gate on To-tock-ah-noo-lah. He'd been familiar with the pitch, given it was the upper pathway to finish his and Mason's free Heart Route. But to be up there in a position like that, at barely three months since smashing his guts to the floor, goddammit, it was nearly an insult to the rest of us.

Not only did Brad have no business being up there risking falls, but he also had no business doing it by his usual lightning style. Brad Gobright was not eighty percent up the flanks of To-tock-ah-noo-lah in an everyman's wall-style ascent; he was up there doing it in a single push, in a day. With his search and rescue friend and Valley local, Christian Cattell, Brad had set off just before dawn, and now, at golden hour proper, live-and-direct from the best piece of rock in the world, Brad was shining like Bennu bursting through the sky at Godspeed. Wrapped in California gold, his best color, Brad wrestled upon the high pitches of Golden Gate that day, the same way he always had. Which is to say, gloriously. Sunrays from the heart of the solar system cast a wax over the entire affair, while the Valley locals and Tom Evans alike had to double take from their telephoto lenses. Nobody could believe his audaciousness. Only a month earlier they'd seen him hobbling with crutches and that cursed back brace.

Brad did not make his goal of a successful free-climb on Golden Gate that day, but as evening came, and darkness thereafter, he did make more believers from the few remaining skeptics. Somewhere in that atypical operating system he ran,

Brad Gobright had found magic. And the longer he executed his craft, the more unanimous the consensus. It was baffling, it was inspired, and it was unheralded, but it was contagious.

As early as 2012, while camping illegally in Squamish, Brad and Jim Reynolds ran in the same circles. It often happens. In the climbing life, the roads are paved by familiar faces. Though they were only acquaintances at the time, Jim remembers their first encounter.

While a circle of friends worked at the beginnings of a campfire, chopping wood and cleaning fish they'd caught from the riverbanks nearby, Brad almost unnoticeably darted off with just his raggedy shoes and chalkbag in hand. An aside which piqued Jim's attention, especially when, just thirty minutes later, Brad returned drenched in sweat and his trademark, snickering satisfaction.

Jim, observant as always, had to pry. "So, hey man, noticed you stepped out for a bit. What was that about?"

Brad looked at his future partner, though he didn't know it then, and answered, "Yeah, um, I just had to run another lap on something, since there was still light out, so I climbed the Apron."

Rock On, a classic 5.10a up the mini-lith called the Apron, at the base of the Stawamus Chief, had been a favorite of Brad's solo circuit. A climb, like Epinephrine in Red Rock far south, that Brad had wired to the point of blind execution. Five hundred feet tall, he'd take it car to car, or campground to campground, up and back again in as little as twenty-five minutes by the end of that season.

Inspired by the mastery and bravado it demonstrated, Jim cheered at the effort, simply replying, "Dude, that's badass."

Jim introduced himself to Brad formally, after which they both folded back into the gathering of friends for that night's campfire. But seeds had been planted. For years, Jim had looked for those majestic traits Brad Gobright possessed in his various partners. And mostly, that search came up empty.

Years and many thousands of pitches would pass between them, with occasional run-ins at seasonal crags patching the gaps, but finally, in the spring of 2016, they came together. Jim Reynolds and Brad Gobright were, in retrospect, designed for one another, and, for the beautiful two years between 2016 and 2018, they had more than just two lives running parallel; they had a partnership, which became a friendship. Jim had many of Brad's anti-establishment, dirtbag sensibilities and his own quirky make-up that endeared them to one another. Two parts pirate, one part nerd, a few shakes of the mystic and monastic, all in a manic, heavy metal raging exterior; Jim is a profound amalgam. Most importantly, Jim wanted to live life as big as Brad did, which is to say, bigger than most of us care to dream or try for.

Back to May 2016. A week after Brad's heroic efforts on Golden Gate, he and Jim linked up in the meadow below To-tock-ah-noo-lah with a new look on the Big Stone. It wasn't a free-climb they were after; it was speed.

Speed climbing, the expeditious, concise deconstructing of holy sacrament on God's biggest stone, is an offense to gravity itself. A pursuit so dangerous, so flagrant, that once in its clutches, most learn it is not history they are grabbing but something else entirely. One desperate hand over the other, many a poor soul has found in their clutch but one thing: the tail of that almighty, untamable tiger. Simply put, speed climbing the Big Stone is a path of no forgiveness.

All hazards considered, it's hard to keep a spirit like Brad or Jim's bound by convention. Eyes wide open to the risk, but infatuated with the concept of endless—fluid movement on nearly a vertical kilometer of granite—they had their first playdate on The Nose within just under six hours. A week later, they'd gone down to five hours and twenty minutes. Another week after that, four and a half hours, with, quite egregiously, the addition of another thirty-odd pitches. A blistering, 4.5-hour Nose burn wasn't enough that day. They decided to add the entirety of the Salathe Wall on top of it.

On just their third or fourth day of ever climbing together, Brad and Jim took the Big Stone for two of its biggest and most famous routes in less time than it takes the earth to cycle on its axis. This, for Brad, was just four months after having destroyed his body back in Boulder Canyon.

But the young man had a vision behind it all. You could almost see him contriving it all to the detail, for months, in those quiet moments back in Boulder, in the hundreds of minutes clawing at the smallest edges of that hangboard. Brad wanted to rage, not just climb. Not rage against an institution, or against the proverbial machine—he wanted to rage, as in live, as in express himself, outrageously, to the hilt. Because when you're climbing through thousands of feet of vertical history—eons of earth systems crystallized by time itself—you are, if tuned correctly, taking on more than the three-dimensional. You're playing the eternal game. Or at least something like it. All those forces, the concentrations of mass and gravity and the unthinkable periods of time which compacted those layers of granite into their exact shape, were sitting there, rebounding electron waves right into the pulsating capillaries of Brad's fingertips with every move he made. Enough contact like that, say, sixty pitches' worth, and it's not just your physical corpus that's raging; something deeper is, too. I think deep inside, Brad was on that plane. I think he also just loved the exacting freedom of grinding out thousands of feet of kinesthetic, vertical swimming. I think he loved it for all the superficial, or topical, grandiosity it could give. Feats that supreme are, at the least, sensational and it is no shortcoming to enjoy that, too.

Brad's vision wasn't just two runs up To-tock-ah-noo-lah in a single day. It was three. Three was elite. Three was historic. Three had only been realized twice before. Once by Hollywood Hans Florine and Steve Schneider in 1994, and only again by legends Alex Honnold and the late Sean Leary in 2010. For all the exquisite company Brad had already climbed himself into via his recent ascents in the history books, a triple linkup on the Big Stone was among his most coveted, especially with his injuries considered. Given Brad was not able to train to his peak performance due to his ongoing recovery, it was the big linkup, voluminous style of climbing that caught his attention. Because of that, he called up his old friend and speed-climbing aficionado, Scott Bennett, to put a ribbon on the sum of their intrepid ventures together.

From the Naked Edge speed record over the past two years to the gigantic linkups they had done in Zion National Park only a few seasons prior, Scott and Brad had a history of uncanny ascents between them, a chemistry that Brad would only ever find in precious few other partnerships. Cool as you like, Scott and Brad walked to the base of The Zodiac route on To-tock-ah-noo-lah, laced up their shoes, smashed a fist-bump, and started the clock just past 2:00 in the afternoon.

Up on The Zodiac, Brad excelled with a cool, focused pace. Tapping into the "slow is smooth, smooth is fast" ethos, Brad moved with balletic efficiency up numerous 5.12 pitches, putting them at the summit well before sundown. Just five and a half hours after beginning, the duo was already making their way down the East Ledges descent, a mosaic of cutouts one must downclimb, hike, and rappel for more than a thousand feet. Usually taking hours, Scott and Brad charged down it in thirty minutes.

Back at the base, rehydration was first order. For their first climb of the day, they'd taken no water up The Zodiac on a rumor there was a stash somewhere near the top. They did find that water near the summit, but along with it came the discovery that bird shit had soiled the lids and bottles to a point of bacterial untenability. They had blasted up one big wall and back down again in six hours at that point, and they'd still not had a drop.

Once recharged, Scott and Brad set off into one of Brad's favorite styles of climbing on his favorite route. The Nose, at night, by headlamp. On The Nose, Scott and Brad shared leads, with Scott of greatest utility in the technical aid-climbing pitches, where he was, and still is, a master at economic, safe movement. Brad, with his fitness and electric charge, would obliterate the moderate terrain faster than anyone, which he did.

Focused on the task at hand, the boys didn't exchange much more than necessary; words were the tools of the planning and reflecting stages of these types of grand operations. Action carried the day, and, as it turned out, the night. At the belay exchanges, communication was often short and compartmentalized to a discussion of the next pitches above them, the gear required, and the logistics for sound passage. Still, in the whitened orb of the headlamps, with a snow globe effect occurring each time they chalked up their greasy mitts, moments of deep awareness came, too. Passage by night, a quiet, intimate affair, still had its romance. Especially for Brad.

Somewhere in the depths of midnight, on some anonymous sheet of granite that glowed before him, Brad turned twenty-eight years old while scuffed up through the protection of his climbing pants and hand-jammy climbers' gloves and soaked with sweat in his burgundy crew-neck tee. Almost a decade after having been kicked off an amateur climbers' team in pursuit of the Big Stone, he was up there doing what only two parties had ever done before. Questions of his direction, the duty of being a good son to his loving parents, the balance of his intimate relationship with his significant other—all of that and any other burden he'd carry on flat ground in the lowlands of life below fell quiet to the uniform sound of his panting breath. Thousands of feet off the ground, on a piece of stone formed millions of years ago for just that perfect, if only momentary splendor, Brad's troubles were cast aside. Brad, a tiny orb of light in a giant Ahwahne Valley of darkness, under a cosmic sky, was precisely where he was born to be.

Near five in the morning, just at the earliest embers of pre-dawn light, the boys hiked up the energy-sapping switchbacks at the base of To-tock-ah-noo-lah to the ends of its western flank. Lurking Fear, a steep, gigantic sweep of granite, stood above them as the third and final climb of the day.

On the route, the crux was as much the exhaustion as the movement itself. Staying awake at the belays, or avoiding a lapse of focus while on lead, were themselves herculean feats. The good news: they had enough time in the bank to climb at a calculated pace and still make their margins. The bad news: the longer they kept that pace, the closer they came to full-system, mind and body shutdown.

In the meat of the climb, Brad was on lead for a consecutive number of 5.12 pitches, whose vertical steepness felt, by that point, as if they tilted into the terrain of the overhung. Frayed and repeatedly runout, Brad recalled a rare, and very palpable discourse with fear. A fear that he would exorcise, as he had with many of his childhood demons, by course of action more than intellect. Brad knew better than to think too long for the paralytic effect of fear on the system. He knew fear enough to respect it, but he knew of himself even better. Somehow, pressed to the last caloric unit of glucose in his blood serum, he fought off the shakes of body fatigue and the quivering pulses of fear and made it, with Scott, to the final pitches. He'd gone to the limit, to the precipice of those fabled ultra-endurance level hallucinations, and in that space had found exactly what he expected: he could become broken, could stand face-to-face with the person deep within, and where most find a chasm between who they are and who they truly want to be, Brad found no conflict, only peace.

Twenty-three hours and thirty minutes after beginning, on June 16, 2016, Brad's twenty-eighth birthday, he and Scott Bennett topped out on Lurking Fear at the summit of To-tock-ah-noo-lah, after having blasted up The Zodiac first and The Nose, as an *intermezzo*, by night. Three routes up the Big Stone in under twenty-four hours, only the third team on earth to have done so.

Brad and Jim Reynolds took a handful of laps up The Nose that spring, enough to get them near the three-hour mark. But with summer comes crowds and the heat. For Jim especially, the heat alone is akin to kryptonite—it can take him from a wall jock to a peon in seconds flat. Due to that, and the upcoming summer trip to Squamish Brad had planned with his girlfriend, speed-climbing on The Nose took a pause.

Earlier in the summer, in the middle of June, while Brad was being overwhelmed by the tourists in the Valley, I'd had a chance to climb a linkup in the high country of Tuolumne—a connection of routes on the Drug Dome, Mariuolumne Dome, and later, Cathedral Peak, that I thought, from a layman's perspective, was somewhat proud on aesthetics. My venture, of course, involved a rope and a partner. When I texted him photos and a brief message, Brad returned with a usual affirmation, which I appreciated considering how many other things must have held his attention. Inspired, I'd like to think by what I shared with him, days later Brad drove up to Tuolumne and did his own linkup, first with the iconic Third Pillar of Dana, which he then linked to Drug Dome, Mariuolumne Dome, Matthes Crest, Cathedral Peak, and Eichhorn's Pinnacle. All of Brad's climbs, of course, were ropeless.

Brad, for his part, always had a difficult time with the mass of "tourons"—as he and many other locals called them—flooding the Valley from Memorial Day weekend until Labor Day. He struggled to see honest taxpayers as anything more than cogs in the great wheel of capitalism, as consumers who came to the Valley as if it were a theme park rather than a tabernacle for the divine. The way that the masses insisted on 24/7 access to their creature comforts, and that they looked at men and women of the rock tribe as zoo animals rather than humans reclaiming the wild within their own nature, always dug into Brad. But so did the fact that he had such a hard time with them. In fact, apart from the forty-fifth president of the United States of America, Brad didn't really care to loathe anything or anyone outright. He could see that those base instincts reflected something amiss within him, and as much as he disapproved of the tourons themselves, he struggled more with his reactions to them.

As complex as this relationship was for Brad, the idea of loathing or not loathing the average tourist wouldn't stop him from making a quick buck. The spring of 2016 is when Brad Gobright came up with the illegal but splendid idea to use the tourist's naivety to his own advantage.

On more than one occasion, Brad would park his car near the Choo-look pullout, one of the main attractions in the Park, first thing in the morning before the day's rush. There, he'd wait for some poor dad in a minivan to pull up—wife and kids in a shitshow beside him—desperate to park. That's when Brad would motion the poor bastard to roll down his window, at which point he'd make his pitch.

"Oh, trying to get the family to see the falls, are ya?" he'd start off.

"You got it," was the usual response, often with an overwhelmed

237

expression as cars honked from behind.

"Well, you're in luck. I'll give you this spot right here, sir. Just gonna need twenty bucks and we're square."

They say a good salesperson never gets too busy with price unless first establishing value. Often, with cars honking behind and the stress of the moment building up, Brad would finish the pitch, completely nonchalant.

"You know, I'll be fine if you don't want to. I'm good. Already here, all day. But you—"

Having walked right up the car window at this point, Brad would usually look into the van and note the cacophonous riot of the family, desperate for a stop.

"—you might drive another two hours before you find a spot."

And just like that, one time after another, it was on. Nonplussed, cool as you like, Brad capitalized. Symbiosis was, at least, a beginning. Sure, he was turning a profit, but at least he was having interactions. And enough of those interactions, enough times looking those poor soccer moms and dads in the eye, they eventually added up. He saw humans, as flawed as the rest of us, just trying to connect to something bigger than themselves.

Gas tanks full, Brad left Ahwahne with his girlfriend in July for a two-month road trip in Squamish. In the nearly two years they'd been together, life had always been itinerant. Brad worked sometimes; she worked most times. They lived together; they lived apart. Things would ebb and flow. But this trip, this was the first time both were explicitly on a trip just to spend time with one another. Of course, with how plugged in they were to the community, they had friends to see and things to climb while on course, but overall, this trip shined for Brad and her both for what it meant between them.

The summer of 2016 was also when Brad had his first

Outdoor Retailer Trade Show, where he was heavily booked for appearances on behalf of his sponsors, and when he made it to the microphone of the *Enormocast* podcast, whose host, the Southern California native, Chris Kalous, had partnered up with Brad and Mason Earle back in Bear's Ears National Monument for that group onsight of Winner Takes All, way back in 2010. Since then, Chris had formed the leading podcast in the industry. After Brad's episode was published, it did even more to put him in the hearts and minds of the climbing community.

The trade show lasted the better part of a week, after which Brad returned to Squamish, where he and I met up for one of the handfuls of climbs together in our later years. Much like with Tuolumne, we'd be on the same route, in the same season, within days or sometimes even hours of one another. But I'd seen him on the ground a fair amount. Almost every time he came home for the holidays, or over the course of his many injuries, we had caught up.

That summer, in the time we shared, it was obvious to me, as it was to his mother long before, that his relationship with his partner was doing for him something no amount of climbing or accolade in the climbing world could. It grounded him to the fullness of the human experience. One night, as he and his lady visited for dinner, Brad was simply alight. The joy in his heart was like nothing I'd seen from him. Just that spring alone, he'd been in the climbing gym in Southern California, back brace and all, and, while he looked a new version of himself then, something about the glow around his partner just made all the difference. Together, we caught up as old friends, chowed on pizza, and laughed. Brad showed us the footage of him taking that terrible fall on Viceroy, which would later be memorialized in Cedar and Taylor's *Safety Third* film. Right then, with gobies across his hands and the seasoning of a dozen years in Ahwahne, he looked a million years removed from the kid I learned how to trad-climb with.

Almost to prove the point, one of the many routes Brad "casually" climbed that summer in Squamish—considering he was still taking it easy on his back and ankle—was The Shadow. A patent perpendicular fold of two alabaster sheets of granite high up the University Wall of the Stawamus Chief, spread symmetrically in that classic open-book layout, The Shadow was first climbed by Brad's hero, Peter Croft. On the magnetic pull of a route like The Shadow, Croft had once said, "It's so beautiful, so obvious, you can see it calling to you all the way from town."

A classic route, once again, the covet of many, that took Brad only a few sessions to master. The day he led it clean, with old friend Bronson Hovnanian at the belay, his now-friend and regular photographer, Dan Krauss, snapped a picture so good it ran as the cover shot to the upcoming *Rock and Ice* issue, for which Brad had the centerpiece profile. The kid was on fire, even in recovery.

My vision of him was soon affirmed by his mom and dad, as Pamela and Jim visited Squamish just a week after I had. Together they also partook in a festive, glorious week of reconnection. It was the beginning of a new era, though they wouldn't know it then.

Over the next few years, Brad would make it a point to get in touch and keep in touch with many from his earlier years in life. And he made it a point to reintegrate towards family. No longer out there simply burning for climbing alone, Brad was, and had been, validated. Because of that, and with the blessing of some moderate income due to his climbing success, he had both the time and the means to build a fuller life. Pamela recalled just how precious that trip to Squamish was for her and Jim alike. Whether riding the tramway up the Sea to Sky Gondola, hiking up the Stawamus Chief, or watching Brad while climbing at the Smoke Bluffs—her son was thriving. Seeing him climb with tact, make plans with financial agency, and walk with the love of another human in his hands, all of it filled Pamela's heart in ways that only parents can fully comprehend.

In September, after their two-month trip in Squamish, Brad and his girlfriend returned south. Years had passed since his girlfriend had joined the climbing scene at full abandon, and in that time, certain questions of her own direction had arisen—questions of herself that the climbing life alone could not answer. It's a part of the cycle for many of us; we all seek rounded lives. Because of that, her directions would begin moving toward her next steps, professionally and academically, back into the fold in the pursuit of reintegration. Brad, however, was one of the lucky few, at least for the time being, to marry passion and profession. With that profession came certain expectations. Places to be and times to be there, which increasingly kept him and his partner at a distance.

In Ahwahne, every September, the Yosemite Facelift is an annual event where climbers the world over gather on the ostensible mission to clean up the place and demonstrate good stewardship to the Park Service. For many in the community, it's also an excuse to see friends, to celebrate the collective way of life, and to kick off a fall season that usually winds from California to the rest of the western states.

As went the climbing press in 2015 and 2016, Brad was one of the hottest items on the market. Because of that, he had a keynote slide show and interview during the Facelift's nightly community gathering. A slideshow that he absolutely crushed. With iconoclast, raconteur, and climbing legend Timmy O'Neil at the microphone as host, Brad wowed the crowd to ecstatic cheer with his trademark blend of quick wit and that self-debasing, boyish charm. Laced right in between the impossibility of his biggest accomplishments and most attractive to all in attendance was his pure heart and quiet humility. Brad endeared himself to the masses, not only as the most comical parade this side of the Mississippi, but as the most genuine, too.

A week after the Facelift, Brad had a chance to keep company with one of the legends of the Valley climbing scene, Mr. Hollywood Hans Florine, who not only had the speed record on The Nose of To-tock-ah-noo-lah at that time, but who also had a contract lined up to film a motivational short piece for what Brad considered to be capitalistic no-gooders, Chick-Fil-A. As earning an errant buck however and wherever you can is as much an Ahwahne climbers tradition as waxing a tall tale by the campfire is, Brad was all too eager to join. He'd be getting precious time to pick the brain of the speed record holder, and he'd be getting paid to do it.

So, for two days, Brad and Valley-local big wall climber and inspiring human spirit, Miranda Oakley, paired up with Hans and his filming team. Brad and Miranda knew one another from the local circles over the years and had climbed The Astroman together in the past, which gave them an easy camaraderie. Together they endured two days of awkward, incredibly cheesy plot-forming and filming with Hans and crew, which eventually took them up The Nose in a seven-hour push. The film was meant to serve as a motivational piece, to be presented at team-building events and board meetings alike out there in the corporate world, touching on themes like teamwork, discipline, and even excellence.

Surprisingly, when the filming crew asked Brad for a "try-hard" face on the wall, or to spice up the dialogue with contrived fear or tension, Brad hammed it up, in Miranda's recollection. He took on the role as professionally as they asked him to, which was no small feat. At one point, Brad, Miranda, and Hans spent twenty minutes looking over the topo (climber's map) of The Nose, assigning who would get which leads and discussing their operational tactics.

While the camera crew had them on a hot-mic, Brad had a realization, saying, "This is probably the longest I've prepared for any climb in my life." A statement, which while comically true considering all the giant things he'd done, was taken as pure gold by the producer.

"That's great," one of the crew spouted out, "Give us more of that feel, for sure. Make it seem impossible."

Two days, a lot of patience, and one summit up To-tock-ah-noo-lah later, Brad was a paycheck the richer. But it wasn't just coin he was after. He'd also leveled up with critical beta from Hans regarding tactics for the speed record. Brad and Jim were barely below the three-hour mark at that stage, which meant they had some ways yet to go. Apart from sharing it with a few friends, they weren't putting their ambitions out to the masses. As far as anybody in the area knew, Brad and Jim were just taking speed laps to get better at other linkup projects.

But the wheels were turning. In November, just after the election, I was in Ahwahne with a friend, and we sat with Brad for breakfast at the Lodge Café one morning, where Eric Sloan, inter-generational big-wall master, guidebook author, steward, and Valley local, pressed Brad for a little motivation. Walking up to the table, Eric gave his usual hellos, enveloped with his gentle smile, and then asked Brad about the speed record.

"I heard you and Jim recently went below three hours. You plan on going for it?" he asked.

Brad, in his usual downplay, responded without commitment, "Well, yeah, you know. We're just having fun up there at this stage."

"Well, you should go for it, if you ask me," Eric began warmly. "I think you guys are good for it, for sure. It'll be cool to see some of the locals have that record again. And, from what I hear, Alex wouldn't mind having that record broken anyway. Rumor has it he'd like to do it with Tommy [Caldwell], but he can't really go after his own record, since it could be seen as a bit of a nod against Hans. If you guys do it, not only do you have the record, but he's free to try it again, too."

I've no doubt that Brad had much of this already figured out. He and Alex had become friends in the past few years. And where Hans and the dark horse legend, Dean Potter, had a notoriously bitter rivalry as goes speed records, Brad and Alex already had something of a refreshed, whimsical one-upmanship. They pushed one another, but never at the cost of a friendship that, over the coming years, would deepen.

Non-committed, but with that undeniable snicker, Brad looked up to Eric and replied, "Those are interesting ideas you bring up. Guess I'll just have to talk with Jim and see how he feels. Things are winding down for now anyway, I'm going to train for harder free-climbing this winter, now that I can take some whippers again. I suppose we'll see where it all stands next spring."

Eric smiled; Brad grinned. Plans were in motion.

On a frigid winter day in February a few months later, Brad's plans for The Nose speed record took a detour. With a focus on hard multi-pitch climbing, Brad and Alex Honnold had teamed up to climb Rainbow Country, a challenging variation up the Rainbow Wall in Red Rock Conservation Area, Nevada. There, clean, giant walls deep in the canyons sweep vertically in dramatic fashion. Just the kind of place guys like Brad and Alex would frequent. This was an additional reason why Brad had moved back for another season. On better days, they'd even run laps between the other cardinal routes on nearby formations, in the legendary linkups they'd both been known to enchain. On this day, though, cold and half-frozen at thirty-eight degrees Fahrenheit at the base, those linkups were on the backburner. They simply wanted to climb a single route and avoid hypothermia.

Arriving at a frozen wasteland, Brad and Alex climbed the first few pitches on Rainbow Country only to submit to the conditions. Tiny, microscopic edges for feet and brutal, nail-biting crimps the size of credit cards came up just short of sadism; because of that, retreat came swift. On the nearby, even harder route, Dreefee, a fixed line hanging some 400 feet, called out to the two of them. Rather than lead and fall from Rainbow Country's crux pitches, risking injury and overall decline in morale, they figured they could climb with the protection of mini-tractions (self-belaying devices) on the fixed line. Not a bad trade-off. That Dreefee was harder didn't matter. With a rope fixed above them and no commitment to top it out, it was much safer, and more enjoyable, on top-rope than it would've been to stay on their original plan.

After putting in an hour of climbing, Alex rappelled first. Brad stayed up for another lap, and, as those short winter days deep in the canyon rushed to a close, he came down about the same time the sunlight did. The fixed lines didn't quite reach bottom, however. Brad and Alex's rappel took each of them to the end of the rope still about fifty feet above the ground to a polished ramp of varnished sandstone. It couldn't have been any harder than 5.6, and only in a few small sections, according to Alex. Stuff those characters don't even blink for. But with the frigid temps, faded daylight, and lack of focus combined, Brad took one wrong scootch that sent him ball-to-floor like it was a goddammed slip 'n slide. Alex, who was already at ground level, barely had enough time to register that unwitting, "oh-shit" sound of Brad's. By the time he'd looked up to survey conditions, Brad was making impact.

According to Alex, Brad knew he'd broken bones immediately. For God's sake, he'd already done it three times in the same decade. Surprising, though, was how cool he was about it. There were no tears or abject shouts of despair; Brad did not fall into self-pity or a fit of anger as he had in the past. Sober as a judge, he just looked over to Alex, thought about those emergency medical bills he still had stacked up at home from his Viceroy escapade, and said something along the lines of, "I hope we can scramble out of here without having to call for an actual rescue."

Alex, whose more human attributes are often outshined by his unfathomable rockcraft, is a champion friend to have when your back is against a wall. For the next four hours, he guided and carried Brad to safety. Without a headlamp, losing course is almost a guarantee when navigating the braided trails to and from that canyon. Cautiously, with only his and Brad's phones to provide light, Alex would charge down the trail a hundred feet at a time with both of their packs shouldered. After dumping the packs, he'd run back, piggy-back Brad, who bear-hugged him around the shoulders, one quad-bursting step after the other until they reconvened with said climbing packs. Rinse and repeat for the next two miles.

A few hours later, friend, local route developer, and America's top sport-climbing magician, Jonathan Siegrist, arrived on scene with his girlfriend. With snacks, sweaters, and headlamps in hand, they were a sight for sore eyes and sore legs. Jonathan's girlfriend offered to carry the climbing packs while the boys rotated on hauling duties carrying Brad, who, by this point, was more pumped in his forearms from having bear-hugged on their backs for hours than he'd ever been while up To-tock-ah-noo-lah. In the dark of a below-freezing desert night, hours later, all parties were exhausted.

Figuring he could manage well enough, Brad took a test drive in the parking lot, driving on one foot, and declared he'd be fine to sleep it off.

"Yeah," Brad lifted his brow while thinking it over in idle, "I mean, it's probably not a big deal to wait for morning."

Confounded, Alex, Jonathan, and his girlfriend shrugged their shoulders with hands in the air. What could you do or say to make him go to a hospital right then? Probably nothing. The gang parted ways, and the next morning, Brad checked himself into the local ward for medical imaging. He'd broken his foot and ankle all over again. A break in the chain of his bone structure and climbing structure that would prove harder, and longer, to come back from than his injury just one year earlier.

By May, it had been three months off the wall and, aside from unhuman level crimping strength due to his time on the hangboards, pretty much the only thing Brad was excited for was the emergence of a new film tour. *Safety Third,* that indelible film that made Brad truly famous to the masses—at least in the outside-sports communities—had arrived at long last.

Kicking off the tour at the Telluride Mountain Film Festival, Brad teamed back up with Cedar Wright and Taylor Keating to run the gamut of venues and amphitheaters where the film premiered. With almost immediate praise for the quality and quirkiness of the work, the Reel Rock Film Tour—the biggest name in climbing film production—hitched on the wagon and bought rights to show it in their upcoming twelfth iteration. Things were moving quite quickly. Almost overnight, Brad Gobright was, for all hyperbole, equivalent to a household name. Not a bad distraction to have while on the mend.

But Brad stayed humble; pure, as it were; always himself. While his name was catching fire in media, he kept his profile small, actually moving home from Las Vegas by summer in order to work with kid's day camps at the local climbing gym.

Spending time with his parents, occasionally even his sister when visiting in from Napa—where she had become a winemaker—and generally making amends with his childhood loathing for Orange County, Brad recovered more than ankle health that summer. He recovered his sense of place. And the community, from the locals at the rock gym he'd grown up at, to the new ones popping up regionally, all loved him.

Brad did not struggle for well-wishers, and, while he never cared too much about his place in public opinion, you could tell it did a lot for him. If anything, what he appreciated in his new status was simply the respect that came with it. For too many years, whether by the dismissiveness or the condescension of others, Brad felt like his was a voice unheard.

As went the romantic life, however, things had not been perfect.

From the accounts of various friends, as early as January of 2016, certain imbalances had been stirring between him and his partner. Though they had strengthened for periods of time—such as after Brad's back break, and on their road trip to Squamish— some difficulties were not overcome. Life will have its say with us, which means that parallel paths will, at times, begin to diverge. For a while, there had been a bit of on-again, off-again uncertainty in the relationship. At least that's how it has been told in the eyes of their peers. But in 2017, after they moved home to Southern California after spending the winter in Vegas, those divergent paths would further branch apart. By the time fall and the Facelift came about in Ahwahne, they were no longer together. Which is not to say Brad was alone.

We'd spent time together that summer, and, more than the incredible display of patience he marshaled, considering his foot took twice as long to heal as the previous injury, what I saw of Brad was an assuredness in his own skin that had been years in the making. Plugged in to a life he had always envisioned, climbing-wise, and back home for the summer and enjoying it, he lacked for little.

In addition to the joy of his day job, working with kids at the climbing gym, and the adulation of the locals, even things at home had been going swimmingly. Brad and his father, Jim, often two sheets of sandpaper running in opposing directions, found themselves closing in on harmony. Brad helped with summer home improvement projects in the yard, and, for utter shits-and-giggles, they spent the afternoons shooting air canister bullets at pesky birds who would defecate on the cars in the driveway. Life with his mom, Pamela, of course, never had much of a hitch. She'd always been his biggest advocate since pre-school. She still was. As he was of her.

At the end of August, with his growing reach on social media, Brad posted not of his exploits, but those of his parents. In a simple but heartfelt message, he bragged online about the fact that his nearly senior-citizen parents had just completed a jaunt up Tumanguya (Mount Whitney) in preparation for their hike across the Nüümü Poyo (John Muir Trail) in the weeks to come. But most of all, he bragged about how pleasant it was living with them while his ankle healed. A revolution from the 2012 experience.

Since the spring of 2016, when not injured, Brad and Jim Reynolds were whittling down time on The Nose. What began as an exploration in speed, as a quest for "feeling perfectly in flow" over humongous portions of granite, became something much bigger. While Brad and Reynalds both had reasons, they also had goals. It is only natural, when going from six, to five, to four, down to even three hours, to use a standard of measurement. For the boys, that standard was the speed record. Were they always trying to break it? No. Were they in the fall of 2017? Absolutely.

While a trademark function of Brad's character was his disregard for competition, ego, bullshit pursuits, and bragging rights, he was not Christ, or Buddha, or any other holiness. He was a guy who followed his heart. That's where the purity was, in relationship to how it aligned himself to his core, not in relationship to how we of the general public felt about it. Besides, it's a speed record, not a moral litmus.

In retrospect, it is never acceptable not to come home from the mountains. We all know that. Brad would have submitted to that as much as anyone else. But, for who he and Jim were at the time, it was a pursuit. As mentioned earlier, speed climbing at the pace of record setting is, for all intents and purposes, of the blasphemous ilk. Risks run beyond any true sense of control, even if there is a counter-argument that one is never in control anyway, not even in our lives in the lowlands. Ask the family members and loved ones of those lost in the game, though, and you'll think more than once before taking your rack to feathers before short-fixing, and especially before simul-climbing. But, at the end of the day, it is the choice of those who do it, even if the consequences, which are often forced upon others, are not.

Somewhere in that rush, in that frenetic, revelatory sequence where Jim and Brad went from six hours down to three, they went for the whole show. They went all in. Admittedly, for Jim, it became about more than just feeling something like perfection, or freedom to move, or any other idyllic, fleeting whim. They knew the risks, and, more than being the buckshot, gung-ho pirates they've been painted as in *The Nose Speed Record* film, they took their time to weigh them all. They did not go into the final stages of the record blindly, nor without their own calculus.

For Brad and Jim, the story of The Nose speed record comes down to two separate but equally virtuous pursuits. First, both were at a stage in life where they fancied the notion of partnership, of doing something together, with others, that one could not do alone. Jim was recently out of a long-term relationship and Brad the same, so that aim seemed more likely on a rope than in the court of romance. They were interested in taking a journey of the impossible with another person and committing to the entire process, not just for their individual successes, but for that of their partner, too. Fair enough. Goal number one celebrates a collaborative approach to life.

Second, an explicitly more punk rock, rebellious tilt. They wanted that record because they saw it as unfinished business. The Nose speed record, especially for Jim, should rest in the hands of those who call Ahwahne home. It belongs to the dirtbags—the monkeys, the pirates, the tribe. However pleasant they were as friends, even heroic characters like Hans Florine and Alex Honnold (the record holders at the time) were not traditional Valley dirtbags. They had mortgages and cars and vans and at least six figures in their respective bank accounts, and, compared to the heroes of yore—say, Dean Potter, Timmy O'Neil, and Sean Leary—Hans and Alex were just a bit too polished. Mind you, these are the types of differentials that matter for nothing in the large plot of life. But for Jim, Brad, and for the sake of chasing records, they played.

So, with one eye on a quest for partnership and the other on winning back for the proletariat what was long ago lost, Brad and Jim had the causes they needed. Causes that—when separated from the absurdity of the whole competition at large—were and still are worth celebrating. Even if the game was not. That was the narrative as they saw it. And while many of us can agree that there is nothing gained from glorifying deathly pursuits if they feed the ego alone, let us also agree that there is no better person to root for in such narratives than the outcast and the underdog. To enable the lesser among us is the way of Hollywood as much as it is the way of Christ's Sermon on the Mount. For theirs is the kingdom, after all.

And so, on October 21, 2017 at 6:30 a.m., with a lime green shirt and the least amount of gear possible, Brad started up the familiar first pitches of The Nose. The lower half of the route, up to the King Swing at the top of the Boot Flake some 1,500 feet above, was Brad's block to lead. For the delicate, tricky nature of the first four pitches, up to Sickle Ledge, Brad and Jim always short-fixed rather than simul-climbed.

Short fixing, arguably the safer of the two methods, risks only the leader's well-being. Once at an anchor, the lead climber will "fix," or secure, the rope tight for the second climber to jumar the pitch (mechanically ascending the rope with tools). In this case, the second climber has eliminated any risk of falling. The leader, apt to get moving while the follower is ascending the pitch below, then climbs ahead without a traditional belay. Should the leader fall, the full remaining length of the rope, which is not fixed to the follower's line, determines the size of any potential fall. Anywhere between 50—100 feet of extra slack is often commonplace. Which means the leader always employs a strict "do not fall" approach.

If in a pickle, a lead climber can plug in a piece of gear and attach their harness or slings to it, effectively taking a safe break provided they have the time to do so. One must first, and always, operate on the notion that you are at least a few moves away from threshold, or falling. If you've got a burn in your arms so bad you cannot place the piece of gear in the first place, it'll do you no good to try. Ultimately, the leader is protected by their abilities and by their knowledge of themselves in relation to the route and the moves above them. Assuming the second climber had arrived at the anchor by this point, the traditional belay system will be restored, and the leader will fall only as far as their last piece of protection. This system cycles and recycles, one pitch at a time.

Simul-climbing, in effect, does not have a cycle. Both parties are always moving. The leader will continue so long as they can, given the pieces of protection they have, and the follower will always be moving beneath them, climbing rather than jumaring. Both are only protected by the pieces the leader has placed in the wall between them. Because of this, the standard rule is there must always be at least two pieces of gear between them, in case of a fall or in case one of the two pieces fails during a fall. It's baseline climbing redundancy.

In simul-climbing, you do go faster, but fall potentials are almost always in that fifty-plus-foot range, often, even further. And here, it is the second climber's responsibility to never fall, too. If a lead climber falls, it can be hazardous, but for the most part, it will only have the effect of yanking the second climber upwards to balance the weight in the system. If the second climber falls, especially without advanced notice, the lead climber is invariably ripped off the wall as a result. Falls of this nature can be disastrous and are avoided at all costs. There are a few methods to protect against worse case scenarios, such as using a mini-traction device or building temporary belay stations at crux segments—essentially switching systems momentarily— but over 3,000 feet, even in comfortable terrain, things can go wrong. Risk is as much in the time of total exposure as it is in a single hard move.

With all that posited, Brad and Jim always short-fixed the first four pitches to Sickle Ledge. After, once in the famous Stoveleg Cracks leading all the way to the Texas and Boot Flake above, simul-climbing was the name of the game. In fact, apart from a few crux segments, such as the Great Roof, the Glowering Spot, and The Changing Corners pitch, the boys would simul-climb all the way to the top. From Sickle Ledge, that's roughly 2,500 feet of continuous climbing in a style that, short of free-soloing, is regarded as the most hazardous.

Brad and Jim knew of these risks. They'd chosen all of this, and, to the best of their ability, had calculated every inch. For us then, from the pedestrian viewpoint, it should be noted that while speed-climbing at this clip is patently hazardous, beyond reason, it is also excellence in motion. Their operations up there are right in line, rank and file, with launching humans into space or pulling g-forces into submission on a Formula One racetrack. With such risk, with so much at stake, to operate with such high focus, function, and execution is the very definition of high performance. It may be a fool's game, but no doubt about it, when done right, it is another branch of human excellence. There are few, if any, more dynamic or artistic expressions of human potential in relation to the natural world.

Thirty-six minutes after leaving the Ahwahne floor, Brad barreled over the second landmark on route, Dolt Tower, 1,000 feet off the ground. Drenched in sweat from climbing more in a half hour than most parties climb in a day, he came face to face with Remy Franklin and Michael Swartz, two climbers who had camped on Dolt Tower the night before. As memorialized in The *Nose Speed Record* film, the boys asked Brad if he needed any coffee, orange juice, or water. Brad deferred. Only a split second later, though, realizing he'd forgotten his own water, Brad changed course and asked for a drink. Short on breath, Brad tried to chug a slurp from a gallon but immediately burst into a cough. Too rushed to give it another go, Brad handed Mike the bottle, somewhat self-consciously, and scurried to his right to enter the next panel of rock, saying only, "God, I hate the Stovelegs."

Noting the difference in style, Mike replied from the layman's point of view, "Well, they are pretty fun if you clip gear."

Brad sped along and out of frame as Remy laughed a moment

later and said, "Mike, I think they climbed three pitches in the time it took us to drink half our coffee."

Jim arrived just moments later, soaked head-to-toe in his beet-red shirt. Just forty minutes since beginning, they'd already climbed one-third of the route and passed half a dozen parties in the process.

One hour and three minutes after the start, Brad arrived at the top of the Boot Flake. Absolutely knackered, nearly seizing, he fixed the line and caught his breath while Jim ascended the rope. Two minutes later, Jim was raging in the horizontal pendulum known as the King Swing. Traversing fifty feet from a blank section of wall to a nearby crack system in something more akin to an astronaut's spacewalk than a rock dance, he lunged and caught the holds leading to an outcrop called Eagle Ledge. Jim darted up the pitch, essentially matching Brad at equal height on the wall, just fifty feet to the left of him. Climbing another thirty feet higher, Jim arrived at his first anchor, short-fixed the line, and continued into the dodgy Grey Bands while Brad took the pendulum ride toward Eagle Ledge for himself.

From here, the leads and much of the pressure were all Jim's. Decently square on time, from this point forward there could be no logistical fuck-ups. To make history, there could be no ropes getting stuck, no snafus, and Jim would need to blast, just full-on rocket-ship-pace his way up that behemoth. We're talking about exposure and dihedral systems up an ocean of granite that make the regular among us quiver. He was vertical pioneering like a bat out of hell in spaces so hallowed and high from the earth that on more occasions than not, for most climbers, this realm onsets a humbling, reptilian vertigo. It can make you doubt your senses, it can make you question up and down and even your perception of belonging to the horizontal ground you once called home. Jim, at full tilt and abandon, put all that was blue-collar within him to the task.

As the boys neared failure, support came from the Valley floor. Down there, in the meadows at the base and beside the snaking Merced River, a handful of Valley locals and cheerleaders had gathered to spur the boys on. Shouts and monkey calls, the ubiquitous climbers' hoots for generations running, bounced off the high corners of The Nose's upper pitches as Jim led into the final 600 feet at pure exhaustion. Aghast at each anchor he arrived at, Jim's spirit did for his ascent what his physical body alone could not. He was dying to rest, but somehow, he pressed onward. Upward.

In fact, in Brad and Jim's system up The Nose, it was Brad who managed more rest. During the exchange at the King Swing, where Jim had taken over the lead, Brad had five minutes of downtime while Jim took charge. Three pitches later, at the base of the Great Roof, the most technically demanding and time-consuming lead on the wall, Brad rested for almost ten minutes at a belay anchor while Jim wrestled with the lead. It just isn't the kind of terrain you simul-climb. In fact, since they began simul-climbing down at Sickle Ledge some 2,000 feet below, Jim had not stopped. Only at that tree, the old pine stuck to the summit, would he find rest and, he hoped, a new record.

Jim and Brad climbed almost within inches of one another up the final headwall. The final bolt ladder that took first-ascensionist Warren Harding an entire night to drill by hand, while hanging out the business end of a chafing swami-belt, took the boys just minutes. Pulling hero moves, one hand over the other, across six-foot gaps between bolt hangers, Jim and Brad ditched all formality of clipping protection between them in the final push. Two-thousand and nine-hundred feet of life-swallowing air beneath them, and one-hundred feet above them, the elemental sludge of their own mitochondria nearly jumped across the cell borders and climbed the rocks for them. Exhaustion did not matter.

Fifty feet, thirty feet, fifteen feet, the final ramp. One final push, through the gauntlet of hellfire and lactic acid in their legs, in full sprint, Brad and Jim took the record from 2:23:46 down to 2:19:44. Together, they'd achieved the impossible.

Brad learned viscerally something he'd always known but had only a few times applied in his climbing life: that partnership, and friendship, could itself endow as much or more meaning than the acts of climbing alone. For a guy who had done so much solo, it changed his perception. Something that he had already learned from his partnership with his now-previous girlfriend, he learned again. That as humans, our best is togetherness.

Part one: check.

For the underdogs and outcasts among us, consider this. It was no secret that Hans Florine and Dean Potter—the representative of the local monkeys—did not suffer love lost. Competition drove Dean especially into places he preferred not to go. Once, famously, Potter had analogized Florine as little more than an overexcited, competitive dog humping his leg, slave to a burning desire to be the alpha among them. Each time Potter set a record, Florine came bouncing back, always doing so in a way that offended more than it inspired. Hence, from Potter's viewpoint, the humping dog.

Their analogy, not mine.

For years their rivalry carried on, horns locked. A seemingly absurd untenability between two of the best climbers—clashing egos on a stone that was made to transcend the pettiness of human contrivance in the first place—persisted until Dean's tragic death in 2015.

But in that contrivance, Hans had the record. And for the boys, for Brad and Jim, it was high time the tables turned. Winning back the title for the home team drove them faster.

So there, at the top of To-tock-ah-noo-lah, two hours, nineteen minutes, and forty-four seconds later, as the owners of the most coveted record in adventure climbing, Brad and Jim reveled. Even though Alex would take the record back—this time with El Cap aficionado and legend Tommy Caldwell—only eight months later, Brad and Jim's moment of glory up there could never be taken. It glowed, both for partnership and for justice served.

Hans Florine, if only a fictitious enemy of the proletariat, would never hold The Nose speed record again. As accounts and inside jokes go, it was Hans who was getting humped, and Jim Reynolds and Brad Gobright, the monkeys, would be the last little dogs to do the humping after all. In the eyes of some folks, that was history done right by Dean. It was due comeuppance. For the locals, for the Camp 4 monkeys, for the kids sleeping in dingy cars rather than Sprinter Vans, and for those slumming it in boulder fields, if only for those fleeting eight months, the record was home.

Part two: check.

On October 21, 2017, the dirtbags reigned supreme.

Alex was one of the first to call Brad after he and Jim set the new record on The Nose. Excited, congratulatory, the tenor of his and Brad's relationship was of another key entirely. They were friends far more than rivals. But even friends gotta zing a little. Three days after Brad and Jim set The Nose record, Alex texted Brad. Epinephrine, the 2,000-foot grovel-fest up the Black Velvet Wall that Alex once called "too blue-collar to put a speed run on," had a new record holder. Brad's timestamp at fifty minutes had been chopped to forty-five. All things considered, Brad laughed at Alex's impulse, congratulated him on his record, and called it a fair trade.

"Let me have The Nose for one season!" Brad said, "I'm done trying to climb fast for a while."

But that didn't stop Brad from an immaculate ascent up Father Time, that new, old-school classic that maestro Mikey Schaefer had established a few seasons earlier. Two-thousand feet of stout, sustained, adventurous, and delicate climbing stacked hand over fist, Father Time was a free-climbing statement unto itself. Brad had, after all, only gotten back to the pursuit of hard free-climbing—an entirely separate discipline to speed climbing—just a few months prior. That ankle, and his fitness in that medium, were only just rounding the bend.

As if that wasn't enough, a month later, back in Las Vegas after the most successful Ahwahne season of his life, Brad pushed out another stellar performance. With less than a week of projecting the route, he climbed Dreefee, the same route he had top-roped a few pitches of during that fateful, ankle-breaking day with Alex in February. Sustained climbing, small gear, hard as fuck on the fingers with 5.13 (+) crux moves, if Father Time didn't announce that Brad Gobright was back to his best, Dreefee surely did. The young man was on fire.

It wasn't fire alone, though—Brad was tapped into a providence too. Days before leaving the Valley, he contemplated climbing Tis-se-ack rope solo rather than free-solo. He'd done it once before, although that was before the monstrous rockfall off its Northwest Face back in 2015. With every ounce of his body primed for what realistically would've been another record of some kind, something inside him shifted gears. A voice, surely something he'd even hesitate to label for his humble, inner composition, kept him off the way that day. Whatever it was, Brad listened to it. He followed it, too, wherever it took him. In this case, that wasn't to another big-climb as a substitute, either.

Brad bailed on Tis-se-ack, not to climb, but to spend his final day in Ahwahne for that season simply walking the meadow. Hand grazing across tall shoots of wild grass, wind ruffling his greasy black hair, no care in the world, and a deep satisfaction to be in stride with a new, inner tuning, Brad spent his last day of the season in stillness rather than action. Goddammit, if that ain't revelation, I just don't know what is.

The two best years of Brad's life, explicitly, were 2016 and 2017. That's what he said to me, and he said it on social media. In both years, what began as winters defined by darkness, pain, and the unplanned wound into an immaculate web of something far greater. In two years, he'd broken his ankle twice, taken emergency rides in ambulances, and moved from one state to another. Painfully, he'd even had to learn how to move beyond his first true love. He had to learn that part of love is, at times, letting go. There were hundreds of reasons why he could've not only been set back by life, but remained stuck. But he didn't.

Brad Gobright had something magical, and not just on the wall. He had a magical way of being. It wasn't steeped in the intellectual life. In fact, it wasn't about intelligence at all. It was not about learning more content or concepts, though he was proving he could do that, too. It was about attenuation; of diminishing the noise of life to hear only what mattered. The paradox was that expansion came only by first subtracting the unnecessary out of life—something Brad was an unheralded master of. He followed a deep, nuanced, individual tuning, and as result people started paying attention regardless of how ramshackle, clumsy, or even foolish certain elements looked on the surface. People across every spectrum began to realize that Brad's was a most special ray of light. Again, not just for what or how he climbed.

To get back all that was lost, not just in his back break or ankle breaks, but in that mistaken childhood, too. To grow out of his narrative that he was unlovable, uncool, unwise, or unable. To have gone from misfit to esteemed. To have grabbed all that and more in his uncanny rise to the top of our collective awareness. Forget about recovery, that's the precipice of artistry.

HOME

Gilbert Keith Chesterton, a giddy old writer known as much for his whimsical nature as for his strict philosophical study, who was born in Kensington, London, and had been heralded as the Prince of Paradox, once talked about a great story he'd imagined that, unfortunately, never got told. In the introduction to a separate book, he spoke about his imaginary subject as representing all things truly human. As a being cursed with an ignorance of, but insatiable hunger for, the living truth. The man, as it were, was a bit foolhardy but aware, and, being desperate for adventure and his path in life, left his homeland in search of new and exotic worlds. Through great, almost Odyssean perils and wayward scripts, this protagonist endured the seas and at last, one day, sailed himself around the globe to a newfound land.

Mystified with eyes anew, he explored each parcel and plot of this new world, enamored. Colors and shapes and beasts he'd never seen before filled the earth, the sea, the skies. Each day, he woke only with excitement to discover further. Life was at last what he craved, at once full of rapture and at the same time familiar welcome. Almost as if he'd known of it his entire life. Only after turning a cape on the island in his journey one fateful day did our unwitting hero see the truth. There before his eyes was his hometown, the ports he had always known, the village, the people, the smell of fresh rain over cobbled streets. He'd sailed the entire earth, passing lands more exotic than the Spice Islands, but to his surprise, the place he'd been looking for, the place he settled, had been home all along.

Such is the arc of all men's lives, he proposed. Today we see it as the journey not just of men, but all among us, in gender, race, credo, or color. It is a quest of the human condition to find for ourselves home. That, of course, is mostly spiritual symbolism, code for why we go to the wild and high spaces, and clue to the reason our hearts feel at once raptured, but also safe, in the light of a thousand sunsets. For there, behind that eternal beam, in the fabric of the rainbow itself, at the tip of revelation, is a portal to both our origins and our destination.

Every now and then, however, that arc is a bit more literal.

In April of 2018, after a winter in Las Vegas living with friends, enjoying a good run of health, sponsorship, and the perks of industry-wide applaud, Brad Gobright went back to the ancient Ute, Hopi, Uintah, Pueblo, Zuni, Ouray, and Dine deserts of Southern Utah. Back to Bear's Ears National Monument. This time, his quest was more personal. It would be, for him, among his most connected and rewarding trips to have taken.

Brad always had an agenda—goals, if you will. A laundry list of climbs to do, grades to achieve, with reasons for why he lined them in the exact orders of priority he did. But after a winter contemplating the larger plots of life, he was climbing for a different connection. The tail end of 2017 had taken mightily from the climbing community, and Brad, as much as others, felt the wake of those losses.

One of the stalwarts of the Valley tribe—and one of its most accomplished athletes—an inspirational figure and wild spirit if ever there was one, had nearly died and ultimately ended up paralyzed on The Nose of To-tock-ah-noo-lah, just weeks before Brad and Jim had set the speed record. Jim had even been on call for the rescue mission and had shared the dire details of the situation with Brad in moments of his own despair. Face to face with real-life consequences, it was impossible to digest. Then another friend of theirs, one of the community's brightest, and also a former member of the search and rescue team, had perished in a rappelling accident that November. A devastating blow that would pulse through the entire community and, of course, their own family. On the loss of such a dear friend, a fellow of theirs recalled, "...they were just one of the best, period. The kind that shines for everyone. Literally, one of the nicest you could possibly meet. The kind that makes you look at the Universe, and honestly just ask, why? Like, don't you know how much we all needed that light?"

And then, overwhelmingly, there was Hayden. Brad's old friend from Colorado who he used to hang Christmas lights with, and with whom he had climbed Crystal Dawn in Red Rock, had died just that October in a most wretched wheel of Shakespearean tragedy. Of course, it wasn't just what they had climbed or done together that connected them—they were quite rightly kindred spirits—just as it wasn't only Brad who was driven into a mind-numbing, soul-crushing shock by his loss. Hayden was beloved the climbing world over, and not solely because he was among the most elite, high-achieving, and most graceful to ever take to the craft. It was, like Brad, for his heart that Hayden was adored. His eye and his attention were rapturous, his care disarming. In all possible ways he was plugged into life, integrated to people, to cultures, to family especially—which meant, unfathomably, that in all possible realms, his loss, and the loss of his partner who perished shortly before him, were felt even beneath the bones. The grief that passed to those who knew Hayden, and each of these bright fellows, still, very appropriately, resounds to this day.

With that ethos, with that excruciating season of life at the helm, like a weather system that just won't lift, Brad came to the desert without the unfettered joy of years past. Instead, conscious as he could be, he came with a contemplative mind. Brad's priority in the desert was to find his old friend Hayden, and there was no better place to start than the routes that Hayden had, himself, first established.

In the desert, Brad always thrived, probably because it was so much a part of how he was forged. Seemingly plugged in on all levels, Brad climbed for three weeks at a version of his best. He even found success on Hayden's most famous line in the area, the Carbondale Short Bus, named after the tiny van Hayden used to travel and sleep in. At the threshold of 5.13 (+)/5.14 (-), it also was among Brad's hardest routes climbed. But, when I asked him about it, the grade meant the least relative to the experience he'd been provided.

Carbondale Short Bus is dangerous. Its opening section, up into the back-breaking zone, is only protectable by employing the smallest camming devices on the market—devices, which, in theory, are only supposed to carry an average person's body weight, and little more. Because of that, Brad happily pre-placed an opening piece of gear in the rock above him—a style that not only allowed him to climb the route safer, but to enjoy it more. And, more than another tick on his list, that sense of enjoyment was what he had begun to crave. Making the climb safer also allowed Brad to pare down that signal-to-noise ratio just enough while on lead to think of his friend Hayden at the bottom of each breath. A connection he felt present, both on Carbondale Short Bus and the immaculate, almost impossible, Kokanee Corner, a wild multi-pitch voyage up the King of Paine Tower within the Bridger Jack pillars.

Over those three weeks, Brad climbed many of Hayden's routes. Finding only limited success on his quest for hard redpoints, he found deeper success in keeping Hayden's spirit close—the original goal, after all. Besides, Brad knew the trade secrets already: falling made him a better person. Rejuvenated, Brad's time in the desert propelled him back to Ahwahne.

Arriving at the end of April, it took Brad less than two weeks to see one of his long-standing goals come to fruition. While he'd been able to climb the Salathe Wall by a mix of aid- and free-climbing, as far back as 2010, he hadn't been able to free climb it completely. Always just beyond his clutch were those infamous, golden headwall pitches.

On May 3, 2018, Brad free-climbed the Salathe, bottom to top. Headwall glory included. Not only that, but he did it in his trademark style, in a push, over the course of just thirteen hours in a single day. His partner this time around was his good friend Jordan Cannon, with whom he had climbed for years on formations such as The Incredible Hulk in the High Sierra. A dream of a lifetime, Brad reveled for days on that one.

A week later, Brad returned, rappelling in from the top with photographer and friend, Samuel Crossley, for a photoshoot on the headwall pitches near twilight. Having not had any documentation on his blitzing ascent the week prior, it was one of those content missions, the kind of formalities new to Brad as a professional climber. The operation went as planned, a perfect moment up in the high reaches of the Big Stone, where Brad executed more of his craft in front of the camera—but the operation also threw a curveball.

Up on the Salathe for that photoshoot, Brad needed a belayer. His friend, Valley search and rescue resident and altogether generous fellow, Christian Cattell, obliged. Just for kicks, though,

Christian also brought his girlfriend along—because who doesn't like a good excuse to gain perspective from the top of the world's most magnificent rockface? Rappelling in on the fixed lines, with all the exposure it provided, would be a good experience for her, too, he thought. Christian was the inclusive type, after all. So, not including Samuel, who was on his own line taking photos, it became a three-person detail.

After the photos were shot, in a rush to get off the wall, Brad pressed Christian's girlfriend to hurry up the fixed lines before darkness set in. She, being less experienced than Brad at jumaring fixed lines, especially at that kind of vertical exposure, was determined to back up her position by clipping an extra point of protection to her and the rope. Personal safety, after all, is each person's to decide for themselves. But Brad, being hungry or impatient or both, insisted she was being overly cautious, that she should skip the extra rigging and get on with it. Just ascending on the jumars, with no back-up, was plenty fine by Brad's standard.

Brad's point of view, and his means of sharing that point of view, were not taken well by either Christian or his girlfriend. And for that reason, there came a falling out. Unwound by the conflict, Brad jumared up the lines ahead of them in frustration. He wanted off, and he wanted off so bad that by the time Christian and crew made it up to the summit, Brad was already down the east ledges' descent and having dinner at the Curry pizza deck.

The old Brad probably wouldn't have lost sleep on it. But things didn't settle for him. A few days later, with a gentle heart and desire for amends, he called Christian and his girlfriend to apologize. Brad expressed his faults with candor and then insisted they join him for a very rare climber's splendor: a brunch at the Ahwahnee Hotel's weekend buffet. His treat. For a guy who used to steal hotcakes off tourists' plates, going all out and spending coin to show good faith and restore a friendship was quite a gesture. And while it might seem only fitting, perhaps even unremarkable to some as something he should have done, for Brad, it meant a lot. Admitting he was wrong wasn't the hard part. He had no problems acknowledging ego gone awry. It was the stewardship aspect, the care with which he held up the friendship. The maturity of his approach was what stood out. It was further evidence that his focus was on a new wholeness of life.

Spring of 2018 came with more than ascents alone—it came with a new relationship. Brad's ability to connect well with others through his easy, insouciant yolk had strengthened and broadened. And his confidence, the overall freedom with which he walked, did more than get him up monstrous rock faces; it made him attractive.

In May, Brad ran countless laps up the Royal Arches during his 'rest days,' something of a tradition that he'd held for years. In the spirit of the 'resting' component of his recovery day, he'd usually drive his car the short, walkable distance from Camp 4 to the hotel parking lot where he'd weave into the valet zone to self-park, and then, against the local edict, leave his car. The entitled parking trick he employed, in the eyes of the valet staff, was a bit of a dick move. One such staff member, Kat, a studious out-of-towner on a break from her strict career path, found herself flummoxed, but also intrigued. It didn't seem to matter how many times she had to police him; Brad adamantly broke rank.

Over time, though, she saw him as cute, even appealing in his uncaring, rule-bending bravado. And Brad, of course, found her easy on more than the eyes alone. She had a sweetness of spirit which caught his attention even more than her faraway, non-dirtbagging look. Due to this shared attraction, the impasse between his position as a climber and hers as some form of authority quickly melted. Soon, wheels were turning.

Not only did Brad park his car at the Ahwahnee Hotel for

climbing, he often stayed for tea, too. The standard daily custom at the institution was to provide guests with free tea and cookies during the Ahwahnee version of cocktail hour; a ritual Brad had long ago acculturated for his own benefit. That season, however, to partake of the Earl Grey and biscuits, each guest had to show their room key first. A key that, of course, Brad did not have. In a pickle, Brad was forced to make conversation with Kat at last.

Not believing his gall, or his naivety, Kat nearly laughed in his face when he first asked. But with Brad's diligence and his blue eyes employed, she soon cracked. She had some sympathy for his plight, and while she had no idea he was a famous climber, she didn't mind his attention. As she put it, they had about twenty copies of each key for every room anyway. So, after a bit of cat and mouse, bound by a cute favor and many a romantic, passing glance, Brad and Kat let their guards down. After a first date at the Alcove Swing, at the base of To-tock-ah-noo-lah, and a few romantic evenings beside communal campfires, Brad and Kat were an item for the next year running. Love had come again.

On June 1, 2018, Brad came within fifteen feet of free-climbing another long-held dream, the El Corazon route on To-tock-ah-noo-lah. No surprise, he was gunning for the ascent in a single day. Established in 2001 by Brad's hero, the German superstar Alexander Huber and his partner Max Reichel over the course of six days, Brad had been inspired toward El Corazon for a long time running. Since seeing a single photo of Tommy Caldwell free-climbing the heinous, forty-foot roof pitch—feet splayed up and above him on the wall behind his head—Brad always coveted the route. It wasn't just the climb; for Brad, often, it was all about position. To be in that exact place, and to operate well, seemingly in a pocket of Earth that mankind has no business attending, that was the sweet spot.

Brad always burned for positions like that. He wanted to know rarified air. Even though he didn't make the successful redpoint on it that day, he did get into that roof pitch and find that coveted position, and that's what mattered most. His effort alone was gargantuan.

Two weeks later, as tradition would dictate, Brad needed to go large for his birthday. Super-size. With friend and Nose speed-record associate, Jim Reynolds, he enchained the lauded Ahwahne Valley Triple: Waijau (Mt. Watkins), To-tock-ah-noo-lah (El Capitan), and Tis-se-ack (Half Dome) in a day. Logistically and technically, the undertaking is massive. More than 7,000 feet of vertical, incessant terrain. Exactly the absurd kind of behavior that no human being has any business doing. Like the free-soling Hairstyles and Attitudes for Brad, or the upward and downward free-soling of Afanassief on Fitz Roy in Patagonia for Jim. In fact, as the realm of elites goes, to date, only four other parties have linked these three Ahwahne monoliths into successive climbs in under twenty-four hours.

Beginning at 4:30 p.m. on June 15 at Waijau, Brad and Jim simul-climbed copious pitches—football-field-sized panels of vertical granite—in a swooping pulse of outrageous stoke. By sundown, on one of the longest days of the year, they met up with Alex Honnold and his wife, Sanni, for a ride back into the Valley below. In the dark of night, they climbed The Nose, a rote tradition for each of them by this point, by headlamp. But that it was rote does not make it any less spectacular. For how well and how often men of this ilk soar through Earth's unfathomable heights, we quickly lose our awe. Somehow the marvel of it all falls sideways to our sense of the norm. But lest we forget it, life at this caliber is anything but normal. Though it invites all of us to join—though glory and its pursuit is the calling of humankind—

there is nothing normal about climbing God's earth at that scale. It is especially flamboyant to do so by night.

At midnight, as best he could recall, exactly as he turned thirty, Brad was 100-feet runout above his anchor on the Boot Flake. Spot in the middle of To-tock-ah-noo-lah, spot in the middle of the night. For whatever danger and abandon it represented, in that moment, he could've done little more to be truly, fully himself. It's less a matter of what made him happy as it was of simply what made him *him*.

The Triple was among Brad and Jim's best days climbing, period. But, as history would have it, it stood for more than climbing alone. For all its glory, it would also come to define a point of departure for Brad and Jim. As daylight broke and the boys found themselves climbing the final formation, Tis-se-ack, fatigue took a mental toll. In the end, it would take them nearly eighteen and a half hours to finish their objective, which meant, when they started the final climb of the day, that they had time on their side. They could've taken more than eight hours on Tis-se-ack and still made the sub-twenty-four-hour margin. Because of that, and knowing that the worst mistakes often happen by small oversight—the kind of oversight that onsets with sleepless fatigue—Jim expressed a desire for a calculated, mindful passage. Brad, however, played to his own tuning.

In the past, the idea that Brad and Jim had safety margins that could be considered "parallel enough" hadn't presented a problem. But for Jim, risk profiles, or what he concluded as acceptable margins of risk, lay on a spectrum like much else in life. They are not static, but elastic. What Jim was willing to do for The Nose speed record was entirely different based on their practice, their fitness, the route conditions, the season, etc. Hell, what he'd been willing to call safe enough just hours before on Waijau had changed. Jim's approach was as fluid as the situation, which isn't to say that Brad's was completely static. But where for years Brad and Jim seemed aligned enough in risk management to share a rope and many epic tales, Jim at least had found a point of departure. On a few occasions, up on that Northwest Face of Tis-se-ack, Brad had climbed a pitch anchor-to-anchor, full rope length, without having placed any protection at all. Other times he went enormous stretches, and without any redundancy, only placed a single piece. When simul-climbing, that's precisely the thing you don't do. It's just the cardinal rule.

Jim tried his best to express his concerns, but by the time they summitted, near 11:00 in the morning, a blistering eighteen and a half hours after having begun, he was frayed. What should have been an opulent celebration at the top for each of them was instead a muted, dissonant cheer. They were enthused, foundationally thrilled about what they'd done, no doubt. Brad could not have celebrated his life, his birth, any better. But a rift had grown. That, after all, is a part of the life cycle, too. Relationships ebb and flow. It was always in the undertone of Brad's life that with certain highs came other lows. Waves, undulating, as they do in all our lives; waves that Brad was not blind to, but that he surfed all the same.

For all the incredible feats they'd accomplished, Brad and Jim Reynolds would never share a rope again. Not that either of them knew that then. At the time, all Jim knew was that they needed space, time apart to consider their own goals and the methods of attaining those goals. A partnership that had run since the spring of 2016 had reached a conclusion. The question was, was there a friendship that could thrive regardless of the arrangements on a rope? It took time, perhaps, in retrospect, more time than either of them would have liked, to answer that. But the answer was always in the affirmative. Brad and Jim remained close even where their partnership did not.

In July, Brad returned to Orange County for the opportunity to work at the climbing gym with youth summer camps and to touch base with his parents. Unlike years past, when he was desperate for the money, Brad truly reveled in the arrangement. He legitimately loved surrounding himself with the exuberance of youth. He also loved the proximity it put him to home. Hungry to rebuild and maintain his role as a son to his caring parents, Brad was happy to be back. Before moving back to Southern California, though, he and Kat shared a handful of holy moments out in Ahwahne in the latter weeks of June. God as witness, those were their salad days. It was a highlight reel of rose-colored romance. Smitten, butterfly buzzing young love.

Brad and Kat were similar in some character leanings, but in many ways, it was their differences that made them fit so well together. Kat, after all, wasn't a rock climber. She was a naturalist, no doubt, but while she took inspiration among the walls of granite in the Valley, she had no drive to blast up the dizzying heights as Brad had. For her, walks in nature, hikes of more appreciable distance, simpler forays getting lost in the wilderness—aesthetically speaking—these were her outlets. Coming from a handful of years in pursuit of a post-graduate degree, Kat's needs, as goes a balanced life, were less of the adventurous ilk as they were of the therapeutic. Nature was a well in that regard, as it always was for Brad, but for Kat, you didn't need to create a crucible to tap into it. You only needed to seek it.

Watch a falling leaf, let spring water pass through your fingertips uninterrupted, lose yourself in the sweeping dance of wind as it caresses carpets of grass in a meadow. Kat's point of view looked a lot like Brad's from a younger time, like that photo album he shared with me ages ago, back in 2010 after his first full year on the road. Back then he paused a lot. He wandered. He shot nature, and light beams, and contrast from his camera as much as he shot his friends climbing. And, for whatever great heights he'd surmised in his tenure upon the high and lonesome, Brad, like anybody, had lost a little in scope of aperture, for what he gained by singular focus.

Kat was a wonderful counterpoint for so many reasons, her dashing charm and her soft spirit among them. She also had a powerful intellect and a firm, independent identity—something of a commonality in each of Brad's romantic partners. As Pamela put it, "He was always attracted to, and fit best with, brainy women." But most importantly, Kat was a force of grounding, someone who could put him back on soil level for just long enough that he realized that it was not only at the great heights that life was so giving. It was just as kind to the layfolk, to those in the lowlands, as it had been to him up in the skies. He might even collect something of value if he simply stayed there at ground level.

In the time Brad had been up on the stone pushing his limits, Kat had been collecting rocks from quaint beaches, finding watering holes and skipping stones, composing her own map of Ahwahne's secret corridors. By June, she and Brad made a habit to exchange favorite places—a bit of a dating quid pro quo—where Brad would take her to his most inspired outlooks, and Kat would return the favor. Every new spot inspired, but none so much, for Brad, as the day he at last gave himself to the Merced River.

On a perfectly balmy morning during the tourist season, Brad and Kat rented a water vessel on the banks of the Merced River and resolved only to float. He'd spent a decade of his life, between the seasons, in Ahwahne, but he wasn't prepared for that day. A reason he would invariably love it so much. Together, they began high up by the North Pines Campground in the cool morning shade. Gliding, they sat in suspension passing one miraculous bend after another, learning lessons in the relationship of buoyancy, to density. Something Brad always had figured out better than the rest of us anyway. Settled, with no rocks to climb, for Brad, everything looked different, greener and kinder on the eyes than it had ever been before.

Softly, quietly, they soon came to a bend by the Iconic Sentinel Bridge where, to their surprise, they witnessed a bear in its natural glory. Basking, bathing, being exactly as it should. A noteworthy occurrence, considering for years Brad had only seen Valley bears in the campgrounds questing for human leftovers, as some brand of scavengers more than regal creatures. But here, Brad saw in that bear something akin to revelation. The way it looked and sat, just so, beside still riverbanks, perfectly in place. That's perhaps the notion that hit him deepest. A sense of belonging, a sense of home.

By all accounts from Kat, Brad loved that day. Snaking across this ancient, indigenous Valley at a pace he'd never thought to plug into was lifting him. Seeing it from the vantage point of stillness, almost aimlessness, as someone who wants nothing from it, flipped his orientation. By the time they curved the last round near Cathedral Beach near the familiar To-tock-ah-noo-lah Bridge, and Brad laid eyes on the Big Stone, all of it was heart-bursting. Joy he couldn't contain. With the help of Kat, he suddenly saw To-tock-ah-noo-lah all over, all new again. According to her, the goosebumps on his body were so big you could make a topographic map.

Brad looked over to Kat, elated, and thanked her. Later, at any point things didn't shine so bright, or on the odd occasion Kat ever doubted her ability to inspire somebody so categorically inspirational, she remembered Brad's words that day.

"It's so cool you don't climb, because I'm getting to see and know these places I've never been to."

Kat recalled that Brad was a great observer. He may not have always had language to express his internal process, but he was always alert. More aware than perhaps his media persona would have painted in the films he was featured in. That was a point of identity he was conscious of. He knew he came off as the fool in some regard, and, while he didn't care what others thought of him, he did care to be represented fully for his roundedness. What those news feeds didn't show was how Brad was as a friend; that he was a mentor to some, even a guide to others. People didn't see his hidden leadership *en masse*. But it was always there.

As far back as high school, Brad was a captain on the Junior Varsity wrestling team, known not only for his pound-for-pound strength but his inclusivity. When circled for a team huddle before a match, he'd make sure the smallest kids—in weight classes even lower than his—were the ones leading the call and response cheers. He brought everybody in, and mostly, people didn't put that into frame.

Brad was also an excellent boyfriend. Kat recalled he extended himself for her continually, whether when taking care of bills on their Tuesday evening drives to taco night in Foresta or when making sure she slept soundly in his now well-established bivy up in the boulder fields. By that point, many seasons the veteran out there, Brad had, in Kat's words, "fully moved in." At least four sleeping pads, two or three sleeping bags, and many pillows the wiser, he had a proper setup. A king of the castaways in the boulder field is still a kingship, after all.

Brad was also honest, always honest. Kat loved the way he asked about things, and the fact that he was an open book. Over the phone or in person, he'd always give her all the details of his day—even ones she hadn't asked about. He'd never forget to ask her about hers, too. He'd ask when the best times were to call, and he'd ask, above all, what he could do to make her feel the most secure. A particularly cute mannerism, she remembered, was the way he always asked about and paid attention to her feelings. He asked as much with his eyes as with his words, and Kat loved it. Something about him was just so obviously caring, not in the patronizing or Barbie Doll sense, nor in the way that's obsessive, which can often drive others away. Brad's care was of the Old Testament, the cup that overfloweth ilk. The way he couldn't help but cling to walls, for the alignment they gave him to his natural tuning, that's how he was within a relationship, too. He was positively adoring. Brad was a tender heart, and he kept other hearts safe, something few ever saw and only a precious few ever experienced.

He was becoming a much-improved climber, sure, but an even more improved family member, too—a part of his identity that was increasingly important to him. Kat remembers Brad bragging about his sister endlessly. He was so proud of the way she'd come from bottom-up in the wine industry, working for a major brand in Napa Valley of all places, actually making the stuff. Kat, rooted to her heritage, reminded Brad it was all well and good for him to feel that proud of his sister, but it's better to share it. To Jill's delight, he called more often because of that.

At home that summer, Brad spent time with his parents with much less friction than ever before. They asked him about his intentions with Kat, hoping, as parents do, that she might be the one. Not that they wanted anything forced on him. They well knew the impossibility of that by then anyway. Pamela and Jim had witnessed such curves in his character arc over the past few years, they just couldn't help but become excited for what it might mean going forward. Kids, family? These weren't questions of obligation or expectation. They were the greatest sources of joy, light, and blessing that Pamela and Jim had ever known, far more than they were only products of institutions. They simply wanted Brad to feel the same joy.

Brad wasn't in those trajectories yet, and neither was Kat. Largely, Brad still felt that a commitment like marriage was foolish, though he carried no qualms with commitment on a day-to-day basis. Together, on the few occasions that she visited, he and Kat passed the Southern California summertime days drenched in surf, laying on beaches, reconnecting to a region that up until recently, Brad had mistaken for a wasteland. Orange County, past all the talking heads and superficial trappings, was nothing to shake a stick at.

After working the kids' camps at the gym each morning, Brad spent all summer training hard. What began as the forced function of injuries each year had turned into an elective procedure. Brad realized that if he spent a couple of months working out imbalances in his climbing, the indoor sequence of training delivered prodigiously. And it was in these gyms where he and I would meet up. The Los Angeles location of his gym, in particular, was renowned for its sizeable height, making it a great option for proper-steep endurance training. And, as I've written once before, it was in these gyms that I personally was able to see Brad shine.

Life had been busy for me, which meant my outside climbs, even to Ahwahne, had been whittled down to short, sub-twenty-four-hour blitz missions. Long passed were the extended road trips. Because of that, I rarely got to see Brad shine in his truest environment, and only later came to hear of his bursting influence among his peers. I did, however, see notes of it in the gym that summer. In the crowded lead-climbing area, itself the size of a college gymnasium, you could hear a pin drop when Brad climbed. It was incredible to behold. Brad Gobright would put himself on the wall and the whole place fell silent. People, old and young, were all lost in a daze.

At one point, in between sets, a dad and his bashful son, no more than ten years old, came up to Brad to say hello.

Overwhelmed by the moment, when his dad asked him to say a few words, the youngster rolled himself into the closest thing to a fetal curl that he could. With the kid hiding in his dad's lap, Brad broke all the tension and invited the youngster to a handshake. He asked him a handful of gentle questions, smiled with him, and met the kid at his own level before posing for a photo. Welcomed, accepted in all his fragility, the kid smiled bigger than the state of Texas for that photo and then ran off back into his father's arms.

Watching this version of Brad Gobright, so far removed from the places I'd first seen him in life, from those old days getting heckled in the climbing gym, gave me more joy than I knew how to digest. Brad Gobright was the stuff of dreams.

That Brad had become a role model with the under-twelve demographic did not mean he wasn't also an icon for all ages. He was, after all, still hard as nails—a point he proved when he tackled the Minaret Traverse in the Ansel Adams Wilderness of the Sierra Backcountry, as a first order of business, at the tail end of August that summer. For an alpine excursion, essentially off the couch, it was a hell of a litmus. Coming in from sea-level, with no acclimatization, the arduous, all-day demands of a high-country traverse should have at least presented a challenge. Distracted by the beauty of it all, while chasing summits up, down, and around exposed, it wasn't challenge he found as much as that feeling of home. Like a bear at the banks of a river.

A week into his alpine excursions, Brad drove to the Tuolumne area, where he met his friend Christian Cattell on a chance encounter. After having soloed a few days consecutively, through the trade routes on the iconic, tallest domes, Brad was catching sunrays and rest at the Tuolumne Grill, next to the ranger station, when Christian walked past him. Happy to see one another, especially considering they'd buried the hatchet on the difficulties from their episode up on the Salathe earlier in the spring, Christian and Brad quickly devised an impromptu run up the historical landmark, Cathedral Peak.

Never an avid runner, Brad struggled behind Christian, who, with fleetness of foot, set a rabid pace. Together they blasted up the Southeast Face, gobsmacking in delight at the succinct freedom that comes with hand over hand, lucid movement over hundreds of feet of near-vertical, moderate terrain. No ropes between them, they scurried down as quickly as they'd flown up, setting what for them was a proud, if only unofficial, record of two hours and five minutes, car to car. More importantly, they remembered that day for what it reinforced—the friendship between them.

The antics Brad adopted for the past three summers—climbing profuse alpine routes as a primer for the Ahwahne season—were mostly feats that he didn't get attention for. But, attention or not, those herculean days in the big mountains were a forge he would always keep close to his heart. Almost exclusively solo, as Moses and a million seekers in human history before him, Brad went to the high mountains before each big season in his performance climbing to extract a secret nectar. Whatever it was that he got up there, it made him better. Probably not the kind of stuff that lends itself to linguistic articulation anyway.

Brad tapered his approach to hard climbing when he returned to Ahwahne in September. Due to increasingly long summers, the constant barrage of and ever-warming climate, globally, he minded the time. He didn't force it. But a month into the season, on October 26, 2018, Brad squared the account on his project, free-climbing El Corazon, on To-tock-ah-noo-lah, in a single push, in a single day. Once again, the kind of project that takes even the better among us multiple seasons only took Brad a handful of attempts to accomplish.

Largely known for his grand exploits—for those bold solos and nail-biting speed records—the foundations of Brad's craft, in my opinion, were often overlooked. Short of very few others, Brad climbed more pitches in his time than anyone. Thousands upon thousands of pitches per season, upon thousands more per year. In so doing, he built the type of pyramid that breeds success. A reason that things, at least in his later years, up on To-tock-ah-noo-lah went so fantastically. Many were surprised to see Brad up in those spheres of highest performance, because, arguably, his life could still look a bit odd on course. He was still choosing to sleep in boulders when, perhaps, he didn't need to. He still swiped cookies and tea at the Ahwahnee Hotel. As goes the translating of his climbing experience to others, he still had the odd struggle for elements of articulation. But, as I had observed before, none of these ostensibly odd arrangements in life detracted him from the fullness of it.

A certain lack of guile, or cunning, didn't matter to Brad. Up on a wall, in the crux of proper hard movement, you could see he and his body were having the full experience. He moved with subtlety when triggered out of balance as much as he pulled with great strength. When at a rest, he shifted into the most effective position if he wasn't recovering the energy he expected. When on a move that required deep, inner core tension or highly accurate precision, he would execute. That he didn't always decode or run analysis on his operations up there isn't to say he didn't have them.

His technique wasn't perfect. There were, at times, still situations that got the better of his footwork, but he had improved leagues since the old days at the Costa Mesa rock gym, where he was colloquially known as The Butcher. A superlative that, apart from being one of his friend Alex Honnold's favorite egging remarks, he mostly outgrew. Brad, especially with his wide base, was a paramount high performer. Combine that with his iron will, that inner dictum of the heart which compelled him to always try that one extra move, and it's no surprise after all. In some ways, his craft, his guile, was exactly there. He had a way of fooling us into thinking less of him by looking only at a surface-level set of operations. Meanwhile, all along, under the belly, that kid was stoking fires without ceasing.

Much of Brad's experience in building and maintaining that base fitness, at least in the recent years, came by means of his friendship and climbing relationship with Alex Honnold. For quite a few seasons at that point, Brad and Alex had not only gone tit-for-tat on various speed records; they climbed and trained together. In the winters, they often waited out rainy days in the gym, where Alex remembers Brad would hone his mind-bending finger strength.

Alex recalled that there were times when he would be doing a maximum weighted fingerboard hanging exercise and Brad would annihilate him. Where Alex would manage to hang off a twelve-millimeter edge with both hands and fifty-five pounds strapped to his harness for just ten seconds, Brad, who was ten pounds lighter, could hang with ten pounds additional weight for just as long. Not only that, but where Alex would take the prescribed ten-minute break between hangs, Brad would rest only twenty to thirty seconds between his sets, essentially showing a greater strength-to-weight ratio in finger power and a higher endurance at that weight. It showed Brad's copious, raw strength as much as it showed what Alex had always said: that he, himself, was not the strongest climber out there. In climbing, and with Alex, the strong suit is as much in how you put the puzzle pieces together as it is about the innate capacity of any single element. You don't need the greatest individual strength to execute some of the single hardest moves, you just need all the components to work together.

More important than any element of Brad's climbing operations in comparison with Alex's was the simple fact that in their time together, a true friendship had developed. And not only a friendship, but an inspirational partnership.

After the Ahwahne season that fall, Brad moved back to the Las Vegas area, where Alex also lived. Whether at the gym or occasionally just to hang out as friends do, they spent much time together. While day-to-day life blends in memory, Alex recalled one of their best days came at the tail end of winter, now the early stages of 2019.

On February 28, 2019, just four days after Alex and the film team won an Oscar for the Best Documentary of 2018 via the *Free Solo* film, Brad and Alex drove outside the Red Rock Conservational Area to a less-traveled climbing sector named The Gun Club. With only a few dozen notable climbs, it's a small crag. It's short, too. Only getting as tall as forty feet, on average, the limestone cliff is decidedly at a distance from a world-class outcrop. With no King Lines or great prominent feature present at the cliff, it wasn't the "what" of the routes that made it special. That day was memorable for "how" it was climbed, and for "who" the persons were that were climbing it.

After a handful of pitches, moderate by both their measure, climbing up to the 5.12 mark, Alex proposed to Brad, "How would you feel about just ditching the rope to get a bit more volume?"

Brad, understanding they could surmise the entirety of the crag's routes in a single afternoon by that style, quickly grinned. "Sure."

All the conversation necessary for them to uncinch the waistbelts and leave the gear on the floor.

Together, for the next two hours, Brad and Alex climbed nearly every square inch of that wall, only the two of them in attendance while the sun slowly melted behind the saw-cut horizon. Nobody else around, they practiced a shared craft of free-soloing that they'd each begun many years earlier. Quietly, except for small moments back at ground level after having downclimbed a route, they ran train. At times, just a look in the other direction was enough. Other moments, joy was as simple as expressing a small note about the unique balance of a single move or the texture of a single hold, or the freedom to execute a section of wall by two or three different pathways. Brad and Alex free-soloed every route worth a damn that day, without sponsors, cameras, or even selfies. Just the sun and shade and hallowed desert silence— empty, spacious, complete.

Alex recalled, "The Gun Club was such a perfect day because there was nothing performative about it. You know? There's only so many characters in the climbing world, at all, that you can have a day like that with."

Noting that Brad was a rare breed, and friend, he continued, "With so many other friends you'd feel self-conscious, or they might not want to witness that style of climbing. But Brad was so well in tune with it, that it made something that each of us normally do alone more special to share together."

Context considered, just four days removed from being voted the best team in documentary filmmaking, that day glowed by its stillness.

Alex's life was exploding in scale. The movie he and the crew, including Jimmy Chin and Chai Vasarhelyi, had made had just beaten out a roster of striking nominees, including a film on the legendary Ruth Bader Ginsberg. For God's sake, who does that? With the fuzz of celebrity frothing at the periphery of his life, it's easy to see why a day like The Gun Club was so fundamental, why Brad was so fundamental. As irony would have it, it was by free-soloing in the desert—not by merit of the applaud of the glitterati—that Alex found validation. And it was in spending time with his "homie," Brad, rather than with Hollywood superstars, that Alex would find true grounding.

That day at The Gun Club—humble as it would've first appeared on the surface—was tailor-made to Brad and Alex both. It was, in retrospect, as graceful as life itself, a subject which they found themselves holding up in discussion, satisfied, on the return trip home afterward. Whether it was in discussion of Alex's upcoming trajectory as a recognized celebrity—in all the speaking events and promotional endeavors he'd soon be obliged to fulfill—or Brad's trajectory, they spoke simply. They talked about relationships, commitments, priorities, the nuance of something much greater than climbing: a balanced life.

April 1, 2019, a month after their highlight reel day at The Gun Club, Brad and Alex teamed up for a run up three of the keystone formations in Red Rock. Alex, coming from a month of post-Oscar press appearances and speaker events, again needed grounding. Brad, of course, was happy for any brand of all-day climbing and an excuse to see a friend. Beginning near sunrise, the duo hiked up to the Eagle Wall, a striking vertical shield far up the north fork of the Oak Creek Canyon where they romped up the beginner's classic, the 1,000-foot Solar Slab, as an approach pitch.

Brad often remembered the time he and his old high-school friend, Dustin Burd, climbed Solar Slab as an epic, all-day affair many years prior. It was one of those comical cut-your-teeth stories he'd recounted to me a few times before. So I'm certain that on that day, he would have kept at least a quiet joy, remembering how his dad, Jim, had been in radio contact via the walkie-talkies, squinting from a half-mile away with his binoculars as he and Dustin climbed it. He must have been satisfied, pondering the arc on which his life had unfolded, to now be climbing it as an afterthought with a friend like Alex on the way to walls much taller, cleaner, and of such high quality. If not to a parallel universe completely, the Brad Gobright of 2006 belonged to a far and distant past.

Solar Slab, a now-casual jaunt, delivered Brad and Alex to the base of the Eagle Wall, where the historic, five-star Levitation 29 awaited. Classic to the swift simul-climbing style the boys preferred, Alex led the 1,000-foot 5.11 route in a single pitch, clipping only a few bolts each rope-length, while Brad followed below.

With a rapid descent of the adjacent Rainbow Wall via rappelling, they then sped up The Original Route, for another 1,400 feet of quality, at times 5.12 climbing. Brad, one of few who could imitate the means and pace of Alex, also led the entire route as a single pitch of uninterrupted, simul-climbing movement.

Rappelling for a second time in almost as many hours, the duo came back to the foot of the Rainbow Wall, scurried down the dangerous slabs—Brad especially minding his safety—and followed a narrow climber's trail to the base of Cloud Tower. Alex, back on lead, made balletic work of the cryptic, off-balance, crux corner system, dancing as Baryshnikov in his own amphitheater of choice. His grace, though, would have its limits. Two hundred feet higher, after the offwidth which turns into a full-body chimney slot, Alex threaded the needle, climbing through the chimney which delivered him onto the western face of Cloud Tower, under which sit its most iconic pitches.

Having linked all of it together without ceasing, Alex felt the weight of the rope dragging hundreds of feet and through the chimney behind him. He also felt the nearly forty pitches they'd climbed, stacking up against the previous month of cinema touring. It went further than that, too.

As far back as October, Alex had been off the walls due to the *Free Solo* promotional tour. Press events, screenings, interviews—it added up. While he'd kept his fitness at the scope of power and performance by sneaking into climbing gyms in every city along the path of his press tours, he had not kept that all-day, blue-collar fitness. That's the kind of shit you can't replicate for the Big Stone unless you do it. Rope-drag, the work of forty pitches, and the waft of forty feet of rope running to his nearest piece of protection beneath him, Alex came at least marginally undone. Finding an inner reserve, he managed to punch through the crux of the final 5.11 pitch and take it clean to the anchors. Humanized, hyperbolically speaking, at last, Brad made sure to rub it in.

Standard over-achievers, the boys took the rarely climbed 5.12 (+) extension for another four pitches to the top of Cloud Tower, where they could set up a direct rappel to the trail below. Ten and a half hours, one approach route, and three long routes later, they'd shared one of the best days of their lives. Climbing-wise, it was just a fun day, arguably almost in the "active rest-day" category, were it not for those final 5.12 (+) pitches on Cloud Tower. Bigger projects awaited each of them that season, but that day, like the day at The Gun Club before it, glowed for its simple freedoms, for its human roundedness.

Alex and Brad were still on the precipice. Next stages, as life goes, were wide open, and with that expanse came a desire for long days out in the mountains, for long days enable long reflection. Together, between pitches, they spoke about the landscape of the emotional life. Brad had an interest in a local lady, but he also still had feelings for Kat, who had left the country for some travels during the winter. Carefree as their relationship was, Brad and Kat had decided to take a break and pick things back up once she returned stateside. When she left, they were no less in love as they had ever been, but they were also realistic.

Perhaps unintentionally, at least for the emotional complications it would enable, Brad had taken a liking to another partner in Kat's absence. Now that Kat was returning, and spring in Ahwahne was just weeks around the corner, he had some things to sort.

Alex laughed about it in retrospect, saying, "You know, Brad really did just have a heart of gold. Especially in that context. He couldn't hurt a girl even if he wanted to, and obviously he didn't want to."

I'm not sure anyone was looking for answers up there. Alex had plenty in front of him directionally as well. Often, it's just about having someone there to look at it all with. Climbers learn, ideally, to lead with the heart as much as with the head. We hope, perhaps romantically, that our time up there on the line, so doing, will translate through the manner by which we navigate our own emotional, relational, and personal frontiers, too.

Up there atop Cloud Tower, with a long gaze at the horizons of life and with satisfied hearts, Brad and Alex, two guys often written off as having detached or unmoored operating systems, found exactly what everybody else looks for on this planet: human connection. Let the record show the paragons, with all their mastery between them, are just as human as the rest of us.

Brad's final spring in Ahwahne was among his most ambitious. With his unyielding fervor and wide pyramid to stand on, he outdid even his own expectations with a trio of free-climbing ascents on his preferred place in the universe: To-tock-ah-noo-lah. Beginning with a free ascent of the Muir Wall, also called the Free Muir, via The Shaft variation, he employed his usual smash-and-grab tactics, linking thirty-three pitches together over the course of seventeen body-destroying hours. At 5.13c, and with its hardest pitch just three hundred feet shy of the summit, he rightly declared it the hardest thing he had done in big wall climbing. He did not mean that just in terms of grade, either. Lest you are of a completely superhuman ilk, the Muir Wall is among the hardest climbs on the Big Stone. Much of it, no matter how polished your beta (movement sequences), comes down to how bad you want it.

Considering Brad was becoming so damn successful up there, it's important we appreciate these ascents for what they truly were: groundbreaking. That he would end up with more than a half-dozen free-climbs on To-tock-ah-noo-lah—an unquestionably elite echelon—does not mean any of it was inevitable. None of it was guaranteed to him. Our human tendencies skew on acceptance for things past, but make no mistake, every single time Brad pushed a grade threshold, even at a crag, or in a climbing gym, and especially on the high flanks of the Big Stone, he was manifesting the nectar of life. Doing it for thirty-three consecutive rope-lengths, over seventeen hours—that was art. An art of which he was both the conduit and the recipient.

A primary reason so many of us, including Brad, keep or kept coming back, is to remind ourselves that we have the power to reinvent our definitions of what is possible—in this world, in our lives, up on a wall. Pushing a grade, making a goal, at its best, takes us always to the limits of our own becoming. When your fingers are sliming out of a crack, or your feet trembling for that next, unlikely upward pulse, when your body burns with anticipation and abandon at its full metabolic output and contraction, it is one hundred percent, categorically sacred. It's not the answer to life's problems or its biggest questions, and it's not purpose on the long wave, but it is magic. It is a forge where we see who we are and what we are capable of. Up on the limit, we may even see a sliver of where we can go in the other branches of our lives. Even for the professional, even for Brad, boiling one instant of life to singularity, watching your soul, your life force, extend beyond your own body and pull itself up into a position it ought not belong—that shit never gets old. It is soul-shaking, heart-shivering, mega-frequency operations. That's why the result, for anybody who has just had a breakthrough—layperson and professional alike—is an incomprehensible, quivering gratitude. It is not for adrenalin alone that everybody shakes, it is but the latent shockwaves of our souls and bodies reorienting to the same medium of space.

It's important we do not forget that. And, so long as we do not chase it as a remedy for those parts of our lives where it has not the reach, it is important that we continue to keep space for it. As Brad always did.

Brad and Alex's partnership on a rope came to a pinnacle the night of June 9, 2019, when they free-climbed the Pineapple Express offshoot of El Nino, via the Schneider variation on To-tock-ah-noo-lah. As the order of the universe would have, it would be the last consequential climb they'd share. Fittingly, for two gentlemen who prefer to climb without the trappings of media coverage, it was mostly a secret affair. Apart from a lone photographer who joined them for the first few hours of the climb, until nightfall, it was a solitary venture. Fundamentally reduced in the dead of night, they chose the quiet image of two anonymous craftsmen voyaging through Earth's grandest stone in the dark. Just two speckles of flickering light, orbs in motion, climbing by headlamp. A beautiful arrangement.

The year prior, before Alex had been busied by his film and media tours, he had been working on a variation of El Nino (first freed by the Huber Brothers), called the Pineapple Express. On the Huber brothers' original line, a remote, eight-meter-long blank panel of rock, forced them to engineer a peculiar, man-powered rappel. Because of this, their free-climb still carried an

A0 rating, representing the portion of wall in which aid tactics, rather than their own hands and feet alone, were employed. Alex was keen on this new variation, specifically because it avoided all aid-climbing, and, arguably, it was harder.

Alex's previous partner had been the Canadian climbing hero, Sonnie Trotter. In the time that Honnold had been stuck in his obligations, however, Trotter, with Alex's blessing, had nabbed the first free ascent. A celebratory accomplishment for Trotter, which, it turned out, became a fortuitous event for Brad. Fit as he'd ever been after successfully climbing the Muir Wall, Alex asked Brad if he would like to try a free-climbing effort on the Pineapple Express in a single, sub-twenty-four-hour, ground-up push. Honnold couldn't think of anybody else deft and desiring enough to do it in such fashion, which was not just a nod to Brad's ability, but also his being in the right place at the right time. Had Trotter not climbed it or had Honnold not been distracted by his film tour, he and Brad would've never linked up for what became such a classic, memorable passage.

Just past four in the afternoon, Brad and Alex ventured onto some of the stoutest flanks of granite and minuscule edges the Big Stone has to offer. What would occur between lift-off and summit, in the fourteen hours between each, would entail six pitches of 5.13 climbing—including one desperately wet pitch just beneath the top—and five pitches of blue-collar, 5.12 climbing. A total of twenty-six nail-biting pitches would hold their attention all through the night. But, as quietly as they entered the operation, at six the next morning, they soon exited.

It was not without a fight, however. The final 5.13 pitch, wet from the remnant flushing of a recent storm, proved especially robust. Alex described it as the type of pitch you would not feel confident on any day of the week, let alone while soaked. Slimy, incongruent footholds and a tenuous, sustained lieback on insipient pin-scars set you up for a moment of truth—a desperate move off a thin undercling to the only half-decent hold on the pitch. Once, twice, in the early shards of predawn light, Alex, who had been charged with that final crux lead, tumbled off the wall and into 2,700 feet of open Ahwahne air. He even took one attempt to try a new sequence of beta, using a series of half-formed, blunted features on a poor excuse for a prow in an effort to generate a compression sequence. When that availed him only another whipper, he rested one more time, searching within for an equal mixture of adaptability and aggression to steady his resolve. Five minutes later, in the same sopping pickle, he charged out one last gasp, pawing for the only decent hold above the crux sequence, and stuck it. Alex had managed his lead.

Brad encountered the same wet conditions just moments after, and between his carnal grunts and screams, also fell several times—on top-rope—before finally thrashing his way to the anchor in what was an admittedly grungy, primordial series of upward convulsions. Style points were not up for grabs, just memories, after all. The memory of those brilliant colors that now came upon the sky, in their final hundred feet up the wall, those are what counted most. It was a cornucopia of indigo and nautical blues, slowly subsumed by the pinkish, miasmic splendor of sunlight filling the horizon. Their journey, an all-night, mostly quiet exploration under the snow-globe lens of the headlamp, had finished. By 6:30 a.m., with the ropes and gear coiled upon their backs, Brad and Alex found themselves as the only two souls on the planet in attendance for the burst of morning light over God's favorite stone. Satisfied, exhausted, elated, they traipsed down the east ledges' descent handily by muscle memory, laughing, recollecting, talking about life, and then disappeared into the thicket of the forest below together for what would be the last time in their lives.

Alex summed up the experience in a single, appreciative word. "Surreal."

For his *pièce de résistance*, as goes Brad's craft on To-tock-ah-noo-lah, one week after climbing El Nino with Alex, Brad climbed Golden Gate all-free, bottom to top in an artful sixteen-and-a-half-hour push. Recruiting his young friend Maison Deschamps as chief cheerleader and logistical support, Brad began in the dark before dawn, almost perfectly timing his ascent to arrive at the highlight crux pitches 2,500 feet off the deck at sundown. "There, at golden hour, the thirty-six-pitch free-climb—which Brad had so audaciously attempted years earlier while on the mend from his broken back—became Brad's final brushstroke on the Big Stone. This time, though, fit as he'd ever been, it was not simply going to be about getting it done—he was going to enjoy it. On his thirty-first birthday, celebrating another full revolution around the sun, Brad came to the tabernacle that is To-tock-ah-noo-lah one more time for pure artistic vision. For free, unencumbered physical—and no doubt in my mind, spiritual—expression.

He had once declared to me, just a season earlier, that for him, peak performance, his action and his art, found a home together up on the high flanks of To-tock-ah-noo-lah. For years I'd been trying to convince Brad to take his talents elsewhere, specifically to the Canadian Rockies where I'd hoped he and I could romp up a series of classic moderates, if in exchange I belayed him on a selection of alpine test-pieces in places such as Banff or the Bugaboos. My chief device of persuasion was an emotive appeal toward aesthetics, to a spiritual plight. Many times I tried to convince Brad that out there, in the great wide open, far north of our stateside border near the continental divide, he and I might just find the best sunsets and twilights of our lives. That revelation awaited.

He could understand my position, of course; he knew it by heart orientation as a seeker himself. But every time I pressed him, Brad would always look lovingly back at me without so much as a flutter of temptation. Instead, he looked into the recesses of his mind, assured, like a man who after so many years and decades of commitment to his wife, after knowing every square inch of her in her best light and her hidden frailties, wouldn't trade it for anything or anyone. There simply was no upgrade.

It was then that Brad said to me, "I definitely think that climbing El Cap, just being on it at sunrise or sunset, is the most beautiful thing I can do in my life. It's the most beautiful rock out there. And there have been times on it where the sky is so perfect, I can't imagine anything else. For me, that's it. I've had it happen all over in nature, when I get completely frozen by something beautiful, but it happens to me the most on the Captain. I can climb all over the world, but I don't think anything will beat it. It's just the most beautiful thing I've ever seen."

When Brad Gobright free-climbed To-tock-ah-noo-lah in that unfathomable push on Golden Gate, he sought exactly that.

In the end, nearly ten years after having first climbed the Big Stone in a single day on The Nose, Brad had climbed To-tock-ah-noo-lah literally hundreds of times. He and that monolith had a history few will ever equal. A rock so enormous by mass and gravity that it could pull a comet from the sky never had a chance with Brad Gobright. Buoyant, alight, pure of heart, and free of life's gravitas, few but Brad could harness both the masterful and the magical that is on offer up there.

In his time, Brad climbed nearly every free-route and trade-route worth a damn. Additionally, he established the Free Heart Route with Mason, which he then nearly freed in a single day one month later with Alex Honnold. Brad free-climbed the Salathe, The Freerider, Golden Gate, The Muir Wall, El Corazon, and El Nino. At best, in 2019, it was three breakthroughs, three free-routes, in a single season. Essentially in a single month. He did an almost uncountable number of runs up The Nose and the Salathe. And he enchained both routes together in the same day with Jim Reynolds. As if that wasn't enough, he also climbed it three times in a single day, via The Nose, the Zodiac, and Lurking Fear, with his great companion, Scott Bennett. Just as rare in the history books, Brad broke and held The Nose speed record. A feat which such a select few ever had the gumption or tact—however dangerous—to pull off. That single accomplishment alone, The Nose record, etched him into the annals of rock-craft on To-tock-ah-noo-lah. But more important than what he had done up there, no doubt, was who he had done it with.

He climbed the wall with his adoptive brother and guardian, Mason Earle. He'd summited with his friend Miranda Oakley. He'd shared time with the big-wall photo crewmen, Ben Ditto and Cheyne Lempe, his amigos Christian Cattell, Maison Deschamps, and his first partner ever, Russell Facente. He ran laps with Alex Honnold, Jim Reynolds, and dear friend Scott Bennett. He'd even tied in with Hans Florine. And, over the years he had run countless laps up to the El Cap Tower with literally dozens of partners.

Always the constant co-pilot to his ascents was the beauty he had spoken of. Beauty was, to gravity's scorn, the girl he'd courted most. For Brad Gobright, revelation reigned supreme. Behind every smile of every partner, in the warm glow of every soul he shared a rope with, it was there. And it was in the design of it all, too. That it all came from a universe so generous, that it had for millennia, been crafting earth systems in such a way as to put a rock like that on a planet like ours, just in time, on the scale of human history, for it to enrapture the heart, the mind, and the limitless body potential of a young Brad Gobright. That was something beautiful, too.

Summer of 2019 was not all so unlike that of the year before. With Kat back from her travels in South America, She and Brad picked up mostly where they had left off. She was in Orange County again, as was Brad. In no time, they were in stride.

Reconnecting with any of his past romantic partners was, like climbing, not apparently difficult for Brad. In fact, he was one of the rare ones who insisted on maintaining a relationship with the people that mattered to him, regardless if the romantic partnership had ended; he wanted to keep the people he loved close. On numerous occasions, he insisted to take his ex-partner—now living in Los Angeles—out climbing. Being such a kind, caring soul, it wasn't only climbing that Brad was up to when they tied in together. He always asked about the quality of her new life, romance included. Of course, those queries about her life were not meant to be nosy or controlling by proxy; they only reflected the deep care he held for her and her happiness. If anything, he just wanted her to know that he was in her corner, and that she shouldn't settle. The lessons, perhaps, that he had learned most from her, he gave in return. He reminded her of her beauty and her unshakeable, innate worth. He reminded her that she deserved someone who would nurture her talents, who would inspire her, and who would treat her with care, always, especially on the bad days.

With Kat, things were back in play, and apart from his family, it was on her that Brad kept most of his attention. In a propitious arrangement for them both, that summer, Kat had a branch of her family living in Orange County, which meant she had even more reason to be there. Together, they spent time as they had the summer previous, lounging and surfing at the beach, enjoying the little things, sharing favorite pastimes in cute, ever-revolving cycles à la Hollie Golightly and Paul Varjack. It was a perfect extension of the way they had been sharing experiences in the

Valley together from the get-go.

Before leaving Ahwahne that summer, where she again worked for the park service, Kat had shared her favorite watering hole with Brad—a secret outcrop on the south end of the Merced. In exchange, Brad, more than once, had taken her up to The Rostrum at sundown. Perhaps, according to her, his favorite place in the Valley altogether.

"Brad had a special connection at The Rostrum," she shared. Though, in their many sunsets up there, he never said what it was exactly that he was connecting with. Most times, he was so obviously moved by just being there, that in many ways Kat never really thought to ask. She could tell it wasn't something he needed to articulate anyway; it was such an obvious thing, on feeling, on tone, on energy. In a lot of ways, it just had a resonance of home.

Kat didn't need to know exactly what it was that Brad was connecting to on The Rostrum. Electron particles, floods of memories, a specific scent, or the cryptic lacings of the divine which perhaps sang for his eyes only; none of it mattered as much as the fact that it was there, on The Rostrum, that it was happening. Kat understood; if we could drop the need to decode it all, if we could focus not on the whatness of his state but the present-ness of it, we'd be as raptured as he was.

Reflecting fondly, Kat continued, "He used to love taking me up there, especially at sunset. Sometimes we'd flail around on the highlines, if they were up. Other times we'd rappel into the Alien roof, just because he wanted me to see how pretty the rock was. But for Brad, it never really mattered that much what we did while we were there. Even if it was one of those times where we just shared a single beer together—I think the point for him was really just about being there." After an emotional pause, Kat consolidated, "I'm just so glad he had me as a part of it."

In the years that she knew Brad, Kat said that the first thing he did when coming into the Valley—and the last thing he'd do on the way out—was a stop by The Rostrum. Often, it was about more than only "stopping by." A free-solo romp—check that, a mindful passage—was ritual for him too.

"Yeah, he loved it, and he loved climbing it," she said. "It was all about his laps, as he called them. Brad always had to run those laps. To connect with whatever that was for him, on the rock, or in the cracks themselves." Kat hesitated to label the whatness behind that connection Brad found. Like most of us by now, she's just happy to know it was there. When I asked for something comparable, she likened his connection to The Rostrum to the kind of truth that people get from something spiritual, or from reading a favorite piece of writing. What we know for sure is that every time, coming in and going back out toward the rest of the world especially grounded him.

At home, Brad and Kat spent most of their time on the beaches around North Orange County, largely because Kat lived near Huntington Beach. Surf City U.S.A., as they also call it. Being a hub of beachgoers and surfers alike, she preferred paddling out a bit off the map, at 17th and PCH, where crowds and conditions were typically less concentrated. Brad, however, felt otherwise. Surfing between the two summers in which his and Kat's lives intertwined had become something he was decently good at. Good enough that, with his knack for progress and his high standards, he wanted to develop further. Kat recalled numerous occasions where he tried convincing her to paddle out at the pier—a jarring proposition. Notable not only for its higher concentration of waves, but also its concentration of brawling and machismo-filled, brooding locals, the line-up at the Huntington Beach Pier has more the ethos of a Friday night corral in the county drunk-tank than it does anything akin to Duke Kahanamoku and the Aloha spirit. For those reasons, Kat gracefully deferred.

With Huntington Pier off the table, Brad then Googled, *Where do the pros surf in Southern California?* The next day, to Kat's surprise, they were driving forty miles south to San Clemente for a session at the world-famous Lower Trestles. As it turned out, Lower's was a place they would enjoy and return to many times, including for their last hang out in September 2019, just two months before Brad went off to Mexico.

Kat was an apposite fit for Brad, not only because she honored that little six-year-old Jacque Cousteau in him by putting him back in touch with his marine biology fantasies of yesteryear, but because she honored the longing he carried to reconnect to his family. With her Latin heritage abetting her, she insisted that family time ought never be a drudge, but a joy. It didn't matter what they did or did not agree on over the years: family, by definition, was always something to celebrate.

Brad, more than others, was the one most surprised at the frequency with which Kat insisted on family get-togethers. And he was even more surprised when, as a first order of business, she would walk in the house, greet his parents before greeting him, and insist to pour Pamela a glass of Cabernet. Beelining directly for the couch or the backyard table, Kat would take Pamela by the arm like she'd known her for years and dish on life. Family-first, she fit like a glove. Which isn't to say Brad was any kind of an outlier. More than ever before, Brad was truly in his skin while home.

In the recent years, it was ultimately Brad, rather than either of his two long-term girlfriends, who had made the most effort to plug him back in with his own family. Of course with Pamela, there were rarely issues deep enough for him to question her unconditional love. Largely, I think, he felt the same about his dad, Jim. But, as he had been since childhood, Jim was rougher on Brad. Some might say he kept him more honest, too. Jim didn't mind asking Brad hard questions, to which Brad often had a hard time finding an answer. No matter how stern, though, those questions were always asked with loving intention. No doubt, operationally, Brad always knew both his parents loved him. Their full, unconditional, positive regard was always there.

The more impressive part, recently, was that Brad was showing it in return. They say there are few joys more compelling than that of a parent when their children return to the roost. At a certain age, that joy is increased further when the parent realizes that, apart from a simple relationship, the child, in fact, wants for nothing. When a child insists to dwell in the presence of their parent, not for the money they might lend, nor for the shelter, favors, or even the advice they may give, but for that baseline, foundational connection—that is the very fabric of life. For a parent, there is simply no greener grass than that of a child insisting on time spent together. That is because at the bottom of every parent's heart—beneath the age, the lashes of life's pain, the scars of time, and the thickened, cynical skin—lay the same needs for acceptance that are the hallmarks of the child's heart. Fundamentally, we burn for belonging.

In the past few years, right about the time he signed contracts with sponsors, padded his accounts in the bank, found love with his two enduring girlfriends, and found praise and affirmation from nearly everyone in this gargantuan outdoor tribe, Brad began that journey home. For the past two summers, Brad and his father had continually taken small steps closer together. Time shared grilling in the backyard, cliché as it was, or afternoons shared on small home improvement projects kept them close. Any activity predicated on sharing and building something together, however menial, allowed time to restore right relations. Relationships between fathers and sons are among life's tenets; a blueprint of nature's order. Brad and Jim both had respect enough for what nature dictated—enough to restore whatever had, over the years, become a rift between them. Usually, it was more joy than hard work anyway. It was what their hearts longed for.

For all the years that Pamela had insisted on meeting Brad at his level—in her trips to Colorado, Las Vegas, and Ahwahne—these years were among the richest of her life. Brad was now the one insisting to share time with her, at her level. Whatever it was: sitting around, going to restaurants, discussing relationships, helping around the house, Brad was good for it. He just wanted to be with her. Life in the lowlands, perhaps every climber's true crux, their most elusive medium, had become Brad's canvas as well.

Of course, the net Brad cast in his quest for reconnection even extended to his sister, Jill. She noticed it happening even sooner than his parents. In November of 2017, while touring for the *Reel Rock* and *Safety Third* premieres, Brad made it a point to arrive two days early, driving from San Francisco to Napa Valley, solely to see his sister. Confused, Jill was caught so off guard she didn't know what to do with him. Wine was decidedly not his thing. But within hours, she could see it didn't matter. He didn't need her to entertain him, he just wanted to be there with her—a fact she found hard to digest, considering a short drive away there was an auditorium full of climbing enthusiasts ready to herald his celebrity. Her brother, though, that old play pal, the Red Power Ranger when they played make-believe, only wanted time with her.

After that trip, Jill recalled, she gifted Brad a case of Napa Valley's finest—something most among us would've saved for some exquisite celebration or rainy day. Brad, unlike most, understood life wasn't about waiting for special occasions; it was the occasion. That didn't mean to live every day living rip-roaring drunk. It meant share with those you love and celebrate the now. Returning to Ahwahne, Brad went straight to the search and rescue cabins, where he rallied his community of friends and emptied the entire case of fine wine for them to enjoy. According to those present, he was delighted to see others partake in something he could share. Especially sharing about his sister, whom he was so proud of, whose very heart and hands had made the wine.

A year later, it happened again. Brad, to Jill and Pamela's surprise, rode co-pilot on a family trip to wine county at a time when everybody would have thought he'd be out climbing. It was fall, not his off-season. But for a chance to see his sister and share the easy life with his parents, he didn't think twice.

Largely, my feeling is that Brad's return home, spiritually, was at least partially influenced by what he witnessed in his longtime friend and adoptive brother, Mason Earle. In the past two years, Mason had developed a debilitating, impossible illness. It was an illness that, after scores of tests and many darkened months, the physicians weren't even sure how to diagnose. Crippled, disabled, Mason suffered deeply. What would eventually come to be called an ME/CFS illness in short order took his freedom, his self-expression, his artistic pursuit on walls, and, in many ways, his community. What remained in the aftermath, largely, was only the infrastructure of family and a few dear friends. Brad's heart broke for Mason. But, because of his situation, I think, Brad also came into a deeper awareness of what mattered to him. As it works in life, we take blood from stones. What Brad extracted from that situation he applied on the home front.

The night of Pamela's sixtieth birthday, the last Saturday of September 2019, Brad was scheduled to be the key speaker at the Yosemite Facelift's nighttime gathering. Center stage, under the lights, wooing a crowd that already loved him, it was all right there, his to hold. Down in Orange County, Pamela dressed up at home, donned a red blouse accentuated by a favorite neckpiece, and walked into her living room, where she expected to play host to a small gathering of friends and loved ones for the evening. The dinner table in their mid-century-modern Eichler home was festooned with a cornucopia of flowers and dining sets, upon which a cardstock printed menu sat, folded between the linen napkins that rested above each table setting. One guest at a time, Jim and Pamela uncorked the wine and curated their favorite tunes. With the sun just beginning to fade in the evening sky, it was, by all measures, a beautiful gathering.

At the apex of conviviality, a few glasses in for the hosts and guests alike, just when Pamela would have courted the perfect buzz and looked around the room, pondering, appreciating the richness of souls gathered at her residence, Brad and Jill walked in the front door. A full, dual-sibling surprise.

If you've had the privilege to give and receive love, you know exactly the tender, soul-squeezing flush of emotion that overwhelmed her. Holy spirit level rapture, with more fuzz and electricity than any cell in the body can rightly conduct, pierced her. Pamela detonated. A deluge, arms to ribs to heart to eyeballs, everything beautiful and fragile of the human condition shot through her neural pathways at the speed of light. Pamela wept, overtaken entirely by the single greatest force of the universe: love.

Brad walked straight into his mother's arms and hugged her from his core—probably for longer than he would have had Pamela simply been able to let go. Call it a mother's foresight—Pamela would not be robbed of an ounce of that moment's tenderness. In her arms, catching her tears in his shoulders, Brad and Pamela both quivered at a realization so profound it nearly went unspoken. For that moment in time, there was no other place in all the world, no landscape nor mansion nor summit itself, that he or she could have possibly wanted to be a part of. Brad and his mother, in one another's arms, were exactly where they wanted to be. Nothing on earth could have afforded a righter orientation. Bonded together. Mother and son.

Soon after, as Jill and Jim encircled their embrace, it was full. Mother, son, daughter, life partner and husband, all together. All in one embrace, with the peripheral cheers of loved ones around them. This was sacred. It was the history that bound them, the love that held them, the sunset that surrounded them, all of it, just there, in that one, single, hallowed moment. This was life to the lees.

While this was Pamela's moment, it was Brad's, too. After years climbing the wild out of life itself, venturing off to the highest spaces, living a most novel, exotic journey in physical space and time, Brad, like Chesterton's unlikely hero, had taken the long voyage of the heart.

From the moment he stepped out that door in 2008, wittingly or not, he was always on that path. Perhaps he, like many of us, just didn't know it. For life happens in revolutions, after all. No matter how far he went, he was always moving in return. It's just the order of things. Travel far enough east, and you come exactly back as you were, only having done so from the west. So, it was some surprise, even to him, that he was there that night.

Not at a campfire, nor in a theatre full of climbers, surrounded by their adulations; not on the biggest wall nature fashioned; not under a boulder with a sleeping pad; not in the arms of another woman did Brad Gobright find his truest fit. Though these avatars waited just outside that door. It was not in any earthly delight, as it were, but right there, in his mother's arms, and only a moment later in the collective arms of his beloved sister and his father, that Brad Gobright found out what his heart had always sought was, in fact, always there. It was in the most fundamental love.

It was in the most fundamental truths, too.

That revolution is not only defined by its venture, but by its return.

That as much as our spirits long for the wilderness, they long for a place to call home.

BLUE

The last time I saw Brad Gobright in human form—gigantic, heart-melting smile and all—was in a climbing gym. Precisely as he had been dressed hundreds of times before, and on that first day shooting for *Safety Third* on the Naked Edge, Brad was dressed in blue: one of his two prime colors. When playing make-believe Power Rangers with his sister in the old treehouse as children, Brad was fire; he always wore red. I believe it was the color that suited his early years, and the color that was true to his passionate, radiant glow. But on a wall, when climbing, when caught by nature's loving gaze or wrapped by the waves of oceans—in the hallowed swirl of his infinite eyes—Brad was blue. It's what he wore that day on the Naked Edge, it's what he wore when he free-soloed Hairstyles, and it's what he wore that random, September afternoon in the gym—his favorite, a Gramicci shirt, a hue true to his deeper, matured tuning.

Two days removed from an impromptu trip to Tijuana where he had a wisdom tooth pulled for pennies on the dollar, Brad was romping a hard training session on the Moon Board. Having no prior knowledge that he was in town, it was to my total surprise when, while talking to a friend, I heard a familiar voice call my name from behind.

"Hey…" Brad's voice rose in inflection. "I know that guy over there."

Turning about-face, I glanced by the guiding of Brad's voice and locked eyes with his Prussian blue pearls, and that giant smile of his lit up a moment later. Brad and I met at the midpoint of the short distance that stood between us, walking with arms open for what became one of the last hugs I ever felt from his embrace. Excited, surprised, we kept arms upon each other's shoulders for a few moments longer, simply inspired to have rare contact. I asked him what brought him into town and, pointing at his absent molar, he clued me in.

"Yeah, I figured it was cheaper than going to a dentist in the States," he laughed. "And it was cool to score some tacos before the operation."

Recovering the space life had put between us, we quickly found connection and, moments later, were already making plans for a way to hang out somewhere outside. He was resplendent, matured in a way I hadn't seen, satisfied on a level you could palpate. Of himself and his position in life, Brad was sure.

The conversation was short, five minutes at most, but it was round, too. Full. In parting, he asked about my partner, as he always did. She, like Brad, had also endured a wretched back-break in 2016, within months of his own accident. It came by different circumstances, but Brad always asked about her well-being from a caring place. He insisted I give her a warm salutation, and then he opened his arms for a hug one more time with that giant, assured, and holistically bright smile. And the truth is, it took me by surprise. In those arms, so much love and carefree percolated between his shoulders that, on a heart level, it took some of my breath away. Sure, his clutch was powerful, but it wasn't the physiology of it, it was the core of it. His entire energy read nothing of shame, of a troubled past, misfit eras, or a misunderstood plot in life. Those themes, and the energy they trapped within him, were long past. It was only love and warm, glowing humanity that he drew between his shoulders. I told him how proud I was to see him in such a sound place in life, then we wrapped. Brad and I hugged one final time, the last time, held it with sincerity, and then went back, each toward our own directions.

"Glad you had a good time in Mexico," I said as we stepped apart, still smiling.

Excited as ever, Brad dipped his hands in his chalkbag and replied, "I'll be heading back in a couple of months. But hope to see you between now and then!"

One foot smudging into the first position of his next boulder problem, Brad grabbed the starting holds, set his shoulders back, and then postured onto the wall, initiating a movement sequence that took him up in seconds flat. As excellent as I'd ever seen him move, he floated, not a hair of gravity in his orbit, all the way to the finish hold.

The summers Brad spent working kids' groups did much more than deliver him a window to train his rockcraft. Sure, it was a world-class facility he had access to, but it was also a new community. Since 2017, Brad had come into the acquaintance of, and then later, the caring friendship of, many at that gym. One friend, a gregarious, caring, self-made businesswoman named Julie would become a kindred spirit. For her fantastic persona, her benefacting ways, and her contagious optimism, Julie was a trusted friend to Brad. She was also a mentor.

Julie was born from struggle. From a darkened past, fraught by trauma and loss at the nuclear family level, resulting in an adolescence bouncing between guardianships, Julie rose above a terrible youth to become a successful, independent woman.

She had also become something of a matronly figure to a core group of gym climbers, who, while not the world's best, rivaled any outfit of climbers for the title of the world's most enthused. As climbing has always drawn the misfit and outcast into the fold, this group was no exception. Because of that, Brad was not only a figurehead and success symbol, he was right at home.

Since seeing *Safety Third* in 2017 at the Reel Rock Film Tour, and subsequently meeting Brad in person, Julie had taken it as something of a personal mission to sponsor Brad. He was humble, sincere, exceptionally talented, and often down on his finances—a recipe that Julie felt compelled to facilitate. In short time, she and Brad became close friends, she a mentor to him in his career expansion and he a mentor to her in climbing. Apt to spread her resources, Julie often paid Brad to lead weekend trips to local crags with the motley crew of locals where he would often ropegun (lead, equip, and anchor) routes and teach climbing techniques. It endeared him to others, it built friendships and community, and it helped his bottom line.

Eventually, in the summer of 2019, Brad asked Julie if any events were on the horizon. It wasn't that he needed it financially as much as he wanted it personally. On one hand, he was spurred by that peer group, by those friends, and often, taking weekends to climb with the layfolk, the non-professional rock-dwellers, did for him what volunteering and mentorship programs do for many. It lent perspective, which unsurprisingly fostered gratitude. In addition, Brad asked Julie about that trip because, for the first time since the autumn of 2014, Brad was getting serious about guiding.

Brad knew his highest grades weren't going to last forever, nor was the limelight. Because of that, he'd recently rethought his conclusions on professional guiding. Considering the hardships he'd faced on his last go-round, when he abandoned the AMGA course, Brad was keen on the accrual of real-life experience to make up for what he considered to be his book-based deficiencies. A test run, as they agreed to call it, seemed a perfect start. Whereas in the past, Brad had rope-gunned on the single-pitch level, he would, in El Potrero Chico, Mexico (the proposed locale of the group's next trip), guide Julie and her friends up entire multi-pitch escapades. Julie had worked with a litany of guides in her tenure of mountaineering experience and agreed to pay Brad the industry standard plus some, with the caveat being that she'd unbiasedly critique Brad's skills, teaching style, and overall tenor. After a shake of hands, and then a bigger hug in its place, the deal was done.

Julie went home, sent the emails and itinerary to the group of nearly twenty gym climbers, booked the housing arrangements and the flights, including Brad's, and called her local peers at the Potrero. The sleepy village of Hidalgo was going to host a legend.

Two days before leaving for Mexico, nearly two months to the day that he had surprised his mom for her sixtieth birthday, Brad came home. The first evening, they simply caught up. Brad had recently taken a trip to the desert for a photoshoot with his sponsors and was excited about how it had gone over. He was especially pleased to have spent time with his friend and fellow climber, Alice Hafer, who he excitedly saw as a trad-climber in the making. Over dinner, he explained to Pamela how he longed to foster more relationships with women in the sport for the equanimous, level energy, and insight they provided.

Brad spent the next day mostly alone. Understanding his needs for personal space and self-care, he simply did as little as possible. When Pamela asked if anything was amiss, he calmly replied, "Nothing wrong on my end, Mom, it's just that I've got to spend a week being switched-on and living with nine other climbers, starting tomorrow, so I'm taking an introvert day to be ready for it."

Pamela missed the opportunity to spend more time with her son that day, but if anything, she was impressed by the level of self-awareness he presented. It wasn't all doom or gloom; instead, Brad shared how elated he was to be a part of the roster for that trip to Mexico, that he was looking forward to it. He knew himself well enough, though, to seek the inside experience as a primer for the social experience he was booked for. Mostly to himself, Brad spent that day in his room, seemingly at a measure of peace.

In the morning, on his way to meet the gang in the town of Mission Viejo, in Orange County, Brad and Pamela honored their long-held ritual and shared breakfast burritos. For years running, the two of them would catch a last meal, usually breakfast, before Brad went off on his next big adventure. It was Pamela's way to ensure he was in a good headspace, to share parting wisdom, to hold him in her gaze just that little bit longer. A local Mexican joint down the street—ubiquitous to Southern California with its homestyle *comida casera*—proved fitting. There, Pamela recalled that Brad was refreshed, and generally only dwelled on the good things of his orbit.

They spoke about his life after professional climbing, on future steps in his horizon, where Brad shared from the heart. He talked about guiding as a means of income and even expressed the worries he had behind pursuing the certifications required. But, more than the financial directions of life, and more than his goals in hard-climbing, Brad Gobright wanted love again. For Brad and Kat, the summer had been gangbusters, but in the past two months, some space had grown between them—not for any specific rift or for lack of chemistry, though. Somehow, with life drawing them each in their own direction, they'd just lost some of their spark. Kat was still developing her career, after all, a path that took her away from Southern California that fall. Whatever the space between them, Brad was still quite enamored with her, or so it seemed to Pamela, and he said that if things didn't circle into favor with her, it would be a priority to soon find a life partner. Someone to take the longer journeys with.

Brad also shared plans for spring, which seemed soon enough around the corner. He'd been pitched an idea by a crew of reality television producers, wherein he'd be recruited to speed-climb his old trade route, Epinephrine, and for which he would be compensated handsomely. He told his mom that he'd sought advice from Alex Honnold, his close friend, and had taken some initial meetings to hear it out. He also shared he was on the hunt for a motor vehicle upgrade at last.

"It looks like I'm selling out, Mom!" he laughed. After many long years in the shitter, Brad was ready to transition to a road-ready Sprinter Van. He even talked about his dream life with a partner in said Sprinter van.

"I hope I meet a girl, soon," Brad shared with his mother, safe, secured, honest.

Pamela was grateful for the sincerity and assured Brad that he would find all the things he longed for in this life as he always had. At the close of their meal, she lingered a little longer still, looking into his eyes, no doubt watching the wind play with his hair, harnessing the secret joys that only parents—likely even only mothers—feel. For it was out of her womb, after all, that this ball of blue eyes and divine light was born. There, at their last goodbye, it saturated. The boy she'd given birth to had become such a bright, generous young man. Behind his disarming blue eyes, in those tiny fragments of insecurity that remained—the ones only she could see—she felt pride, too. She could see him evolving before her, finding his fit, slowly, gently engaging in life, and inspiring others.

At last, she hugged him, told him to be safe, swallowed the

lump in her throat—the one that was always there when saying goodbye—and reminded Brad that she loved him. They hugged, hearts moved, and Brad answered, "I love you, too, Mom."

Upon first sight, Brad was taken by the grandeur of the Potrero. For its size, sure, but also for the way it manipulated light. He was always fascinated by light, for as long as I could remember, as was the case that day when he took that small road up through the town of Hidalgo into the foothills which crest the bosom of the Potrero Chico in Nuevo Leon, Mexico. Standing, towering, glaring thousands of feet above him were the castled spires and jagged limestone walls; grey, blue, bronze, iridescent depending on the angle, lush with vegetation and grandeur.

Being his first international foray with travel for the sake of climbing, save for trips to Squamish, he was unsure what exactly to do with himself. The rocks, quite literally, are just right there— as close, if not closer, than To-tock-ah-noo-lah is to the road. So, while the gang was settling into the giant, well-accommodated space Julie had booked, poolside and all, Brad placed the few items he'd brought on his bunker and paced the premises until making his decision. He was a climber, after all.

Others in the gang joined, jaunting up the short round of the hillside, along the road, past the humble hostels, the public pool, and into the canyon, where they came face-to-face with the calcified limestone and its substrates. Pitches were shared, many of which were but simple musings for Brad's appetite. He helped hang lines, he belayed, he encouraged others in their climbing, and then, as time allowed, when the gang was keen on an afternoon fiesta, Brad took his shoes and chalkbag and free-soloed Yankee Clipper, a regional classic on a roadside cliff.

Nearly 1,500 feet, most of which was 5.10, and a final, headwall pitch at 5.12a, Brad took little time to feel it out in Mexico. That said, most in his circle said he showed no signs of restlessness or compulsion that day. His solo seemed natural, organic, unrushed, even composed.

The next morning, Brad packed up his gear and reviewed the climber's topo for another moderate, regional classic. Space Boyz, an eleven-pitch 5.10 (+), which he was committed to guiding Julie, her partner, and two of their friends up, was on the menu. After stretching out the cobwebs lingering from the jetlag, the time shift, and the boozy late-night libations the gang was known for, the time had come to climb. Breakfast and morning coffee complete, an hour later they walked into the canyon.

Smooth sailing on the wall, Julie was most impressed with the care with which Brad showcased his knowledge. On his leads, he slowed down prodigiously. He spoke on technique, on position, on balance, and he demonstrated them all, too. Whereas the day before he had climbed Yankee Clipper—essentially the route next door—in a smooth two-hour jaunt, he turned to a new direction completely with Julie and the crew. Speedy still, by most layfolk's cadence, it took them nearly eight hours to climb and safely rappel Space Boyz. Brad was clear, directive, a guiding voice at each anchor, and he taught carefully, mindfully. Especially on rappel. Climbing higher by vertical swoop than she ever had before, Julie was impressed and empowered, ultimately singing Brad's praises for the way he provided and guided such a full, fun journey.

Brad glowed up there, from his situational awareness to his emotional awareness—exemplified by the ways he guided Julie's fear management and inner dialogue—he demonstrated poise, stoke, and aptitude. At the top, with a joy so grand and a view so clean it cut all the way to Heroica Matamoros, Julie and the three others, along with Brad, gathered for an indelible photo by selfie stick. Cheesy, righteous vibrations oozed off their faces on top of the known world, looking out across the spoils of Mexico. Far back in the distance above them, at the tip of El Toro, the vertical shield behind them, El Sendero Luminoso stood radiant, calling Brad.

In the evening, back at the gorgeous domicile that Julie had commandeered for the crew as a basecamp, which was outfitted with a pool and backyard barbecuing station, the gang made like the locals and partied down to the belt-buckles, Ranchero-style. They brought their own soundtrack from the States, sure, but no doubt some strong cumbias and Norteña-sounds pulsed from those speakers that night. It was a proper little *discoteca*. Julie, wanting to honor Brad for joining, teamed up with others in the group and hired a local butcher and cooking crew who staged in with an entire pig, slow-roasted Saltillo-style, an ode to northern Mexico's premier pork purveyors. Brad, eyeballing an unbelievable upgrade from the food quality of the Yosemite Lodge Buffet, was at a loss for words. Supremely stoked, a dirtbag's paradise stared back at him on that table setting. Sound system thump-thumping, tequila bottles stacking, glasses clanking, it was, at least for a prime couple of hours, an inspired night, and one which Brad loved.

Somewhere near midnight, Brad called it, earnestly asking Julie and the kids to do the same. It wasn't that he was a humbug, nor was it a matter of not having fun; Brad was just exhausted. For years running, he'd made a habit of sleeping by 9:00 p.m., usually for his all-day, gigantic pushes on the Big Stone. Staying up till the Bruja's hour was way past his capacity.

Laughing, but serious as he retired for the evening, he looked over to Julie, who was a few pints in and happier than ever, and said, "This is amazing stuff, but you guys are wild." Not wanting to pass judgment, he wrapped up, shortly, "I guess I've just been on the big wall schedule for too long now."

Brad drug his tired feet back to his bed, rolled in passively, and switched to lights-out. Another day of guiding stood at the other end of his REM cycles, which, with his fatigue, onset immediately.

Relatively early the next morning, one at a time, the Orange County gang slopped out of their quarters at the pace of molasses. One by one, tired feet sauntered to the communal kitchen, where Brad was already set with pen in hand, scribing the day's plans. Julie was set to do some one-on-one climbing with him, and Brad had the guidebook open, having bookmarked a dozen would-be suitors for her first-ever lead down in El Potrero Chico. While she and the gang shook out the cobwebs, treating tequila-induced hangovers with muddy cups of brew and dives in the pool, Brad stepped out to the backyard and called a special someone. More than a thousand miles away in California, Kat was taken with disbelief to look down at her vibrating phone and see Brad's caller I.D. lighting it up.

"Hey, you," he began. "Thought I'd say hello from Mexico!"

Kat smiled, happy to hear his familiar, caring voice, and asked him about the trip.

"It's going great, actually. Big reason I thought of you was because I ate an entire pig last night."

"Ha-ha," she laughed, thinking he spoke idiomatically.

"No, really. It's not a joke. These guys got us an entire pig last night, and I loved it. Ate more than I should have, but I just kept thinking about how fun it would be to rub it in your face," Brad jested.

Kat, being plant-based in diet preference, understood the *schadenfreude*.

They laughed for a short few minutes, catching up and discussing whatever the near future held for each of them. In little time at all, it was obvious the reason Brad had called had very little to do with the pig. What he wanted was to keep her close, if only by phone and distant contact. Nothing had gone wrong between Brad and Kat, after all. And, at the end of the day, Brad, and his mom, really weren't sure why he and Kat weren't together. For whatever cryptic cause, they just *weren't*. Based on the phone call and the sound of his voice, Brad did want Kat to stay close, though, that much was apparent. He missed her.

Shortly after, Brad and Julie were walking side by side, passing the entrance arches of El Potrero Chico, bathed in light which shone between a few sparse, wispy clouds. Into a shaded canyon near the public pools and the *nicho*-shrine of Our Lady of Guadalupe, the Virgin, Brad and Julie tied in for a short, two-pitch climb. Brad danced up the approach pitch easily, then belayed Julie to the anchors. There, he instructed her on how to set up an anchor and how to belay a partner from an above position. He reminded her of the safety standards for proper clipping of gear, and to keep the lead rope from ever running behind her in case of a fall. After double-checking her knots and her safety gear, Brad gave her a spirited talk, reinforcing her strengths, and then charged her with her first lead in Mexico. In her brief tenure with vertical climbing, she'd only ever tallied a handful of leads, so the experience was fundamentally engaging, new, and challenging.

At the top of the second pitch, not long after, Brad quickly met Julie at the anchor, congratulating her on her successful lead. Julie, still buzzing, admitted to Brad that she was terribly overwhelmed, that she felt naked, that her nerves hadn't yet steadied. Going down by rappel was going to have to wait.

Equal parts elated, disbelieving, and trembling, Julie was out of her skin. To be in Mexico, learning the skills, then actually applying them—and doing so with her dear friend, Brad—flooded her with emotion.

"I'm sorry, Brad," Julie stammered. "This is just such an

exposed moment for me. Not just with the heights we're at, but with the emotions I'm feeling."

"You know," Brad responded, "You did such a good job! I could tell you were nervous, but you really stuck with it, and that's inspiring, Julie. Don't forget that."

Brad paused in reflection, then continued, beautifully. "You know, I didn't tell you how great it was yesterday, on Space Boyz, and how happy I am to be guiding you guys. I'm nervous too, you know. A lot like you. Maybe not for lead-climbing that often, but I'm pretty scared of this test I've got to take for the guide certification."

Julie listened and looked on in amazement as Brad continued.

"I've never been a good student, you know. I'm not very smart, not like a lot of people. And I've always been scared by tests. I'm afraid I won't pass, and I'm afraid I'm not going to be good enough. But I really want to change my direction, you know? I think watching you on your lead climb, just now, reminded me that it's okay to be vulnerable. You help me see it's okay to be nervous, too. That it's good to try things when you think you might fail."

Julie, dumbfounded, could not believe that she had any possible mode by which she could inspire the mighty Brad Gobright. But hearing his words, and watching his face come clean with honest emotion, it was all there.

Julie was disarmed by the way he chose to mirror the emotional exposure she felt from climbing by sharing his apprehensions on life. More than the climb she had just led, Brad's choice to bring a deeper connection into the experience had deeply moved her.

That night Julie recalled a special glow—what felt like an extra mark of conviviality in the air at basecamp—after she and Brad returned from their fantastic day climbing. It was an all-time, community warmth, wrapped up in a bubble of collective cheer, good food—tacos, of course—and blue-collar suds to wash it all down. The dryness of climbed-out hands, the sting of lime juice on the fingertips, and that glowing, warm, remnant electric charge buzzing in her fingertips from having climbed all day alighted her. Brad, just beside her at the dinner table, exuded a deep satisfaction too, but she caught fleeting moments of distraction in his gaze—something she noted, at the time, with only a little concern.

Between the laughs of the dinner table and the day's storytelling, Brad's mind was elsewhere: on home, his future, the guiding test, his relationship with Kat—it could have been any of these, or the aggregate of them all. It could have been as simple as feeling a need to step away for a day, too. Brad was good with a crowd, but it also took a toll on him to stay switched on socially for consecutive days in a row. Being responsible for other people's safe passage up these multi-pitch routes—all while being the center of attention—could've easily left him longing for a reprieve. For Brad, that usually came from a long day out on something tall and mighty.

Hastily, almost pining for a scratch at a familiar stimulus, Brad's thoughts turned toward how he might climb a bigger, harder route at the Potrero during the group's oncoming rest day. And in that thought, the call of El Sendero Luminoso just behind him rang above the group's warm, incandescent cheer, over the dinner table and the buzz of drinks and clanking glasses. Figuring something of his own calculus, Brad decided that nearly anybody would do, as goes a partner, and put out a message on social media.

At the neighboring campground, one minute later, two Ticos, Juan and Gino, were among the first to see his story and laughed with excitement.

"Hey, *cabron*," Juan jested at Gino, "I think Brad Gobright is going to be on Sendero tomorrow. He's asking about possible partners to climb 5.12–5.13 with. I mean, he must be thinking of Sendero, right?"

Gino perked up, seemingly agreeing to Juan's rationale, as Juan continued, "Holy shit, man. It's going to be awesome."

Juan laughed back, conciliatory. "We better get an early start."

A block away, a climber Brad had never met before, a hotshot kid named Aiden who was still in his mid-twenties, was among the first to respond. Brad took him up on the offer to partner up, and, with less time than it takes to toggle between apps on a phone, Brad locked in his plan. Coming back to the conversation, Julie asked him what he was doing, at which point Brad disclosed his machinations.

Immediately concerned, solely on gut feeling alone, Julie expressed her views.

"I'm just not sure that's a good idea," she told Brad. "Please, please promise me you'll be careful."

Brad nodded, not with cockiness, but blindly enough that Julie still carried concern. She'd been charged with keeping him safe, even by his folks, who shared he'd never really been out of the country on a climbing trip. Worried, she kept her eyes locked on Brad until he understood she wasn't just saying it on rote practice.

"I'll be safe," he said.

Considering how detailed he'd been in the past two days with her, Julie took him at his word. The night wound into a haze— with slurps of swill, more stories, laughs, and cheer, everything blended into a long, harmonic chorus.

It is a terrible fact, a rudiment of the sport, an unbiased truth of life in and on the mountains: in climbing, people die. In the eyes of those who perished, or the fewer still who somehow survived, sentinel events never seem as close or inevitable in the moment as they do upon retrospect. Nobody goes up there, operationally, to court death. The knowledge of its proximity is more commonly accepted but filed away behind the stream of conscious operations. But still, death comes. And, in the mountains, it rarely does so as a matter of fact. Events are often grey, blurred, skewed, and they only dissociate, rather than coalesce, as time moves from them. Truth, as a matter of fact, at the level we recognize it in our life in the lowlands, is a luxury few entertain in the wild.

Will we ever truly know what happened up there on Sendero Luminoso? Perhaps not. But still, Brad's family, and those of us who knew Brad, are forced at some level to accept what cannot be undone, even if it can never fully be known. What we do know is that alternate—even conflicting—narratives exist for the events of November 27, 2019.

The morning began familiar enough: the Orange County crew was primed for a rest day, which allowed Brad his window. With his new partner, Aiden, in tow, they walked the easy path up the canyon toward the 1,750-foot El Sendero Luminoso. Quickly, through the third-class, rocky scrambling at its base, they stood face-to-face with the giant, fifteen-pitch climb, equipped only with a dozen or so quickdraws, an eighty-meter rope, their belay devices, a few slings, and a humble daypack stocked with a small reserve of water and nutrition bars. Juan and Gino, the Costa Ricans, had gotten an earlier start on the day and were already three and a half pitches up.

According to the boys, you could just *feel* it. Before Brad even arrived at the base, the energy on that wall was sharp, like something special was marinating. So, you can imagine their inspiration when, still not completely positive of the identity of the figure at the base below them, that figure darted off the ground in a bright Prussian blue shirt, linking the long first and second pitches together in one massive, 260-foot lead. Gino thought it must be Brad.

Brad sped through two of the most sustained pitches as a warm-up, dividing the dozen quickdraws he had brought as equipment over the expanse of the twenty-eight bolts. Skipping protection and running it out in the face of a monstrous wall, was, after all, *modus operandi*. The Ticos stood in awe, assured of his identity, which they confirmed when he arrived at his first anchor atop the second pitch. In the time it took Aiden to follow such a robust lead, the Ticos made it up the fourth and fifth pitches, which took them to the bivy ledge, also known as La Quinta de Santa Graciela for its spacious, accommodating floor.

At the Quinta de Santa Graciela, Juan and Brad shared their first interaction, both belaying their respective partners up the wall. At a loss for words, starstruck even, Juan made the best small talk he could. He simply didn't know what to say.

"So, how's the Potrero treating you?" Juan asked.

"Oh yeah, great so far," Brad replied. "I've never done a climbing trip like this."

"*Chido, amigo*," Juan affirmed. "You think it's better to free-solo on granite or limestone?"

Brad laughed, unsure, which made Juan feel self-conscious for even asking. A moment later, Brad continued, "So, where are you from?"

"Costa Rica!" Juan proudly offered, taking in a yard of slack from Gino below.

"That's great!" Brad smiled. "I went there with my family once, a long time ago. It was pretty awesome."

The small talk continued gently until, in Juan's words, it was obvious that he better just stay quiet and belay Gino, before he asked more dumb questions. Juan recognized that the feeling of inferiority he carried was only on his end. Brad was welcoming, encouraging, affirming. He cast no judgments. But, Juan noticed, he was also distracted.

"I'm not sure if that's how he always was, because, you know, I don't know him," Juan later shared. "But even if he was stoked to be there, he did seem distracted. Like his mind was somewhere else. I'm not sure how else to say it. He was just in another place."

What took Brad Gobright, king of the present moment, out of that exact spot, away from the air that filled his lungs? What possible permutation of thought stuck to his wings? What on earth sullied the young man who seemed, at least on a wall, impervious to mortal, emotional gravitas? We'll never know, but that sense of tension or minimally just being off-kilter continued. Brad and Aiden soared past the Ticos after that belay, summiting in the time it took the Costa Ricans to climb another five pitches. With such a brief interface, it's hard to surmise much of anything about the mood or Brad's real presence of mind. He was climbing well, seemingly on autopilot. And as for Aiden, the only remarkable thing the Ticos remembered was that, when they asked him how the climbing was going, he replied, "It's great, but this stuff is way out of my league. I've never done anything like this, and probably wouldn't if it wasn't Brad on the other side of the line."

One side of that quote reads benign enough, even inspirationally. Brad brought out the best in people, and Aiden was climbing well. He wouldn't have been on a route like that any other day were it not in the wake of someone more accomplished to help him get there. Another side of the quote, as the Ticos digested it, was less optimal. Neither Aiden nor Brad were wearing a helmet. They had minimal gear, and Aiden seemingly had even less experience. He didn't seem, to them, comfortable in the environment, nor understanding of the scale at which he and Brad courted risk. The Ticos, by contrast, had a proper daypack, much more food, two space blankets, two sweaters, and two more liters of water. Nobody thought twice about the disparity in the moment, though; the Santa Graciela Ledge was true to her name. The views were outrageous, the climbing was a dream, and it was all happening, goddammit. Whether you were Aiden, Gino, or Juan, it didn't matter—the one and only Brad Gobright was up there, executing his craft, runouts and all.

Hours later, the afternoon came swiftly. El Sendero Luminoso is a north-facing wall, after all, often blocked from sunlight entirely. At the tail end of November, less than a month from the winter solstice, days are short. They're also cold. Wind sweeps up that face, harshly, aggressively, ominously, especially when a storm approaches, as was the case that fateful day.

For what it's worth, in Juan's recollection, there's the shamanic version and the forensic version of that sequence. In the shamanic version, things were already turning toward disaster.

"I don't know," he explained. "The best way I can put it is that the energy of the mountain changed. Clouds came in, quickly, and things got much more serious."

That Juan has an account of things that consider nature's energy, the feel of the day, those intangible—or more mystic— elements is not to discredit his forensic account. In fact, as a first order of business, as soon as he and Gino got off the wall that day, eventually rescuing Aiden, the two of them returned to their campground and wrote down a first-hand account of everything they'd witnessed. They understood that time would take the clarity of their memory, and for what they had witnessed, a full account of events, from their lens, was requisite.

What the accounts agree on is that Brad and Aiden did, in fact, summit. No falls for Brad, he onsighted the King Line of the formation. Aiden even climbed wonderfully, only failing to succeed on a scant few moves. From there, the boys began their descent, following the usual means of rappelling the entire 1,750-

foot face they'd just scaled.

As Brad and Aiden came into view, Gino and Juan were at the anchors of the tenth pitch. Gino rappelled first, leaving Juan at the anchor at the same time Brad and Aiden arrived. The duo were simul-rappelling, each on one strand of the line, a style in which it is imperative that both members weight and unweight the system at the same time. If one person comes out of the system before the other is ready, they will create a seesaw effect. This is ultimately what happened an hour later.

Brad was ahead of Aiden, meaning lower in the rappel, and was racing toward the anchor, where Juan sat. In an apparent rush, neither Brad nor Aiden had rightly equalized the rope for their rappel, and Brad's end was short of reaching the anchor. No back-up knots in the line, Brad zipped down to within two meters of the end, until he heard Juan, who was yelling profusely, "STOP!"

"Dude, your rope doesn't reach, man!" Juan shouted as Brad came to a halt.

"Oh fuck, man," Brad quickly replied. "Fuck me. Thanks."

Had Juan not been there, who knows what could've happened right then and there. The last of Brad's provided nine lives exhausted, the two stopped their rappel, ascended the rope all the way back to their anchor, and then re-fed the lines into equilibrium, to the point where both ends reached the anchor where Juan was still stationed.

At the next rappel, atop the ninth pitch, Brad and Aiden caught up to Gino and Juan. Just as quickly as before, they skirted past the Ticos in an apparent mission to flat ground. A storm was still brewing, after all, and neither Brad nor Aiden had cold weather clothing or even headlamps. Like much of the events of the day, these were simple oversights. The problem, often, is how they add up. Were Brad and Aiden rappelling so fast just to beat the darkness? Unfortunately, we don't know. But as much as things up there were fast, they were also loose. In addition, the Costa Ricans noticed Aiden's rappel set-up with some concern. Brad, while not backed up, at least had a Gri-Gri, the industry-standard auto-locking device. Aiden had only an ATC and a poorly constructed back-up. When they asked him about it, Aiden responded it was meant to serve as an auto-block (a specific weave of cordelette around a carabiner, attached to the rappeler's harness, used in like fashion to a prusik knot), but the problem was that Aiden's auto-block was neither woven correctly—to enable a locking action on the rope—nor was it the right equipment. Rather than using a cylindrical, woven cordelette, Aiden was using a flat-webbing Dyneema sling. Even if woven correctly, that sling would not exert the same "catching" mechanism. Its shape came at a detriment to its application on physics.

"Dude," Gino said as Aiden passed. "I don't think you've got that set up right."

"I think you might be right," Aiden responded. "But it's just there for back-up anyway."

Downward, Aiden and Brad flew, rappelling at a rate that the Ticos saw as outrageous, bold, and dangerous. At the top of the seventh pitch, according to the Ticos, roughly 150 feet from the Santa Graciela ledge, Brad and Aiden fed their rope through the rappel rings and cast it down. Brad's end of the line was stuck in a pile of shrubs to the climber's right when facing the wall—Aiden's end was not stuck to anything. Brad and Aiden would not have gone willingly into that last rappel had they known there was no way to make the ledge. Their eighty-meter (estimated at 263 feet) rope, when divided into two parts, would never cover the approximate 150 feet they needed to get to Santa Graciela. The system was always going to be short by about forty feet. Because the rope was not cast down at its midpoint, as fortune would have it, one end came up about thirty feet short of the ledge, the other about ten feet.

Testimony from the Costa Ricans agree to this point and the

following. Somewhere in that rappel, both Brad and Aiden fell. One of them rappelled out of the system, causing the other to seesaw down, and eventually out of the system, too. Additionally, in their eyes, when Brad and Aiden set off on the last rappel, it was Aiden who was lower, rappelling ahead of Brad, who was on a more focused mission to unstick his rope from the bush.

Moments later, while Gino and Juan were roughly 250 feet above Brad and Aiden, a terrible, bone-chilling scream from hell unfurled, followed shortly after by two thuds—the sounds of both bodies impacting the Quinta de Santa Graciela ledge below. It is worth noting, according to the Ticos, one of the two thuds was distinctly louder and later than the other, affirming the notion that one of them had fallen much further than the other (roughly thirty feet, as opposed to ten).

Right about here, however, accounts from the Costa Ricans separate, if only a little. Gino heard the scream and had time to look down before disaster struck completely. Juan's account begins just a few seconds behind that. Gino claims to have seen Brad clinging onto the wall in a fight for his life, just moments after the scream occurred, before losing his grip and falling to the Santa Graciela ledge below, a ledge Aiden had already fallen to. Juan can only confirm that he saw Brad hit the ledge and roll over the brink. He didn't see Brad hanging in desperate circumstance from the wall as Gino had. But, more importantly, in both Juan and Gino's memory, Brad was the last to fall, not the first. For them, Brad's fall was the result of the system failing, and not the cause of it. In Juan's memory as well, Brad was still in that system when he fell. Juan claims to seeing Brad still attached to his blue rope via his Gri-Gri when he made impact on the Santa Graciela ledge. Though neither of them witnessed Aiden falling first, the default of their testimony regarding Brad implies that was the case.

In the community I call home, death is not unfamiliar. Our friend Ian, who was a part of that 2008 To-tock-ah-noo-lah team that booted Brad, tragically lost his own life in 2015 in the remote reaches of Turkey in a BASE-jumping accident. There were scores of eyewitnesses, including those I would call dear friends, and somehow even then the media got it wrong. Accounts of what happened, how it happened, and even what he was doing while in Turkey were "telephoned-gamed" into oblivion via the internet, social media, you name it. All of that to say, I understand, especially in the aftermath of a catastrophic event, facts, for whatever reason, slip between the details.

I'm not sure who put out the first press release or who nabbed the first interview, especially with Aiden, in the aftermath. But within days, a story had percolated. Even as early as a day after the fall, on November 28, 2019, *Outside Magazine*'s online branch had run an article giving a summary, and had quoted and sourced interviews directly from Aiden, with an official accounting of events—a story that ran counter to what the other two eyewitnesses, Juan and Gino, attested.

I'm not in the business of judging anybody's journalism, period. But, one can spot holes in the current public narrative without looking too hard. And, before anything further is stated, please understand I am not claiming to remotely know, truly, what on earth occurred, but I do believe that for Brad's legacy, at the very least, we ought to consider what two other gentlemen have said they saw that day. A look at the sequence of events that afternoon, as told by the two Costa Ricans, is meant to be less of a true-crime tangent as it is a simple matter of asking complete questions.

Facts or not, many swallowed the narrative that Brad rappelled off his own rope with a certain ironic ease—at least it seemed true to his reputation. Silently, in most hearts, it just made sense.

Others went further still, online and in the comments of news feeds, suggesting he had it coming. Part of this, regrettably, seems to branch from the danger-prone *Safety Third* caricature he carried. The truth was Brad, when not guiding or climbing with loved ones, was not a consistently safe climber. On the spectrum, relative to most, he took huge risks. He and Jim Reynolds parted ways exactly because of that. Other people in the community, similarly, either never climbed with him, or tapered off their climbing with him precisely for that reason. But that he was not safe does not make him ours to judge; it does not damn him a halfwit; it does not endow our unchecked acceptance of events. What's clear from those who were close to him in his final year is that he wanted to be—and was evolving into—a safer climber, at least at times.

According to Aiden, as quoted in the *Outside* online interview, he and Brad had tried to rappel from the top of the sixth pitch down to the Santa Graciela ledge. By his accounts, it was only fifty feet. There, they hastily cast the rope ends down, with Brad's end getting stuck in some brush and Aiden's side laying true, easily down to the ledge. According to Aiden, they both sped off, Brad first, down this fifty-foot, mini-rappel, when Brad accidentally rappelled off of his end, which was quite a bit shorter than expected. Further, according to Aiden's interview, they both fell about twenty feet, both impacting the sizeable ledge, where Brad, subsequently, continued to fall further.

Problems with this testimony are two-fold.

First, the distance of pitch six on Sendero Luminoso is not fifty feet. By all accounts, it is a ninety-foot pitch—a fact that appeals against the credibility of the accepted testimony.

Second, the real-life application of events, as told, would mean some spotty arithmetic. If, per Aiden's interview, they only needed to rappel fifty feet, and, when Brad fell through the system, they each fell roughly twenty feet down to the ledge, this would, by definition, mean that Brad's end of the line was literally only thirty feet long. I can swear to you now, even in the dark, (though it was not dark at the time of their rappel) with no headlamp, no climber on Earth would cast a thirty-foot coil of rope down his end of the rappel and not notice it was egregiously short of length. There is no possible way Brad, even at his most distracted, could've cast only thirty feet of rope down a fifty-foot rappel—a rappel which doesn't exist on that route. The most important part of this critique is that it does not rely on anybody else's accounts of the day; it, by definition, cannot sustain itself.

The remaining critiques of events do hinge on others' accounts, and thus become subject to thought and counterpoint. But, if reasonable doubt is the aim, my belief is they do serve their purposes. Firstly, on credibility, Gino and Juan were clear-headed. Gino had taken a hit of pot on the ledge at the fifth pitch earlier that afternoon, but it had been hours since then. Juan had not indulged. For me, that's reasonably clear-minded. Additionally, neither, as best I can tell, have any incentive to share their version of events, other than the fact that they believe it is what they both witnessed. They do not benefit from our adoption of their events, financially or emotionally. They were not cast aside by anyone and are not in need of any redemption. In fact, they are heroes either way. It was, after all, Juan and Gino who rescued Aiden off that ledge and rappelled him safely down to Earth. It was they who comforted him, who gave him water, food, and clothing as he sat shivering in despair.

According to Gino and Juan, Brad and Aiden were rappelling from the top of pitch seven. The mathematics already presented earlier sustain the idea. The distance between Santa Graciela and the top of pitch seven is roughly 160 feet. When a plumb line of rope is thrown down, bypassing the zigzag of the bolts, that length is closer to 150 feet. Brad's eighty-meter (estimated 263-foot) rope, when divided in two (for rappelling) would have covered approximately 131 feet on each end. Add in another meter or two of rope-stretch (the effect of the climber's weight on the line while rappelling), and the mathematical estimates begin sounding similar to the accounts provided by the Costa Ricans. In addition, Gino and Juan both attest to hearing two separate thuds of impact, after the scream, supporting the notion that one of them fell further than the other.

In the Costa Ricans' interpretation, Aiden fell through the system first. The mathematics of their account would suggest that his end of the rope was ten to fifteen feet short of the ledge, with Brad's being closer to thirty feet shy. From Gino's account, after that initial scream—what he believes was Aiden falling out of the system (by lowering out of it with his ATC)—Brad was roughly twenty to twenty-five feet above the ledge, struggling to hang on before he fell. Juan, for his account, cannot confirm this entirely, as by the time he looked down, Brad was already falling to the ledge. Juan does believe it accurate, though, agreeable to what he saw just a split second later. Juan describes that when he did see Brad, he was already falling, and, in his estimation, that fall was at least twenty feet. Juan maintains that he saw Brad make impact with the ledge, and, when he made that impact, he was still in the system. Only when he rolled off the ledge, slowly, did Brad's rope pass through his Gri-Gri, unchecked.

Here, in this detail, is where anyone looking outside-in will question the rationale. We are told, after all, that Gri-Gris are auto-locking. The notion that Brad would have fallen down that cliff and not taken the rope with him, if he was still attached to it when Aiden (hypothetically) fell, challenges us. It's the biggest leap one would have to make to adopt the viewpoint. Gino and Juan are the first to admit they don't really get it, either. It's counterintuitive, but no more so than Aiden's narrative.

Personally, just in my experience, I've found that anything less than a 9.2 mm rope can escape the Gri-Gri's locking system without much trouble. According to the manufacturer's website, anything below 9.4 mm diameter will take the device's efficacy from what they rate at three stars down to two. Anything below 8.9 mm is strictly incompatible. They also warn that even when a rope's diameter is within range of compatibility, "The compatibility between the Gri-Gri and the rope used is dependent on more than just the diameter. The ropes texture, sheath treatments [...] the state of wear [...] play an important role in the performance of your Gri-Gri, in belaying, and also in descending." There's a reason we're instructed by Petzl to keep a brake hand on at all times, in case exactly that happens. If what the Costa Ricans say is true, I could see it as at least possible, even if unlikely, that Brad's Gri-Gri may have not engaged as he took his final fall. If Aiden fell first—as the Costa Rican suggest—Brad would have been near the end of his side of the line already. It's not unrealistic to think he may have only had ten to fifteen feet of rope, perhaps even less, left on his end. A distance short enough that if Brad fell to Santa Graciela the way the Costa Ricans said he did, if he rolled slowly over the brink, not at terminal velocity but at more of a frozen skid, it's not unreasonable to think his rope could've stuck to one of the many bushes or blocks on that ledge and slid out of the Gri-Gri.

The truth is, we'll never know. What we do know is that we have differing accounts. We're told, by the Costa Rican account, that by the time Gino and Juan came down to Aiden, meeting him at the Quinta de Santa Graciela ledge, Aiden had pulled the rope through the above anchors. According to the Ticos, Aiden was out of the system, having disengaged his ATC device and coiled the rope in a corner. He wasn't even in the same spot he had impacted the ledge in the first place. As goes forensics, the scene had changed, so there was no way to confirm or deny either scenario.

Aiden's account also said that he was using a prusik back-up for his rappels, but, as mentioned earlier, Juan and Gino saw it otherwise. They can confirm this because when they got to the ledge and rescued him, they gave him their own prusik set-up, with an actual cordelette, rather than a Dyneema sling, precisely because he didn't have one. When they made it to ground level and were all pulled in different directions by the local authorities and the triage response units, Aiden actually walked off with their gear still on his harness—gear they can prove was theirs for the markings on it. They have contacts and eyewitnesses who can confirm that two days later, Juan and Gino reconvened with Aiden at the campground just for the gear swap. Unfortunately, for the purposes of this narrative, we do not have Aiden's participation, nor his firsthand accounts. Attempts to establish communication with him were unsuccessful, leaving us only with what had already been said, sourced, and quoted by him.

It's important to state that while looking for clarity, we are not looking for blame. What occurred that day was unthinkable, appalling, impossible to bear. There are no villains, none of this is black and white, dualistic, or conclusive. It doesn't matter, to me, who rappelled through the line first. Both were guilty of gross oversight in the management of their safety; both made mistakes.

There are, perhaps, at least two lenses to reconsider the day's events. The first is the most fundamental. That is the macro-level lens, in which both men were equally responsible for the results of the day. This is the place where responsibility, blame, or any accounting of the day is shared. It is on Brad and Aiden both that tragedy took place. The other lens, a more microscopic, focused view, is one we employ to seek clarity on the details. It is not used to dispense blame, or guilt, though it may be where we discover something akin to causation. It is where the truth lies, and it is where any possible manipulation of truth will dwell also.

If what the Costa Ricans say is true, and events went against the accepted narrative, I would not use that as evidence against the character of the minority opinion—in this case, Aiden. Were the circumstance put on me, were such tragedy found while I was on a rope with a partner, let alone one who was beloved the world over as Brad was, I would not be surprised to find myself divided as my instincts battled for self-preservation. I could easily relate to a character who, in such pain and confusion, would generate a testimony that makes sense to their own mind. Professionals in mental health and trauma have for years told us that, in spite of any good and strong character we may have, our brains will disavow us the truth if doing so serves us through the trauma in moments of radical, unfathomable pain. I'm not saying that anyone deliberately lied, but I can understand, very easily, very humanly, why a person might.

However it happened, it did happen. Both men fell and hit that ledge that fateful afternoon, but only one would survive. Shortly, almost instantaneously after impact on the Quinta de Santa Graciela ledge, Brad Gobright—beautiful soul, majestic kid, pure-hearted, inimitable powerhouse of a climber and gentle son, brother, and lover—rolled with his momentum off the ledge and fell, by the hand of gravity, the force he'd disobeyed so many times, down the remaining roughly 650 feet of the Sendero Luminoso into a jagged corridor and gulley. His blue Gramicci shirt, a last vestige of his beautiful aura, surrendered to the abyss which surrounded it, and he fell deeply, irreversibly, into the next frame. Sounds quieter, emptier, and at once sharper than anything the Costa Ricans had ever known filled the north face in a hallowed, desperate swirl of loss. As for Juan's shamanic interpretation, that mountain, the high shield known as El Toro, and the whole of the skies and their baleful clouds, darkened into an indominable squall. Brad Gobright, the kid who crawled out of the womb eight weeks premature only to brighten the world by the most unlikely course, had died. Even the mountains mourned.

More than 1,400 miles away, in Orange, California, it was the day before Thanksgiving. At the Gobright home, food was being prepped, boxes were being checked; it was, by all appearances, not the kind of day you'll never forget. Having not heard any word from Brad in the past few days, since his arrival in Mexico, did not worry his parents. That much was common; he wasn't the type to phone in with daily updates. In addition, knowing he was in the fold of the Orange County gang, whose human-sized ambitions—as goes climbing goals—would have kept Brad on a leash, eased Pamela's tendencies toward motherly concern. She just hadn't ever thought he'd end up in any form of real danger, let alone utter devastation out there.

Within moments of Brad's death, however, the hard facts of life were on a direct collision course with Pamela, Jim, and his sister Jill. The complete shattering of their delicate human hearts was inevitable. Even worse, it was coming in fully on a blind side. There was simply no preparation for the deepest pains of their lives.

On the wall, even before rappelling down to rescue Aiden, Gino and Juan called their friend, local guide, and search and rescue point-woman, Carla, who has had the dubious luxury of heading more than one body recovery in the Potrero. Carla called the local authorities, which prompted local news channels, the military, and anyone in authority or with curiosity and a smartphone to stream in, *ad nauseam*. By now, word had gotten around at the base of the wall, which meant it had also spread further—to the whole of the campgrounds within in minutes. By the time Gino, Juan, and Aiden were at the base, the news had caught fire.

Devastated, devoid of all hope, Julie had the impossible task of breaking the news to Jim and Pamela. When a phone call didn't go through, she found the nearest community member in Orange County, a friend and kind spirit, Matt, who absorbed the tragic news while driving full-speed to the Gobright residence. Matt had the equally unthinkable task of giving the worst news imaginable to a pair of honest, kind, untroubled parents. But the news was spreading, and for the pure insistence that they hear it from something like a direct source, Matt kept foot to pedal while Julie stayed on the line, until arriving at their home. It was 7:30 p.m. on the dot.

Pamela answered Matt's knock at the front door, eyes unsure, until Matt's face broke in a swell of uncontainable emotion. Everything, every cell, every ounce, every functional, waking part of Pamela's being, her entire life force, separated from itself by the working of a pain so deep, so fucking unspeakable, that it transcended these three perceived dimensions we call our mortal coil. Pamela wept. And she did so from a place deeper than words will ever touch.

Jim came to her side, overwhelmed so much by shock that even grief could not find a means for expression. Jim's pain was so severe it couldn't even be expressed. Not because it wasn't there, but because it was orders of magnitude more profound than any outward display, any word, any tears, even any anger, could possibly equivocate.

As parents, however, Jim and Pamela learned long ago that their lives were about more than just themselves. Brad's loving, preternaturally joyful sister, Jill, was at a house party up in wine country, and Pamela and Jim needed to get the news to her before anyone else did. They called Jill, who walked out of the crowded party to a small tree outside, and then told her to sit. The words did not want to come out of Pamela's mouth, nor did Jill ever think she would have to bear them. But on the helpless, other side of that eternal, pregnant pause, it was there, it could not be denied.

The truth, with its piercing, merciless decree, had been spoken. An unfathomable ordinance, detonating across the plains of such delicate, innocent hearts.

Truth is, no third-person narration will ever remotely touch on the agony, emptiness, or soul-crushing despair that the Gobright family endured that day. Pamela and Jim told Jill to find her long-time partner and to call back when they were on the road together, heading home. Instead, Jill crumbled, shattered. Paralyzed into oblivion, Brad's sister wept on the floor just outside the vibrant halls of a crowded holiday party for the next ten minutes, alone, until her partner found her at last, having heard the news from the rumblings of everybody's smartphones. The tiny, intimate window for the family had passed.

Word from social media, including from Alex Honnold's heartfelt but wide-reaching post, had gotten out. From Mexico to Madagascar, from the halls of a crowded house party in Sonoma to the entire phone book in Jim and Pamela's church, the news had spread. Even 1,000 miles off the coast of California, on a remote sea vessel, Brad's long-time mentor and friend, the To-tock-ah-noo-lah cameraman himself, Tom Evans, sank into a cloistered depression. A newsfeed from the BBC had come in over the signals, and with it, the details of Brad's death.

Before the first wave of tears could even dry, the Gobrights' loss was public item number one. It was everywhere. Pamela and Jim's phones rang, irrespective of sleeping hours or common decency, irrespective of their need for space and privacy, for the next week straight. A sad, surely unintended side effect of the social media and news media web that we have all spun. Within hours, Jill was on her way to Southern California, and shortly thereafter, the Gobrights were en route to Mexico.

Thanksgiving Day, 2019 was spent in desperation. Brad's death was conflated into the news cycle so ubiquitously that neither Jim, Pamela, nor Jill could string together coherent thoughts on their pain without being interrupted by continuous phone calls. Family, with all their best intentions, and community folk were a part of the inquisition, too. It wasn't just newscasters. To quell at least a part of this frenzy, Pamela started a group chat, some forty to fifty members strong, between friends and family, where she gave status updates as she received them. Down in Mexico, that morning, they were just getting the first recovery missions underway.

By evening, plans had been made, the State Department had been called, Julie had corralled a team of translators and facilitators down in Nuevo Leon, and tickets were booked. On Friday morning, on board the first plane out of the gates, the Gobrights flew to Monterrey, Mexico, into the heart of darkness. An ominous mission, to face death square on its own canvas, and to find the ghost of their dear son and brother, Brad, lay before them.

At the arrival queue, heartbroken, Julie waited with her team of locals for Jim, Pamela, and Jill to touch down on the tarmac. Moments later, walking past the baggage claim and customs, the Gobrights stepped into Mexico feeling the thick, humid waft of smog and sub-tropical air, heavy as the pain they carried. All together at last, words were few. Julie broke in despair, still unsure of the accounts of what had happened, which left her assured only that in some tragic twist of fate, Brad's death was ultimately charged to her ledger. Of course, without a doubt, that is not—and was not—the case. But Julie's great challenge was, and would be for years to come, to understand that truth and to disassociate her pain from her guilt. A long and frightful journey of the heart. On that day, though, the journey was impossible to even begin. She provided the Gobrights with every possible assistance, lodging, food, transport, communications with the bureaucrats, anything and everything—a testament to her kind heart and her courage for simply being there.

Sadly, much of the Gobrights' stay in Mexico was a convoluted fog of bureaucratic red-tape and shady, back-end deals. They barely had time to grieve. It's not Ahwahne, but the Potrero Chico does have its own ornate beauty—a beauty that Pamela and Jill would have longed to connect with more for pure resonance to Brad's spirit, were they not so inundated with logistical clusterfucks. In Mexico, things operate differently. But, it wasn't just with the Mexican authorities that the workflow to get Brad home was interrupted; according to the family, the U.S. State Department was not of great assistance, either.

After the accident, Brad's body needed to be rescued and then identified. After transport from the hospital to the morgue, his remains needed to be identified again, by the parents, and a DNA test was also requisite from Jim and Pamela, along with proof of birth and citizenship. Once identified, transport and transport fees needed to be squared through the morgue and the government, at which point crossover logistics needed to be arranged with the U.S. State Department. Perhaps to no surprise, not a step was passed in this flowsheet without a middleman of some kind.

Because Brad's body had been recovered on Thursday before the family had arrived, Julie was the one charged with the first identification of Brad's remains. Still reeling, Julie rejected the idea, fundamentally considering herself unable to walk into a room and see the physical wreckage. Heart fractured, though, she understood the necessity of it and courageously obliged— knowing full well that seeing Brad would only further her own pain and scarring. Brad's body was so corporeally damaged that, in general terms, he was not recognizable. But for his gear and for his blue shirt, Julie was assured, her dear friend was now at rest.

By the time the Gobrights arrived a day later, Brad's body was already at the morgue. Julie had put them together with a trusted driver, long-time friend Joe-Bert Guadarrama, a local climber and gentle spirit who, in the words of Pamela, only ever had stars in his eyes for Brad. Joe-Bert very caringly guided the Gobrights for the next two days across floods of traffic in the city of Monterrey, to the Potrero, and everywhere in between.

On Saturday, after having spent hours bouncing between offices and telephones with the government, Pamela and Jim were required to take a DNA test to confirm their position as parents before Brad could be signed away. His body needed to be identified, once again, by someone in the family this time. But, too terribly pained, none were able. Joe-Bert, with his kindness extended, offered to do so in their place. After confirming it was Brad's remains at the morgue, the family fell apart in another uncontrollable wave of grief. Being in the same building, the same room even, with their beloved, fallen son and brother, took light from their souls. In terms of steps to get Brad home, and for the helpless finality of it, they hoped the hardest part was over.

But the local office had other plans. Even though every step had been followed, the admins at the office insisted more fees needed to be paid.

"That's not the policy of this institution," Jim objected, incensed. "I'll call the police!"

To which a secretary snidely looked back and said, "And what will the police do for you here in Mexico, sir?"

Unequipped for such extortion, Pamela and Jim broke down in that office. Jim, long past the end of his rope, paced the building in a fit of rage. The office was asking for $1,500 with no guarantees that the transporters wouldn't also impose their own "off-record" fees for their services. After thirty minutes of argument, despair, and untenability, Pamela begged.

She walked straight up to the desk, emptied her wallet, which had a mere one hundred dollars, and cried for sympathy. "Can't you see the pain we are in, miss?" she cried. "Our son has been taken from us, we haven't eaten, we haven't slept, we haven't felt anything but pain for the last seventy-two hours, and we just want to take our son home. Please, for all that is human, take what I have and let us have our son!"

Joe-Bert, Jill, and others in attendance emptied their wallets on the desk a moment later, only adding up an additional fifty dollars, after which they sat, waiting. The gatekeeper at the desk collected the money, quietly said something to her co-workers in Spanish, and then stamped the paper. Onward, to the next step.

Of course, hyperbolically speaking, it wouldn't be Mexican bureaucracy if it wasn't consistent in its corruption. The transport servicers at the next step demanded excess payments, too. Unable to retrieve any further money from their accounts for having maxed them out already, the Gobrights were short on cash. No surprise, of course, these extortive payments were not accepting of debit or credit. Cash is king in cartels as much as anywhere else. No paper trails, after all. Baffled by the endless corruption, the Gobrights had no way out of that last pickle—that was until Joe-Bert, a caring example of true light in humanity, emptied his entire savings account on the Gobrights' behalf. A debt which, of course, the Gobrights wired back to him the moment they returned Stateside.

Finally, the Gobrights drove up the Potrero for a meeting with the locals—and with Juan, Gino, Julie, and Aiden—on the eve of their departure. It promised to be an emotional, dire affair, and, before jumping in, the family at last had a window to walk into the Potrero itself. Brad's body may have been committed to the process of transport, but his spirit was very much still in that sacred canyon. The weather was just beginning to clear from the same storm systems that rolled in the day Brad fell, and light and skies shifted into something deeply personal, illuminating, heart-breaking. The Gobrights walked into the canyon and, for the mere twenty minutes afforded to them before their meeting began, opened themselves and their pain to the force of nature around them. Pain and light and fear and grace and despair, all in a transcendent, skin-chilling oscillation of waves, pierced their hearts as clouds and skies and light beams refracted from the high pillars of the Potrero into the flooded irises of their tearful eyes. So little was spoken; so little could be.

"Some lights just shine too bright," Pamela said to Jill as they unclenched a hug that had overtaken them. "Some lights are just too pure."

Jill agreed between her tears and involuntary spells of grief. Together, the family stood heart to heart, hand in hand, having gathered all they could from the force of life around them, from the presence of Brad beside them. Unfathomably, they attended to the task of forward motion, simply by placing one foot in front of the other, together.

Between the conflicting narratives and the volcanic swell of grief, often expressed in crosstalk and conflagratory anger, the meeting that night was, perhaps, as or even more painful than any step the family had been forced to take. What happened exactly and how long the conversation carried in the end, those details will remain privy only to those involved. Words were not kind, spirits were trembling, doubt and fear and guilt and loss swirled across people, narratives, scenarios, and character types. At one point, with Jim having left the room enraged, with Jill broken, with the Costa Ricans flummoxed by opposite accounts, Julie in despair for a lack of coherent narratives, and Aiden tethering between the defense of his character as a natural scapegoat and the defense of events as he saw them, Pamela realized the impossibility of it all. For everyone's sake, she'd have to accept that the truth of what happened would have to fall secondary to the truth that Brad was gone. Whatever the events, however that rappel ended in the death of her son, constitutionally, she was going to have to accept the finality of it, and, perhaps, the mystery of it, too.

With the meeting at its most fractured impasse, Pamela stood up, looked over to Aiden, and gracefully let go.

"I want you to know that for whatever was said here tonight, and for whatever it was that really happened, for the things that only you and Brad will ever know, I do not blame you. If there is any guilt you carry, for whatever reason you carry it, I want you to know that I do not wish it upon you. For any and all pain in this, Aiden, I, we, forgive you. So be free. And if you find that you cannot be free of this, if you find you carry anything, for whatever reason, within, I just want you to know that my prayer for you is that you find a way to forgive yourself, too. I want you to know that that is what we hope for you."

With her unearthly grace, Pamela took Jill's hand into her own, wiped away her tears, and walked out of the room. Outside, Jill and Pamela found Jim, and soon they piled into Joe-Bert's car to return to their hotel room. The next morning, with all arrangements in accord, the Gobrights said goodbye to Mexico, to Julie, who they thanked profusely, and to Joe-Bert, who they called their "angel" in it all. Joe-Bert stayed true to the commitment he made to the family and drove alongside the transport vehicle that afternoon, and the next day, following it and Brad's remains all the way to the border, where Brad was put in the hands of the U.S. State Department, and, finally, carried home.

Julie awoke the next morning worse than she'd felt all week. The Gobrights had left for home, and Brad was assuredly in transport. But in the Potrero she stayed. There were remaining loose ends to tie off and, after all the recent efforts, people to pay. What was supposed to be a vacation for Julie, of all things, had become one of her greatest traumas in a life already flush with darkened trials. It's one thing to pick up the pieces of our damaged, scattered selves after a seminal event, with the stroke of time, or spiritual practice, or by the hand of community. It's another thing entirely to survive the immediate aftershocks before the wounds have dried. Feeling alone now that the Gobrights and the media circus had mostly skipped town, there was a haunting quiet. She was, after all, still in the emotional epicenter, still in the Potrero. A place, with all its wounds and brittle glass, where even spirits bled.

Julie was devastated. Fundamentally, she needed hope. Her thoughts returned incessantly to Brad, her dear friend. His kindness, his spirit, his vulnerability about his fears that he shared just a few days earlier at the anchors of their climb together—it all rushed back.

Thoughts of his smile and his deep blue eyes.

Thoughts of his sincerity.

Thoughts of his ambition.

Thoughts of his lifeless body.

She couldn't shake it.

More than anything, that image, what she'd been forced to see when she identified the body—that poor, lost living being—recurred. As if an addict obsessed by thoughts of a vice they simply, with all willpower, could not shake, Julie was tormented. With every blink of her eyes, there it was. There he was.

Julie needed something, *anything* else. The morass she was in was too thick to survive otherwise. Staving off a complete psychological breakdown, with her friend Rojo, a local route developer, she made a determined call: she would hike up to the base of Sendero Luminoso on a quest to find something of Brad's spirit and a modicum of peace.

And that, to her surprise, is when the impossible happened.

Julie recalls walking up to the base of the climb, Sendero Luminoso, so burdened by pain and physical depravity (she had not eaten or slept soundly in days) that each step required a strength she hardly knew she could access. On a fair day, it would take maybe thirty to forty minutes of labor and some third- and fourth-class scrambling to reach the base. That Sunday, it took that much time to progress just halfway. Finally, near the base, where the local authorities had still taped off the area as a suspected crime scene, they stopped. Overwhelmed, Julie sat and began to cry, and, in a slow crescendo, cried more.

Even though she wanted to forge further, Rojo encouraged her to stay exactly where she was. Together, they stayed, just beside the base of the Sendero, while Julie unwound in her tears. Time passed, and with it, the wave of grief, until, quietly, she picked her head up, looked around, and found a surprising clarity.

"This was something I was completely unprepared for," she later shared. "It was just so peaceful, so quiet. It was such a different world up there at the base."

Julie's heart began to open.

"And I looked up at Rojo, and I just said, 'My God, it's so beautiful, and serene, and, I just feel like this is exactly where I'm supposed to be.'"

Rojo sat beside Julie, both of them tuning in to a new sense of perception where, as Julie describes, "We just listened, clearly, to the chirping of birds and the sound of the wind through the trees. And it was suddenly so overwhelming. This force, this presence of life and awareness. It was just so undeniable."

Julie's mind, the embers of the rational self, swung from clarity to confusion. At the precipice of revelation, she also questioned its viability.

"I'm just not that type of person, you know," she began,

sharing her suspicions. "I live a rational life, and I don't follow my horoscope, I don't believe much in big signs or symbols, or at least I didn't then."

Julie looked up, eyes fascinated by the glorious wall above her, and lost any vestige of self-composure. Unwound, held, cradled by a new awareness, by what we'll call the sweet embrace of life, Julie submitted herself to that moment, trusting it could heal; trusting it was designed to.

"My goodness, I remember thinking. It's just so incredible up there. You can see the wall. This entire beautiful wall. And the sun is shining on it, and it's wrapped in this angelic, beautiful light. And I remember looking up at the climb and thinking of Brad, and how much he and that wall had in common. And right there, in that exact moment, I swear to God, this giant, bright blue butterfly just swirls around me. After me, it moves to Rojo. And this thing just starts flirting with us, encircling us, and I just looked over to Rojo and said, 'This is just so perfect. It's the most beautiful blue I've ever seen in my life.'"

Julie's heart, at first unwound, had now melted. Fully connected, her eyes awakened. What flew in front of her was, by all accounts, a rare *Morpho peleides*: a blue-morpho butterfly. Native to the tropics, from Mexico to the northern reaches of South America, they are large, fist-sized, regal characters who dazzle by their mythic, vivid, iridescent blue wings.

"After a moment, it landed right in front of us on a branch, like, right there, face to face. It looked me dead in the eye, slowly flapping its wings, completely engaging with me. It was not threatened, it was not scared. It was just there, for minutes at least, dwelling with us. I looked over to Rojo, still not connecting the dots, and just said, 'I feel like Brad is with me right now. I don't know. I can't explain it. I just have this overpowering rush, this crazy feeling.' I looked over to the butterfly, peaceful, perfect, and it's just right there, looking me in the eye, still sitting with us, and I was so captivated. I said to Rojo, 'Have you ever seen something like this?' Rojo hadn't, of course. Monarchs, he'd seen, but not these butterflies, and not like this."

After another minute, feeling more peace than she'd ever known, Julie describes that she and the butterfly came to an understanding: the moment to move on had come. The butterfly slowly batted its wings one more time, then gracefully lifted with the breeze, submitting itself and its tender blue aura to the abyss that surrounded it, and moved deeply, vividly, irreversibly into the next frame.

Julie looked over to Rojo, "Do you think...? Could it have been...? It's just too weird, ironic, that feeling—I—I—I—I don't know."

Rojo smiled at her, took her in his arms, and Julie came to an inner submission. "It's just one of those things I can't explain, you know? It's either the strangest coincidence, or the workings of a higher power, some kind of higher source. I mean, I'm not one of those people, I never have been. But I can't deny what happened, even if I don't have language for the way it felt, in terms of how to describe those visceral, gut feelings. It was different than the five senses alone. But even truer."

Julie steadied herself, almost laughing with joy as she reflected on her conclusion.

"I know it was Brad. It was the Brad I always knew. Not the caricature, but the full, evolving version. It was him, there, gently saying, 'It's okay, Julie. I'll sit with you, right here, right now, until you feel okay. Until you see it's all okay.' I just know it was him."

The blue-morpho butterfly, while small, is among nature's most magnificent beasts. It is captivating and incandescent. Its blue is deep, regal, mesmerizing, and is so on the virtue of its millions of tiny, microscopic scales, which bend light in multiple directions. Ultimately, it is this bending of light coupled with its innate, azure tonicity that provides its remarkable, iridescent glow. For all its splendor, though, the blue morpho is often a hidden gem. It is not always visible to the naked eye. When not in flight, it blends into the world around it by the closing of its wings, where, on the underside of its magical scales, it is only colored brown to match the soil around it. On the ground, it gives off the look, rather falsely, rather keenly, that it is but another twig or pile of dust, as something inconsequential, or useless. Only when it flies do those wings open, and with them, the colors and the glory of life itself unfurl, just as they did in front of Julie.

As with much of life, it's up to us to choose what meaning we parse from it. The skeptical mind, even within ourselves, will always betray the heart. But the heart, that magical symbol at the core of our being, does not extinguish. It beats. The stuff of life, the indescribable, the sacred, the imperceptible, that is precisely the business of the heart. And, much like our physiological organ, this human heart we all carry is in the business of perfusion. It will, by automaticity, always be there, pulsing those messages of incomprehensible love and connection into our consciousness. Whether we believe in them or not, it continues. It always will. What we choose to do with it, and with the signals that we get in transmission, is our business alone. But from the life I've known, I can say: happy, contented are those who speak the language of the heart.

I wasn't there that day, so it's not my truth to know. But for context and creature considered, goddammit, if that wasn't Brad Gobright, I just don't know what else in the natural order would be.

WAKE

At 2:00 p.m. on January 25, 2020, at the St. John's Lutheran Church in old-town Orange, California, Brad's memorial took place. After a whirlwind two months since his passing, wherein regional climbing gyms and climbers out at campfires alike held small celebrations in his honor, this, the last gathering, was a testament. On the southwest corner of Almond Avenue and Center Street, up the stairs which lead into the hallowed, brick-laden cathedral, a massive number of friends and loved ones gathered. Within minutes, climbers from all over the world, old friends, and family packed the varnished, creaking wooden pews and aisles of the main cathedral, shuffling in by a quiet, constant murmur. Electrons buzzed between the hive mind amid the young, the old, the religious, the non-believing, the agnostic, the spiritual, the musical, and the manifold of other types of seekers. You could feel it, thicker than water—magical, powerful, emotional. All in attendance, the sanctuary of St. John's stood packed at capacity, with some 500 people facing the stage, each ready to honor their own version of Brad Gobright, however well or briefly they had ever known him.

Lynn Call, Brad's old Scout leader, father to his lifelong friend, Roger, eulogized Brad first with touching memories of the old Brad, that rambunctious, somewhat misfit, bright flame of energy who would crawl up trees all day long during camp. He remembered a quizzical but kind, ultimately pure-hearted kid who came from behind the oddsmakers polls in more ways than one, to remind all about the real stuff of life—of the wildness of our hearts and our very humanity. He told the mass of onlookers that for as long as he'd known him, through all his troubles, he knew that Brad was an endless fount of light. That he knew his arc was wide, that the hearts he touched were deep, that the spirits he moved were many. Lynn then looked at the crowd, amassed there in Brad's honor, the likes of the world's best climbers, lifelong friends, creatives, mothers, sisters, cousins, generations of outdoor folk and commoners alike, he looked across the sea of eyes and said simply, "I never realized just how far that light of his beamed."

On the big screen, a small vignette played next, a five-minute montage that friends had put together in his honor. Brad's trajectory, all the innocent and inglorious moments—from clean-cut in childhood to his most disheveled, at the peak of his dirtbagging—played in a series of slides, as literal projections beaming from his eternal highlight reel. One moment he was five, the next he was fifteen, a second later on top of the world. Frame by frame, his giant smile, his goofy grin, his fully saturated, dreamy blue eyes cut the room clean with a palpable, rich tone. Loss, love, pain, and joy all spun like cyclones in the ether, in the collective consciousness of the room, one person at a time, and yet, all at once. All five hundred having their own blossoming elation, longing, pain, promise, and joy. Each memory on the screen, and the personal flicker of each individual's own playback tape, spun across the room to the point where, no doubt, Brad's spirit filled the halls as sure as the Holy Spirit's did at the hour of Pentecost. The buzz of his familiar, brilliant aura was so manifest you could feel it tingle at the bottom of every breath.

After the film, longtime friend, adventure aficionado, and kindred spirit, Scott Bennett, extolled the room on the Brad he knew. Scott spoke softly and gently, weaving pain and pleasure into each narrative as he recalled his and Brad's climbing tenure. Soberly, with the delicate, bittersweet package of gratitude and deep, spiritual longing, Scott spoke of a Brad who he missed dearly, a Brad who he always struggled to keep up with. A Brad who pushed like no others could. A Brad whose operating system burned for so much more than the high peaks alone, for a sheer desire to extract the very juice out of life itself; a Brad who burned for the honesty, not just the accomplishment, that lies behind physical brokenness; a Brad who organized his entire life around the walls, for the passage they provided to scenes of ephemeral, intimate, beauty.

Taking the stage for the memorial sermon, the pastor looked out across the sea of faces. He looked out as a shepherd to his sheep. It did not matter the circumstance in life or the credo that each of these humans had come from—the reverend looked at that full-capacity crowd and sought to guide one and all through the most natural yet difficult function of life: death. He was warm, direct, and, most importantly, inspired. Not just with words, but inspired by the undeniable energy he could feel from the crowd.

Speaking to the collective, outdoor tribe, he laughed as he said, "I can tell that many of you have found beauty and revelation, perhaps more than the rest of us have, by your lives outside. I can tell that you have made a life's work of seeking truth, too."

The pastor cleared his throat, and then reflected, "Brad showed us much of that truth, and much of that beauty. He held it, he climbed toward it, he sought it, after all."

Reflecting on the words, my heart moved to the Brad I knew,

largely consistent with the one presented by others. I thought, as the pastor had, on the stuff beneath the stuff. I thought on the things underneath, or behind what he was known for—about the ripples that are cast by the stone which falls into the water.

I thought on the magic of what he was doing all those years, failing hard, living wild, deconstructing standard operating systems. I thought on how Brad always confounded every system he walked into. How he challenged everything we inherit. Not by rebellious, petulant decree, but by a simple honesty. By staying true. I thought on his sublime foolishness, like that of an Eastern monk or a spritely sage, which granted him joyful passage through so many heavyweight moments of life. I thought about how he made choices, how he had steered himself through life by an unshakeable core—by his untamed, pure heart.

Then, context of the institution considered, I thought to the sixth beatitude, as presented by Matthew. Blessed—happy, in the Latin derivative—are the pure of heart, it tells us, for they shall see God. That's what and who Brad found after all.

I'm certain that was Brad, The Visionary—like Doug Robinson had shared with us all, decades ago—and the Pure of Heart. I'm also certain that when the Carpenter, who gave the Sermon on the Mount, said God, he was not referring only to what people have now, in our twenty-first century, fashioned. God, in Zen, is an experience, more than all else; and She is a fair lady. Designer, architect, wooer of hearts, all present force of both grace and rapture. She is the painter behind the canvas; the rush of water through a glacier-formed, ageless Valley; the tease of the wind on locks of wafting grass; the faces of people in distant lands; and the eyes of unbridled human brokenness. She is the promise behind each sunset, the light at the core of our origin, and our final destination. The eternal creative, She is the force that brings it all together, that connects the dots, the one who can, and did, arrange such a magnanimous weave of five-hundred unlikely souls to the same stage, in the same place, in the same time.

Brad saw this God in his questing, even if he didn't talk much about it; it's why he kept coming back. Because of his pure heart, Brad knew more of the beautiful, more of the divine, than most. And he reflected Her back to us.

When I think of a pure heart, I think not of something cloistered, hidden from the world. I think rather to something exacting, expressive, true to its nature. Like the waterfalls in Ahwahne, raging, flowing, channeling earth systems and feeding life to the world around it. I think of things that are precisely operating to their natural order, to their design. I think of purity of heart as equal to singleness of heart. To will, to desire, but one thing. That's where I see Brad. Reaching up 5.14s with that compact frame of his, running it out over oceans of granite, that was all just the superficial. Behind it all, I see a boy turned young man, reaching for light as water reaches for all life.

After the ceremonies closed, the Gobrights invited the congregation to join in a celebratory banquet in the adjacent hall. Gently, people shuffled out of the pews, back into the bluebird light of day, before walking the short skirt to the banquet hall. Those who hadn't yet hugged or had handshakes gathered into small pockets; warmth radiated across all faces. People cried, others shared stories, more and more, each minute, they also laughed. More than anything, you got the feeling that everybody tapped into a deep, full gratitude, blessed to have known Brad.

Even Mason Earle, old pal of Brad and I both, fought through waves of disorientation to find for himself a familiar smile. The debilitating storm of symptoms brought on by his ME/CFS diagnosis, including barely being able to stand upright for more than a few minutes at a time and being stuck in a constricting neck brace, had little more than a superficial effect on him. Even through his physical and obvious emotional pain at the loss of his adopted brother, Mason carried a quiet, joyful awareness: we were all connected because of Brad. Sure, many had other shared threads, common weaves of life to bind them, but, fundamentally, that day, the beautiful, heavenly host of humans would have never gathered and shared the same space, nor the same rich gratitude, together, were it not for Brad.

That he had such power over us, even away from his physical corpus, put a grin on Mason's face I hadn't seen in years.

Inside the banquet hall, circles of conversation continued, surrounded by a maze of tables and tripods, flush with photos of Brad. He was everywhere. Around the perimeter, winding some hundred and fifty yards into the neighboring kitchen, a line of humans formed in single file, all for the opportunity to express their condolences and their colored, bright memories of Brad with his bereaved mother, father, and sister.

Titans of industry, at least the climbing industry, were there to remember him. Such as his dear friend and longtime partner, Alex Honnold. As were titans of the dirt, old friends who shook out the cobwebs and left the campgrounds, all for a chance to say farewell. Members of the climbing gyms, old faces, new faces, even the faces of those who were at the Potrero, were there.

Brad's two great loves were present, too. His first girlfriend, who had radically changed his sense of self, who had shown him the beauty of being fully, unconditionally accepted, was there, standing strong as best she could, remembering not just her most significant lover, but also her best friend. Brad's other longtime love, Kat, who had restored his lens on life by sharing the magic she found in places like Ahwahne, was grieving, celebrating, attending. She, the woman who encouraged him back home to rekindle a joyful life with his parents, and who had never asked anything of him but to shine as only he could, was there.

All of them, over the course of hours, would wait in that line just to hug and to hold Pamela and Jim and Jill. It would never bring Brad back, but for the family, within the aggregate of those hugs, those conversations, and those memories, inside each set of eyes that grieved and laughed that day, was an undercurrent. A mercurial but vivid reflection of their son. He was there, he was smiling back. A light from beyond the brink.

In the months after Brad passed, Pamela gathered rosebuds like her life depended on it. Thing is, they weren't hers as much as they were Brad's. For months, cards piled in from the postal service, emails stacked up, and phone calls from old friends and distant strangers filled her voicemail. Stories of Brad that she'd never heard from people she'd never met washed over her, almost always just at the right time, just when pain and despair and loneliness would seemingly boil over from the brink. Some moments, overwhelmed by it all, she just broke down. Not simply for the pain of it all, but for the providence of it, too. She just couldn't explain it. Each time she went darker in the night, into the soul, another card or a call would come her way.

Days were long, quiet, terribly unmoored. Heartbroken, she would walk, sometimes hours at a time, in the local canyons where oak trees sturdy the sloping, rolling hillsides, which brim with new shoots of wild grass each spring. Pondering how to float, as Brad always did, amid such a vacuum of loss, she bided her time. She stopped when fatigued, or when, for the emotional pain which stole her vital capacity, she was unable to breathe. There, alone at the tip of despair, each day for months she would read the cards, open the emails, replay the voicemails. Pamela made it her habit to face the void.

Ultimately, these days, which turned into months, sustained

her. They brought her hope and something like fortitude by way of faith. A fixing she would soon need, because, at least in the mystic interpretation of events, her pain would soon manifest into a new physical illness. Seemingly out of the blue, months later, Pamela was diagnosed with early-stage cancer.

Back on the backyard table where she and I first began our interviews, Pamela leads with the heart. It's been more than a year and a half since Brad passed, and three months since her cancer treatments came to a successful close. But looking at her, it's clear—she's still in it. Scars remain, as they should. There's nothing she's trying to cover up in how she presents herself emotionally, that much is obvious. She's real, direct, present. But she's also boundless.

The wind lifts, it reads the landscape and the trees of her backyard by braille, then it reads Pamela, free, unfurled grey hair and all. A plane hums above, catching a ray of sunset on its underbelly as it makes its approach toward the tarmac of the John Wayne Airport down the road, reminding us that journeys are continually being taken by all of us. It's the human condition.

Pamela smiles as she lifts her glass of Sauternes, a fitting dessert after her homemade mushroom risotto, and then leads my attention towards her and Jim's table-sized map of America. Highlighted across nearly twenty states, fifteen degrees of latitude, and the entire width of the country is their path. She and Jim are days from cycling across the States.

"I'm nervous about the passes." She smiles gingerly while pointing at the Cascades. "But, I also just can't wait to be under the sky for that many days and nights in a row."

Jim, the meticulous planner, smiles too with that coy, understated pride and excitement of his own. He sits up, engaged, and shares much of his endless machinations. He's timed it all to the day, the season, the moon, even the hours of road construction on the passes, which will allow them safer passage with less car traffic. He hasn't been the most expressive in the past year, not when discussing his dear son, understandably; but for a big adventure, for an invitation to life, he's out of his seat. A beautiful, inspirational thing to see. Both of them amaze me for their continuity. The spark of life could've been extinguished long ago from the impossible blow of Brad's passing, but looking at these two, I am taken. Yes, there's fracture; there are deep, cavernous divides of grief still circling in their hearts as much as on their faces, but there's also a demand for more. Pamela and Jim's embers still smolder bright, white light.

"I can tell you that Brad always told us how much he loved driving through and climbing in the Pacific Northwest. Especially Smith Rock," Pamela shares. "So, I'm quite thrilled to know we'll be connecting with him there on our path."

"Actually," Pamela points me toward the saddlebag which is mounted on the handlebars of her bike, "we'll be connecting with him everywhere."

Her fanny pack has a clear pocket oriented exactly in the position of a dashboard, and in that clear pocket is a photo of Brad. Smiling lovingly back at her. That image of him will serve as her guide. It is how and what she will navigate the journey from; it is where she'll look for indicators regarding her operating system; it's how she'll keep true.

Dessert and sunset finished, we clean up our plates and pack up for the evening. A new hope swirls about the room, about the empty halls of their house. I can tell that for all the ghosts of the past, slowly layers are being compiled. Life is moving still, and it's clear to me that Pamela and Jim have so much left to give. All of us can learn deeply by keeping them in our gaze, just as they've come to realize the same by keeping their gaze upon what life continues to present, rather than what it has reclaimed.

Jim and I share a last memory of Brad, laughing about a time they bonded over bird-hunting, and then we close with a measure of understanding. I thank him for his attention and involvement in all the difficult places I've asked him to go.

Pamela finishes her glass, face just gently blushed from the effect, and then smiles from the heart.

"Good luck, and trust in the process," she says. "It'll be fun knowing that, while we're out on our bikes, you'll be putting pages together. It'll be nice knowing that we've all got so much focus on Brad this summer."

I'm about to write a book about her dear son. Pamela is about to live wildly once more.

Pamela gives me the kind of loving look of assurance that I'm sure she gave Brad and Jill thousands of times before. Her eyes are kind, believing, hopeful. It's not just that she believes in my task, but, more immediately, she believes in hers. Having walked through fire without being burned, she radiates light.

We hug, the wind lifts once more, and the next day, her journey begins.

Over the course of her and Jim's ride, Pamela will face the world like never before. She'll grind her bike's gears down to their original molecules before giving in to her fatigue. She'll laugh, she'll cry, she'll push ever forward. She'll come to the blunt side of physical exhaustion, and there, in her brokenness, she'll even smile at it; she'll even be thankful for it. In her deepest moments of physical pain, Pamela will soon find she is not undone but rather made alive.

She and Jim will sleep in campgrounds and shared hostels, they'll meet hundreds of fellow wayfaring strangers—men, women, and other genders who have taken to the road on their own vision quest, for their own reasons—and they'll hold one another as they haven't in years. In those people, in those tiny towns, in those long hours, in the grandeur of the natural world, she'll see the face of God again. Because Pamela, for all her fire, has been refined. She, too, has found a purity of heart.

As a primary purpose, Pamela joyfully continues to be a mother for Jill and a wife for Jim. But she's also more. On that bike, she will be reminded that she is the wildling, the raptured heart, the seeker, the young girl who moved across the country for a new light and a new life. A human in search of the great and loving core of the universe. And, on that bike, exactly aware of her course in life and what she's been through, Pamela will soon be reminded that the plain facts of life are this: bright as she may be, she's only got so much time left to shine. A fact that does not cripple her, but frees her. It's what gives her that singleness of heart, that ability to will for only the simplest things. For Pamela, that is to love all in her orbit, without condition.

Brad would be proud of his parents; check that, I'm sure he is proud of his parents. I guess it depends on the lens you operate with. For my gut, though, we live in a spiritual universe, multi-verse, some-kind-of-verse, where energy and life force and sacred shit fly in eternal superhighways right under our noses, much like light waves, radio waves, and all the other things that we well know are there, all of the time, but which are not in our scope of senses to perceive. At some point, for me, life just affirmed this to a level of undeniable, unimpeachable truth. And, while not pushing anything on anyone else, I'd be dishonest to the core of my make-up if I painted it otherwise. I've no need to debate the lens, or attempt any proofs about these orientations of the spiritual suit. When I go deep to the inside space and seek acceptance of all that is, ontologically, and when I sit in lotus to observe the void, I just keep running into what I perceive to be fundamentals. More is mystery than is ever known on these things, anyway; and knowing, spiritually, is not a perfect likeness to its counterpart in human epistemology. Hopefully, that's qualification enough on the lens.

Safe to say, Brad would be, and is, proud of his folks. When they completed the *Nüümü Poyo* (John Muir Trail) back in 2017, he bragged for days just as he did after any of their impressive bike tours in the States and in Europe. In the midst of a global pandemic and a year of deep loss, of overwhelming uncertainty, to have picked up the shattered fragments of their dear hearts, together, and put foot to pedals just to recapture the sun upon their spirits, goddammit, that's the stuff of life! Real-world heroics.

Brad would also be—is also—grinning on his sister. Jill has worked her ass off recently, not just at her job but also on her interior life. Among other things, she's now a winemaker for a prestigious brand in Napa. Creatively, artistically, weaving molecules and earth systems into cohesion; from soil, to grape, to barrel, to the tasting room. She's riding the beam between the forces that cannot be controlled and the expressions that can. Understanding *Terroir* is, at this stage, her métier. And by that, I mean not only the vine's terroir, but also her own.

In 2017, during the *Safety Third* tour, Gramicci published thousands of posters, all from a shot of Brad on The Zodiac on his three-in-a-day push up To-tock-ah-noo-lah with Scott Bennett. In the photo, shot by his friend and Valley wonder-man, Cheyne Lempe, Brad is face-deep in one of the prime headwall cracks with an inaptly named "Pakistani death loop" of rope, hanging large, all the way into the abyss below him. It's the perfect image of both the glorious and the trudging nature of his quest. It's both ornate and blue-collar, much like Brad. He probably signed thousands of those posters, but one of the best of them sits above his sister's work desk at her office in Napa Valley. It's framed, of course, and it simply reads, *"To my sis, with love!"*

Jill's poster is not the first or last note he ever wrote to her, either. Brad's love for his sister was expressed across their lives. For another keepsake, Jill also has a letter in an old scrapbook that Brad wrote to her when he was sixteen, just as she turned thirteen, entering womanhood and junior high school. In it he writes, *I have known you all your life, and I think I know you better than anyone, except for mom and dad. I know you are really bright, and you can be the best at anything you want to be the best at. When you grow up, you are going to have your own business and be really good at what you do... I remember my first day of junior high, I knew I was going to hate it. I also hated being thirteen, but I know you will handle it just fine and do great in school. I remember when you were small... You're a teenager now and not some kid, sometimes it can stink but other times it will rule. But remember this whenever you feel sad, stressed, or pitiful. God, mom, dad, and I will always love you.*

I'm almost certain he'd say a version of the same thing to her if he could stand right beside her today. That, and he'd tell her just how proud he is of her.

For me, that note has a special, soft resonance. Behind his support for his sister, and his unconditional, positive regard, I see one shining fact in Brad's memo to Jill. In spite of that damned AMGA test he was so fearful of, from my point of view, it sure looks like Brad was guiding, years before even he realized it.

It's beautiful to think of how Brad would reflect on those he knew and loved as they carry on today, but it's also important to reflect on who he was for the rest of us. As a climber, for his accomplishments and general humility, he inspired the masses. That much goes without saying. In the eyes of his peers, he was decidedly a climber's climber, even an antihero.

On what made him cool, almost every person I interviewed simply said, *It was the fact that he wasn't.* He didn't try to be. He didn't need to be. That's what was so refreshing.

Brad was always and only himself. A riddling paradox of whim and deep intention, or, as best I can reduce it, a Zen Koan. Historically, the Koan is disruptive but not belligerent, awakening but not comfortable, cheeky but not nihilistic, counterintuitive but not absurd. Finding that recipe in a single moment is the work of the Zen master. Manifesting it as a character type—that is outright one of a kind.

As it has been told to me, the Koan is not just cryptic for its own sake, either. A proper Koan has four parameters. First, a good Koan is an experience before it is anything else; to be understood it must be had. Second, it is fundamentally beyond words; it is not enhanced by linguistic tilt. Third, the experience of the Koan must lead to the heart of the person; it is not qualified by the thinking mind. And lastly, a good Koan reveals the truth of nature as it is; there is always an awakening and a restoration of right relations within it.

When I step back, open my heart, and consider the broad strokes of paint on the canvas, it's hard not to see Brad as precisely that. At the least, he's my Koan.

Michael Kennedy, premiere climber, writer, father to our beloved Hayden Kennedy, and mentor to an entire generation of climbers, once spoke with me about Brad, about these character traits and these broad brushstrokes. Captivated by the lens and what it intonated, he reflected on others he'd known in his life, people often misinterpreted and likely of the same ilk. Having only met Brad once, Michael talked about how bright Brad's character suddenly appeared, how beautiful it was to decode his presentness, even his lack of guile, for the candor it demonstrated. He said it helped him "to see how unique Brad was, and to see how much we can learn when we're willing to strip away the filters."

For me, when I peel back those filters, I see three fundamental pillars in Brad's character. I'm fairly certain there's more, still undiscovered, but I'm assured that I'll learn those lessons from him when I'm ready. Because, as mentioned long back in the opening sequence, when Brad was free-soloing the Naked Edge in Eldorado Canyon, it is on us, not him, to find them. His experience in life was as complete as it could've been for him. Our experience of him, though, is only limited by the aperture we bring to it.

First and foremost, as I see it, Brad was an original.

On originality, as mentioned earlier in this charter, climbing legend, raconteur, and elder, John Long, once said, "A genius is a person most like themselves...It's an impossible task, really, to be entirely ourselves, with all our light and broken glass."

But then you look at Brad, blue-eyed, atop the Naked Edge; you see him lying in the To-tock-ah-noo-lah meadow, a shoot of grass in his mouth; rewind back and you see him in that make-believe submarine, starstruck by the magic of life at the age of six; you see that same look of wonder as he's up on The Rostrum for the umpteenth time, after another free-solo, looking out to the tip of To-tock-ah-noo-lah and the rest of Ahwahne just before leaving for home one last time. Curious, resplendent, carefree. No matter how fractured his heart was, no matter the pains or belittlements he endured, you see it.

Brad was a genius, an original, for being exactly himself, the rarest creature on Earth. Of which there is only ever one. The crux of life, as it were, for the rest of us, is his shining light.

You could say he struggled as much as any of us for becoming. Conceptually, it's a different path than being. Being, as I see it, is the antecedent. No use becoming much of anything if we aren't even sure if it suits our being. Becoming takes work, and there are largely no shortcuts about it. It requires action, undertaking, and an aggregate of events. Being, however, is all about the reduction.

On being, it's been said by many spiritual gurus across every long-standing culture that the path to being is not a process of addition, but subtraction. That's how we get to the heart of it. That's where Largo finds his genius, and that's where I find Brad.

Becoming is the task of effectively taking our being—our original state, our Zen mind, the Holy Spirit within us—and positioning it into the world around us for the benefit of others. It is more a matter of function than essence. You can become a parent, a plumber, a doctor, even a spiritual mentor. But you do not become who you already are. Your being, that essence behind the projected self, is the eternal spark. To return to it, to get to the *no-mind*, the beginner's mind, which is to say, the heart, you need only work life in reverse. That's why every spiritual tradition reminds us of the beauty of children. It's not for their ignorance they are heralded, it's for their understanding.

On being, Brad reminded us of the shit that matters, and the exact shit which doesn't. Effort matters. Beauty matters. Nature matters. We were damned fools for separating the notion of our being from nature in the first place. We are nature, of nature, in nature, from nature, lest we forget it. There is no separation, and the sooner we get that, the sooner we get to be original, too. Brad got it. But he didn't get it all alone; he got it from the elders.

It was in the pulse of his fingertips when he climbed Midnight Lightning, every one of the hundreds of times he did it. That's where he picked up the electrons Ron Kauk and the Miwok elders had left for him to find, just as it was in the fabric of the quartzite speckles of granite that he put his feet into, up high on the Too-tock-ah-noo-lah. That's where Chouinard and Frost had left the same messages.

Call it hyperbolic, but he got it from somewhere. And for how long now have both Kauk and Chouinard been sharing the same message? As climbers, look where we've come. We've gotten up the highest peaks, we've created featherweight carabiners and super-thin ropes, we've got stickier rubber and we've codified every experience, in every medium of the vertical pursuit, into some kind of grade and scale. But, asks our elders, Kauk, Chouinard, and Brad, are we better off than we were when it was all just about finding ourselves in nature? Have we gotten any closer or perhaps further from the core of it all by the trappings we've put on the table? Are we better served by the system we've submitted ourselves to? Or, at least from time to time, shall we not simply cast it all aside for a new experience in this life we think we know so well?

Brad was the ambassador of the new experience. He knew how to cast aside anything, including operating systems, which did not serve his core being. As for the rest of us, we were the fortunate ones, after all, for having been swept up in Brad's wake while he was out doing in life what so many of us couldn't, or wouldn't. And, again, I do not mean the superficial doings. What he did that many of us couldn't, or wouldn't, was to interface as often as possible with the original within himself.

Because of that approach, his greatest show of courage wasn't the runout on the rope, it was the runout of his life. He went to places people simply will not, to both find his being and to express himself to us in his becoming. No money in the bank, no backup plan, no redundancy in any of his machinations. That was the real show he was running, on the real stage of life. The only problem was our lack of sight in the first place. We were too busy looking at the sensational to see the subliminal.

Kat, one of Brad's great loves, reflected sincerely and with great care when I asked her about his resonance on her life. On his plight and his ability to draw his own course, she said,

"My brother [who lived with her] and I both admired his courage. You know, I think we all have a part of ourselves that wants to be a dirtbag, or to drop certain frameworks. We all want to quit our jobs and live in a boulder field, at least we want something like it, for what it represents. But we don't, because we don't have Brad's courageousness."

As she remembered him further, retelling story after story of their time together, sometimes laughing, often crying. Kat continued.

"Brad had a way of making life so clear for us, you know. He showed us what was important. He could restore the lightness of it, where so many of us get bogged down. And, he made us want to live life, completely. Like, just having him in our presence, just him being there, it revived a part of us that was just sitting there, wishing to exist. It was just such a privilege for us to have him in our lives. That he chose us, to be with us, to love us, sometimes I still can't believe it."

Brad's ability to tap into his natural state did not always come naturally, though. He got it from his own heroes, from the originals he kept company with. It just so happens that in his case, that could have been the sea anemone in Hanauma Bay as much as it could have been Steve Jobs. They both said the same thing, just by different means.

"Your time is limited," one of Brad's heroes said, "so don't waste it living someone else's life. Don't be trapped by dogma, which is living with the result of other people's thinking, don't let the noise of other's opinions drown out your own inner voice. And most important, have courage to follow your heart and intuition, they somehow already know what you truly want to become."

Could've been the sagely advice of a sea anemone, dancing to the water's current in an animated film, just as much as it could've been words directly from the co-founder of Apple and Pixar at a college graduation ceremony. Brad, better than most, could see the messages in more than words alone—he saw them in nature. Because of that, he kept his sources of inspiration close to protect that very originality that he so generously shared with us in his time on Earth.

In so doing, he was free. Not perhaps when society was trying to round his square peg into the cylindrical hole, but unto himself, accountable to himself, he was without compromise. That freedom to *be* is what led him to that lightness, to that unsullied flight about life, to that coveted, playful intuition.

No doubt we all crave that freedom. No doubt there are parts of ourselves that are also "wishing to exist." They—we—want nothing more than to be seen, often not just by society, but by our own selves.

Some of us fear our natural suiting; we spend our entire lives looking the other way. It's not always pretty or easy to come to terms with what lies inside. In a struggle to be heard and seen, our inner bearings may express themselves in a variety of misfires, and it is no small task to clear the wreckage of self gone awry. Especially over the course of a lifetime.

But whoever, whatever, is there, I assure you, it is good. You are good. For, as the *Dineh* (Navajo) suggest, just like the rest of us—the winged-people, the four-legged people, the insect people, the ocean people, and the human, five-fingered people—you are of nature. And that which is of nature is never without beauty, purpose, and light. Whatever it is, whatever it be, Brad reminds us that there is space and purpose for all expressions, for all beings, in this great and kind universe.

As for the Impossibility of Being, or pillar number two, I believe Brad Gobright showcased the miracle of life as few others do. For how unlikely was it that a kid born eight weeks premature, the size of a grapefruit, would ever make it to such great heights?

The Impossibility of Being, as premised earlier, is both a truth of the universe and a realization of the heart. It is the fullness that's present, though often unrecognized, at every moment of existence as conscious beings. The realization that so much of the here and now, for so many reasons could have—almost should have—been something other. It is the understanding that the odds were always greater for an alternative life to have happened, for another inevitability to have expressed, so much so that it startles us to the unlikelihood of the now. A now which, whatever the circumstance, is miraculous. Truth be told, the very fact of existence itself demonstrates its own incredibility.

From a physics point of view, there was nothing essential about existence or the universe. A big bang, a spark of life within the Hawking Shuttlecock, none of it needed to happen. Nothingness could very well have continued as nothingness, and no force would have stopped it from doing so, or even lamented the extinguished alternative. But here we all are.

What that implies about the sanctity of all of this shit, the good and surely even what we call the bad, is phenomenal. We are all walking miracles. Down to the single breath, the single cell, and every single one of the trillions upon trillions of agents in the biome, the virome, the kingdom, and the phylum.

Those who can hold that awareness, constitutionally, have the great byproduct in life to not only be in the stream, feeling the flow of that universe, but also to be of service to others. For it is in attending the present moment, eyes wide open to the great circuitry the universe is weaving, that we ourselves can conduct its pulse.

And, as mentioned, without this view in place, Brad's story, all of our stories, are only as poignant as the things which we have done, and not the reasons for which we did them.

Brad is exemplary of this because his story has endless data points where we can see it in action. There are so many, in fact, that it is impossible to calculate even a fraction of them.

But for a cursory look, consider. Just for Brad to have been born, Pamela had to move across the country, as did Jim. Jim likely would not have done so if his early years weren't stricken with loss in the nuclear family. Pamela, for so many reasons, also needed a new beginning. Jim had to go to that bar the night they met, which he easily could not have. Pamela, the same. Furthermore, Jim needed to invite the wrong date to his friend's wedding, then needed to invite Pamela to lunch to make up for it, and his mom needed to plant a seed of love at the picnic table while Jim played catch with the boys. Meanwhile, Pamela could have easily passed on that job, or, among the hundreds of candidates, she very easily could have never been selected for it. She very easily could've not walked the beach that one non-descript day, where her stepmother insisted that she leave a note under Jim's door.

For Brad to have met and climbed with Hayden, his dad Michael had to meet a young Julie, Hayden's mom, on the ski slopes, after his family immigrated from the Canadian side of the Ambassador Bridge. For he and Jim to have broken the record on The Nose, the old guard of Potter and Leary needed to come first. And the Stone Monkeys needed to be inspired by the Stone Masters, which means that guys like Rick Accomazzo and Richard Harrison and John Long needed to have a bastard upbringing in Upland, CA, which means Largo needed to be adopted in the first place. For those guys to move on rocks, John Salathe had to come from Switzerland with his forge, which means that emigration in the wake of WWII had to happen, as did the industrial revolution. The list goes on. For Brad to have met Mason Earle, Johann Sebastian Back and Antonio Vivaldi had to first walk this earth. For Brad to have met Alex Honnold, a great Polish migration needed to happen. For him to climb with Cedar Wright, guys like Copp and Dash needed to first come, and sadly also go. And, for Brad to have ever had a friendship-going-on-mentorship with veteran Tom Evans, the El Cap photographer first had to be reassigned from Vietnam to Memphis after the Reverend Martin Luther King Jr. took a bullet.

All unrelated, on the surface, but all true.

"You can't connect the dots looking forward. You can only connect them looking backward. You have to trust that the dots will somehow connect in your future...because believing that the dots WILL connect down the road will give you the confidence to follow your heart, even when it leads you off the well-worn path. And that will make all the difference."

Another quote from Brad's favorite speech by Jobs, reminding us that Brad did have his focus on the weave of life. He could see it connect, in my opinion, based on his character and the choices he made. Much like his originality, my hunch is that he gathered that insight from his craft. In touching eons of time, crystallized into rock form, often on his ungodly twenty-four-hour linkups up the Big Stone while completely under the sun, moon, and stars, Brad absorbed certain truths of the universe. One being that if you allow it to, the weave of life will always work in your favor.

With that awareness, Brad was granted his most uncanny character trait: the ability to tap into the present moment at a frequency greater than most. Because what on earth could be more fascinating than the present? The place where the dots intersect, the place where wisdom is revealed, the place where beauty is expressed—not reflected upon, but fully, intimately expressed.

Many in the interview process had differing opinions on Brad's capacity for safety in climbing. Not all agreed on the parameters of his risk profile, and not all found the shine of his life so obvious in the face of the danger he courted. Some would even say he didn't have the awareness I assume he did. But all agreed that what they'll carry of Brad long after they've replaced his cautionary tale with the next, inevitable one, is his striking presentness.

Watching Brad operate in the present was mesmerizing. Not just because you could see Brad in action, not only because you witnessed something like faith in action, but because you saw the universe in action, too. Brad's constant interface with the present showed us not only who he was, but also what the universe on the other side of that impregnable present was. And, as the mystics and indigenous hearts have long told us, that universe, the force which precedes life's impossibility, is kind.

Brad allows me—hopefully, allows us—to see life with all the preciousness it has to offer. He shows me that the beauty of our stories is not only that they happen, which is a miraculous feat unto itself, but that they do not happen only for us. Whether we climb To-tock-ah-noo-lah or spend our working hours on some godforsaken assembly line, we are not just rocks falling into water, after all. We are choreographed, intended instruments of the universe put into exact places at exact moments in time, if we so boldly allow ourselves to be, for a purpose. Our very existence is proof that good rises not only from fortunate circumstances but from the entire human experience. Our fractures, pains, and despairs included, we bleed through our human frailties, not only with blood but with endless light.

Brad didn't have to talk about that shit; he lived it. For me, that's cause enough to put the pin on his tail. Because, whenever The Impossibility of Being wells up within me; whenever that awareness and its subsequent gratitude bursts upon my consciousness in a euphoric, fell swoop; whenever I look around at all that is and am overcome by the sweet embrace of existence, I know, just for me, that part of my ability to find and hold that truth is because I first saw it in Brad Gobright. Less by the words he spoke as by the manner in which he lived.

On light, and how it bends, Brad showed me that it moves in relation to how you move toward it. He showed me that it's one thing to be born of the light, but to bend it, forward and backward through time, that's another thing entirely.

If that sounds a bit cryptic, what I mean is this: our light is not meant to go in one direction only. It is not meant to be ours alone. Much like rays through a prism or light through water vapor, which deliver us those most magical sights of nature, our beloved rainbows, our light is meant to go in more than one direction. It can take shape, it can take tone, color, even texture, all based on what that light moves toward and what it shines through. Of those directions, it is my belief that our light can move and bend both forward and backward in time. For as mystic as that might sound, it's all quite fundamental. Brad's truths always were.

On directionality, what I see of Brad's life is that every time he followed his heart, the universe also moved toward him. It enabled him to get there. In fact, it's likely more accurate to say that had Brad not taken any given step in the first place on faith, the place his foot landed upon would not have been there. It came precisely because he needed it.

At every step in his path, whether that was desperately floundering in elementary school or out on his own after closing his gas cap in 2008, it was there. His teacher in fifth grade, Mr. Zuidema, would have always been a decent man, but had Brad quit school, Brad would have never entered his life, nor would Mr. Zuidema have ever entered Brad's. Just as one moved, the other did also, somehow each toward the other. Remember, Mr. Zuidema left a corporate job because he wanted more meaning of life, and there, just when he needed that meaning, was Brad. Similarly, when poor in spirit and in cash on the road during those early days, had Brad not stuck with it, neither Mason Earle nor Scott Bennett would have been there for him. It was precisely in those movements, each heading toward their own center of direction, that Brad and Mason and Scott and Mr. Zuidema all moved toward each other. The light of all of their lives was magnified and cast further because they first moved toward the source.

So, when it comes to bending our light, I believe Brad demonstrates that when you move toward your purpose, the forces of existence move with you, toward you. They magnify your efforts. And, if done successively as Brad did, your shine will ultimately reflect not only to those around you but also to those behind and before you. It goes ahead of you, into all the lives you'll effect, just as it goes behind you, illuminating all the places you've been in order to arrive precisely where you are.

The reason I find beauty and comfort in this correlation is because, firstly, it is reassuring. Seeing life function this way in others' lives allows us permission to seek that function in our own. It provides us a passage to be. When we have seen light bounce and bend off another beside us, it lends faith, and even courageousness, to allow those parts of ourselves that are hoping to flourish to finally do so. Secondarily, the reason I choose to focus on this concept of our light and its many directions is that it relates me to the present, a place Brad so perfectly attended. I see from him that for my light—our light—to shine in countless directions and even to shine across the planes of time, I need—we need—only to remain present. For once again, it is in the present that we cast our beams, as it is in the present that we receive them.

That's what Brad demonstrated, for me. In all those times he was stuck, fixated on something, in all the moments he was willing to look the fool, in all the times he failed on a wall or tried for things that seemed far too ambitious, or when he simply went against so many standards of operations. In each situation, often in those which seemed the most outlandish, he was there, gathering light.

It was there when he laughed with Juan and Gino at the Santa Graciela ledge. It was there in his caring smile when he told his mom he loved her before his trip to Mexico. It was in his voice the last time he and Mason Earle spoke, when Brad called just to check on his illness and to see if in any way he could help. It was there at The Gun Club that evening when he and Alex Honnold paused for the last light in the Red Rock desert. It was in his eyes when he smiled at Kat while they floated down that Merced River, admiring bears and spires of granite in a way he'd never seen before. It was in the light of the moon when he and Jim Reynolds linked Waijau, Tis-se-ack, and To-tock-ah-noo-lah over the course of eighteen long hours and one remarkable night. Just as it was when he apologized to Christian Cattell for his short patience on the Salathe.

Brad shined his light, bent it, when he sat on the Manure Pile Buttress, drinking life to the lees in the lap and loving embrace of his first girlfriend. He found light each time he sat beside Tom Evans at the Yosemite Lodge Café for breakfast. Just as it was when he watched the sun weave its way across the canyons countless times in Boulder with his dear friend Cedar Wright.

It was there when he was lonely in the desert, as the South Six Shooter crept into the light of day, just above the morose, grey clouds of a weeklong storm. It was there when he captured photons from the sun, square into his irises, while up on the Monkey Face at Smith Rock. It was with him when he awoke in his frozen car, crying in quiet desperation, the day he saw school children in Boulder living so careless and free. It was there, bending, refracting, when he told his mom he would never know the pains and passions of true love. Just as it was when he cried for a whole weekend in his room after being booted from the To-tock-ah-noo-lah team in 2008.

Brad was with the light when he rode his BMX bike as a high schooler. It was there when he wrote his sister a loving note the day she turned thirteen. It was in him while he was at school, trying so unbelievably hard to just not fail, to make his parents proud. It was with him when he played make-believe Power Rangers with Jill in the treehouse. And it was the sunray on his back and the illumination in his mind when he was face-down in the splendor of Hanauma Bay, with crystal blue seawater trickling into his snorkeling goggles, which he endured purely because he didn't want to blink. It was with him when he was on the floor, collecting keychains as an infant, exactly as it was when he spent an entire year at ground level where he crawled. It was with him and Pamela the day he squirmed out of the womb eight weeks early, bathed in the wash of amniotic fluid and millions of beneficial colonies of bacteria. It was there when the staff placed all the unlikely four pounds of him into the warm, tender-loving arms of his mom and dad.

Brad Gobright was fashioned by, held by, guided by, and magnified by the light. Forward and backward, outward and inward.

For as many people there are who knew him, there are as many ways he will be remembered. But for me, the lucky chump who had the privilege to meet and learn from him, the guy who met him as a high schooler and watched him grow into a young man, and then into a full expression of himself—he is a star. He's someone to emulate. Not in exact deed, but in matters of the heart.

He's not the most complex character, but he never wanted to be. It wasn't complexity, after all, that he was after—it was simplicity. He's not the intellectual, nor should he be. Just as he's not the simpleton. The fact that he courted danger, sometimes willingly, others not, does not diminish his light, even if that danger or the abandon with which he courted it ultimately took it. He was not perfect in his operations, only perfect in his character. An anomaly, a lover, a brother, a son. A human being, true, brilliant, genius, even with all the fractures of light and the broken glass.

A life lost, that cannot and will not ever be replaced.

What Brad Gobright teaches me, shows me, apart from a burning desire to run full speed at beauty for the entirety of my time left on Earth, is, firstly, that there is an impossibly unlikely world, universe, life, before us all right now.

Second, by manner of how he lived, Brad shows me that this wondrous, miraculous web of life can be and needs to be attended to by the most original character imaginable. It needs you. Not the shell, not the projection; the original. We need you. In full attendance.

Brad shows me that this life is so precious, so unpredictable, that it can shine a ray of light for you or bring a revelation so bespoke it may alter the course of your life at any moment. Its miracles and its arrangements can be nested in the next step you take, or in the first face you see with your own eyes the moment after you put down this book. He shows me that this life is so rich in revelations that upon taking honest stock of it, I should be inclined, daily, to see it with new eyes and to listen to it with new ears. Just as I ought to eat each meal with complete awakening, and as I should take joy in every kiss, celebrate every tear, and burn for every touch. For the sheer tenderness and gift of this thing we call waking, conscious life, I should rejoice. Brad reminds me that all of life oozes with utter magnanimity.

Lastly, Brad reminds me that the world needs not only our fullest being, but very simply, it needs our light. It needs it now more than ever. It needs our light in all directions. It needs it in every nook and cranny and hillside and forest. It needs our light to shine into the future; it needs our light to illuminate the past. It needs it today and it needs it tomorrow, and it needs it in high places and lowlands just as it needs it on the faces of the poor, and the weary, and the lost, and the broken.

So go, as Brad would encourage us. As the Carpenter from Nazareth or the Siddhartha Gautama would say, go, and do not be afraid. And, if you find you are afraid, do not be undone by that fear. Consider the lilies of the field, how they do not worry and are yet provided for in all their beauty and splendor. Ponder the lotus, see how it is enlightened by virtue of only being that which it was ever meant to be. You were only ever meant to be light, so shine. Put your feet in the stream of life, then submerge yourself completely. Open your eyes, open your lungs, open your heart. There was never anything but light within you. So shine it, cast it, bend it in every direction you can. Move toward it with all your might. For you are so precious and your light so unique that we cannot afford to carry on without either.

Go forth, and shine all of your light, all of the time.

That's what Brad teaches me. I hope, deeply, that it's the same for you.

After all, it is the way of the fool that has always found a home in the hearts of the wise.

A NOTE FROM PAM GOBRIGHT

Two and half years ago, after sixty glorious, naïve, tragedy-free years, the worst thing that could happen to a mother happened to me. I could not breathe. I could not imagine that I would continue to wake up every day. The world spun away.

But somehow, I did continue to wake up, and the love poured down on me. The love of my family, my friends, and Brad's amazing tribe. I see it as the face of God, all that love. It lifted me up and helped me navigate the darkness. It gave me purpose, and I started to breathe again.

Only two days after Brad's passing, I received a DM from Lucas Roman. I did not know him, but his words, written eloquently and lovingly, penetrated deep. He spoke of God and love and connection, and how these things are not destroyed by death. I took a breath.

Lucas, thank you for this great gift, for crafting this beautiful story of our beloved son and brother, and for the way you have taught me to see the miraculous arc of our family's story. The "impossible necessary light."

And Brad. Your power and spirit continue to motivate me. I am just so proud of you. I love you, son. I'll be with you "in the blink of an eye," and I'll be ready to grab you and hold you. But I still have adventures ahead in this life, so stay close where I can feel you, okay?

ACKNOWLEDGEMENTS

This book would not have been possible without the participation of an entire community, a community that I would not have had access to were it not for the openness and support of the Gobright family. So, to Jim and Pamela, thank you. Your love and encouragement have been a cornerstone, not just for this book, but for many in life. The world is simply better for the ways you've dedicated yourselves to it. I'm grateful and humbled for your place in my life. To Jill, also, for your support and care in the interview process, and for keeping your parents and the world around you so filled with joy.

Much of the content of Brad's early road trip days and contact with those who spent time with him in that period would not have been possible without the help of Mason Earle. For your wholehearted involvement and your magnetic sincerity, I owe you deeply, my friend. Thank you for helping each step of the way. Thank you for making the community what it is and for lifting hearts, especially these days, in the fog and trials that have been placed before you. You make us all understand the tenderness of life better.

Another cornerstone in the foundation of this book was, without question, Jim Reynolds, who of his own volition took on the task of networking to great effect. For gathering interviews, for going far out of your way to bring stories and people together, for your outrageous stoke and your contagious presence, thank you. Entire chapters, especially the later ones, would have suffered greatly without your contribution. To share time and a rope with you was an honor and an inspiration.

To Alex Honnold, for your great help and involvement, and for the sincerity and care you put into the foreword. Thank you for taking time out of a busy schedule to honor your friendship with Brad. Thank you for being patient, communicative, and willing to pilfer through the old climbing journals to get not only the notes of these many salad days, but also the tone, tenor, and color of them. All the best going forward.

Thanks are due to many others for interviews, emails, photos, reflections, and contributions. This work would not be possible without the participation of you all. To Dustin Burd, Scott Bennett, and Cedar Wright for the candor and hard reflections; Taylor Keating and Chris Kalous for your podcast archives; Russell Facente, Tom Evans, Kevin Mohler, Bronson Hovnanian, James Lucas, Alice Hafer, and Sam for your patience and precious memories; Dan Krauss, Gino Negrini, Juan Ramon, Julie Ann Baxter, and T.K. for helping me see more under the surface; Joe-Bert Guadarrama, Mash Alexander, Matt Blank, Donny Goetz, Wayne Willoughby, Christian Cattell, Miranda Oakley, and all others I may have forgotten, or who helped but would have themselves kept anonymous. I am in debt to you all.

This work would also not be possible without the vision and direction of the Di Angelo team. To Sequoia, thank you for the vote of confidence and the opportunity. Thank you for the deadlines and the direction. To the editors, Ashley and Elizabeth, thank you for your insights, your kindness, your collective strengths, and your individual differences. Thanks for taking the time to get face-to-face and talk of tone as much as technique.

Personally, I owe thanks to my two guides in writing. To Jeremy, as always, for your endless love, for your softness and deep, irreplaceable insight. For how you guide the writing process without ever touching the page. To Michael Kennedy, for your piercing vulnerability, especially when sharing your own drafts; for the way you live your life, especially off the page, which helps me better understand how to live mine.

To my parents, my siblings, my nieces and nephews, and to Grandma; to all my supporting family, Boustanis alike, thank you for reminding me of what truly matters, and to seek balance more often.

Shukran Ikteer.

Lastly, to Nathalie, light to the earth, my salt. For your presence, for your eyes, for your touch.

For taking me in and through and across every landscape available to the human experience, and for allowing me the privilege of returning the favor.

For naked acceptance and love without condition.

—Lucas Roman

PHOTO CREDITS

Introduction – Drew Smith
A Note About Safety – Drew Smith
Foreword – Ted Hesser
Bloom – Chris Van Leuvan
Roots – Dan Krauss
Foundation – Dan Krauss
Approach – Samuel Crossley
Realization – Cheyne Lempe
Solo – Samuel Crossley
Forge – Samuel Crossley
Anchor – Pam Gobright
Recovery – Cedar Wrigjht
Home – Drew Smith
Blue – Sam Crossley
Wake – Sam Crossley

Family photos provided by Pam Gobright

ABOUT THE AUTHOR
LUCAS ROMAN

Amateur wave rider, runner, and registered nurse, Lucas Roman lives in Costa Mesa, California, with his partner of many years. He studies all things, has hopes for all things, and fancies himself an aficionado of low bottoms and hallowed spaces. Convinced of the profundity of foolishness and potency of new beginnings, his writing is an attempt to triangulate that which is ever present but never still: the human condition. He strives for habits that enable singular expressions, which last a lifetime, but never stay too long. He writes for his friend, Jeremy, and his partner, Nathalie.

ABOUT THE PUBLISHER

Di Angelo Publications was founded in 2008 by Sequoia Schmidt—at the age of seventeen. The modernized publishing firm's creative headquarters is in Houston, Texas, with its distribution center located in Twin Falls, Idaho. The subsidiary rights department is based in Los Angeles, and Di Angelo Publications has recently grown to include branches in England, Australia, and Sequoia's home country of New Zealand. In 2020, Di Angelo Publications made a conscious decision to move all printing and production for domestic distribution of its books to the United States. The firm is comprised of ten imprints, and the featured imprint, Catharsis, was inspired by Schmidt's love of extreme sports, travel, and adventure stories.

DI ANGELO PUBLICATIONS
A Modernized Publishing Firm